Windows 2000 Professional

Copyright - Editions ENI - July 2001
ISBN: 2-7460-1347-9
Original edition: ISBN: 2-7460-1235-9

ENI Publishing LTD

5 D Hillgate Place
18-20 Balham Hill
London SW12 9ER

Tel: 020 8673 3366
Fax: 020 8673 2277

e-mail: publishing@ediENI.com
http://www.eni-publishing.com

Editions ENI

BP 32125
44021 NANTES Cedex 1

Tel: 33 2.51.80.15.15
Fax: 33 2.51.80.15.16

e-mail: editions@ediENI.com
http://www.editions-eni.com

Author : José Dordoigne
Collection directed by Joëlle MUSSET
Translated from the French by Andrew BLACKBURN

Introduction

Installing
Windows 2000 Professional

Deploying installations and applications

Chapter 3

Configuring the system

Chapter 4

Configuring the network

Chapter 5

Managing users and groups   Chapter 6

Managing disk resources
Chapter 7

Printer management
Chapter 8

System monitoring and performance tuning

Chapter 9

Backing up, Restoring and Troubleshooting

Chapter 10

Chapter 1: Introduction

A. Overview of Windows 2000 operating systems

Before you start looking at Windows 2000, you must note that this is by no means a completely new operating system. Windows 2000 is an evolved version of the Windows NT 4.0 system that draws on Microsoft's experience in the fields of servers and operating systems. However, Windows 2000 is the biggest server development that Microsoft has undertaken since 1993. This operating system benefits from increased power, increased reliability and increased security. Under Windows 2000, administration is easier. In addition, flexible administration tools can be fully customized in order to assist you with these tasks: in particular, Windows 2000 uses the wizard approach similar to that of Windows 98.

In order to understand the characteristics of Microsoft operating systems fully, a few concepts must be defined.

First, this chapter will describe multitasking. It will clearly distinguish between co-operative and pre-emptive multitasking. Next, multithreading will be studied, and this will be followed by multiprocessing, with a look at how asymmetric multiprocessing can be used to improve fault tolerance

1. Multitasking

Multitasking is the ability of an operating system to manage several programs at once. It allocates processor time to each of the programs in turn, so that they can execute. This means that devices and memory must be shared so that the programs can use them. Multitasking can be implemented in two ways: co-operative multitasking and pre-emptive multitasking.

With **co-operative multitasking**, one of the applications that is running on the operating system uses the processor (together with the associated resources). Then, the application frees the processor, and allows the next application in the queue to use it. Each task depends on the others. This means that if a task goes into a loop, or gets blocked, then it will pause all the applications, and it will sometimes even pause the operating system itself. This implementation is used with 16-bit Windows systems (Windows 3.1x).

With **pre-emptive multitasking**, each application uses the processor either for a pre-determined time period, or until another application is given a higher priority than that of the current application. Scheduling and allocation of CPU time for current applications is handled by the operating system without consulting applications that are running.

Consequently, if an application locks up, it loses its initial processor time and is put to one side, without blocking the system or the other applications. The sharing of the processor and resources (such as printer ports and the keyboard) between applications is managed by the operating system.

2. Multithreading

Multithreading is implemented during the development of a software application, and is managed by the operating system. A **thread** can be an executable unit, or a part of a program. It can even be the entire program if the application does not offer multithreading.

Multithreading means that several tasks can be carried out practically simultaneously, within the same application. With Word for example, when you enter text, the characters are displayed with the required formatting, and any spelling mistakes are corrected at the same time. Furthermore, threads in the same process share the same memory space.

3. Multiprocessing

Multiprocessing is the ability of the operating system to run the applications and to use the processors that are present in the workstation, in order to manage the Windows 2000 system. There are two types of multiprocessing:

− Asymmetric multiprocessing (ASMP): one processor is reserved for the system while the others are used for the applications.

− Symmetric multiprocessing (SMP): execution requests from the operating system and the applications are distributed amongst the different processors. In this case, the system will always have a percentage of free processor time.

The multiprocessing features of Windows 2000 are vastly superior to those of previous versions of Windows, and, as with Windows NT 4, you can use the task manager in order to link a given process to a given processor.

4. Microsoft Windows 2000 architecture

Windows 2000 is a multitask, multithread 32-bit operating system with SMP architecture.

Windows 2000 is made up of layered operating systems and micro-kernel based client/ server systems. The grouping together of these two technologies has allowed two parts of Windows 2000 to be distinguished: **execute** (or kernel) **mode**, and **user** (or **application**) mode.

a. Kernel mode

Kernel mode groups together the set of system components that run in this mode. These components are called executive services and have priority in the use of the processor. The kernel plays a key role, as it is responsible for providing the applications with memory, for choosing the processes that must be run at a specific time, and for communicating with the peripherals. The applications depend on the kernel for all their needs. This means that they do not come into direct contact with the peripheral devices, which prevents them from provoking system failure.

◐ It must be noted that the Windows 2000 kernel is a development of the Windows NT 4.0 kernel and features improvements such as the handling of **several user sessions** on the same machine (which allows Windows 2000 to act as a terminal server). In addition, it allows you to add **processor quotas** in order to meet the needs of Internet Information Server 5 (such as the ability to control the amount of processor time that is granted to each Web site, and the logging of the CPU cycles that are used for each Web query).

Unlike that of Windows NT 4.0, the Windows 2000 kernel supports **WDM** *(Windows Driver Model)* **architecture**. This is a new driver model that allows you to use the same drivers on Windows 98 and on Windows 2000. Whilst on Windows NT 4.0 the applications run most of their tasks in user mode, WDM architecture allows these jobs to be transposed into kernel mode, thus allowing them to run quicker. However, in order to take advantage of this feature, applications must be specifically written for this purpose.

Windows 2000 supports **EMA** *(Enterprise Memory Architecture)*, which allows applications to use up to 32 GB of memory and is a very useful feature for database servers that manage large amounts of data. This is because data can be handled much quicker in RAM than on disk.

◐ In order to benefit from this architecture, your hardware must support it. In addition, the applications must be developed in a specific way. SQL Server is an example of an application that can use this feature.

Kernel mode is equipped with a **Plug-and-Play** module that reduces the time that is required to configure the hardware. In addition, kernel mode offers an **energy management** module that runs on **OnNow/ACPI** *(Advanced Configuration and Power Interface)* technology, and this reduces the energy that is consumed by the machines.

The improvements that have been made to the kernel allow Windows 2000 to operate in cluster mode (two machines that can take over from one another in the case of a problem).

Finally, it must be noted that kernel mode has been developed to support any application, whatever the language that is used. To this end, Windows 2000 uses **UNICODE**, which is a standard that defines a correspondence between bytes and characters. Unlike the ANSI standard, which requires an operating system to be developed for each language, UNICODE allows you to use a single source, irrespective of the language used. This feature means that you can change the language of the interface without restarting the machine.

b. User mode

Unlike kernel mode, user mode groups together protected subsystems that underlie user applications. User mode processes do not have direct access to the hardware; they are limited to a memory area that is allocated to them, and they are processed with a low priority level. One of the major developments of Windows 2000 user mode is the presence of Active Directory in the security subsystem.

B. The Windows 2000 range

The Windows 2000 range comprises four platforms:
- Windows 2000 Professional,
- Windows 2000 Server,
- Windows 2000 Advanced Server,
- Windows 2000 Datacenter Server.

Windows 2000 Professional is a workstation product, whilst the three other platforms are Windows 2000 server products. This section describes these different versions, and specifies for each of them, their role in a company and the hardware capacities that they require.

1. Windows 2000 Professional

The purpose of this operating system is to replace Windows 98 and Windows NT 4.0 progressively. Windows 2000 Professional combines the simplicity of using Windows 98 with the performance and reliability of Windows NT 4.0. In addition, it offers new features that allow you to optimize such aspects as resource access and security in a Windows 2000 domain environment. Furthermore, this operating system supports other features such as Plug-and-Play, energy options, the new WDM drivers, and the recognition of over 6500 hardware devices.

Resource access

Windows 2000 Professional supports the Active Directory client. This provides access to the resources of the directory database (according to the permissions that have been granted). It also provides access to the resources that are contained in a DFS *(Distributed File System)* topology. This allows users to carry out searches in Active Directory in order to find an item such as a printer, a contact, a person or a shared directory, by knowing only one characteristic of the object concerned (such as the name, the location or the telephone number).

Users of portable computers will find it easier to work on documents that are stored on the network. Thanks to **work offline** technology, users can work transparently on their documents via the network in the same way as they would work with local files. A synchronization mechanism that runs upon opening and closing a session ensures that they will always have an up-to-date version of the document. In addition they can use the Networking Connection Wizard in order to set up a secure connection to their company network easily, using a remote connection, or simply by creating a **VPN** *(Virtual Private Network)* via the Internet. Also, **IPP** *(Internet Printing Protocol)* allows mobile users to print documents via the Internet on their printers in their offices.

Simplified installation

When you are implementing a network architecture, one of the longest phases is the installation of the workstations. As network administrator, you will save time when you install Windows 2000. You can install a Windows 2000 Professional workstation without leaving your office, thanks to a remote installation service that is supplied with the server versions of Windows 2000. This service is called **RIS** (*Remote Installation Service*). Other techniques are also provided in order to reduce the time that you spend in installing workstations. These include the **sysprep.exe** utility, which can be used in order to duplicate the image of a disk on other workstations, using a disk duplication tool from a third-party vendor.

Previously, you had to fill in several fields and select several options during the installation process, which meant that you had to stay in front of the computer. The new graphic installation script creation utility allows you to create files that provide responses automatically during the installation process.

File systems

Here again, Windows 2000 is more developed than Windows NT 4.0, which recognizes only FAT16 and NTFS file systems. In addition, Windows 2000 supports the FAT32 file system (which is used by Windows 95 OSR2 and Windows 98 systems).

Furthermore, NTFS has evolved with the version 5.0 that is offered in Windows 2000. This version offers features such as file encryption, disk quota management, and distributed link tracking.

Utilities such as Disk Defragmenter, Disk Cleanup and Scandisk allow you to maintain your disks and to optimize storage of your data.
A major development of the backup manager must also be noted. The new backup manager allows you to backup data to different media such as tapes, recordable CD-ROMs, logical disks, ZIP drives and external hard disks. An integrated backup planning utility simplifies the design and implementation of a backup plan.

Security

Security is important for all computing networks. Windows 2000 provides a marked improvement in this field. Amongst the numerous security improvements, a major advance concerns file encryption on NTFS 5 volumes. This public key / private key encryption technique means that only the user who encrypted a document will be allowed to read it. This is done transparently (the document is decrypted automatically without any user intervention). This function is added to the NTFS permissions. However, this feature does not allow you to encrypt documents when you transmit them on the network.

The **IPSec** protocol allows you to encrypt all IP traffic within the same LAN, as you would if you were using a non-secure network such as the Internet by means of VPNs (*Virtual Private Networks*). It must be noted that the IPSec (*IP Security*) standard was developed by the IETF (*Internet Engineering Task Force*) and allows any system that uses IPSec to communicate, thereby ensuring secure IP traffic.

Although versions of Windows NT authenticate using the NTLM protocol, Windows 2000 uses the Kerberos v5 protocol to authenticate users.

◉ Windows 2000 still supports NTLM protocol for backward compatibility reasons.

Thus, a Windows 2000 Workstation that is integrated in a Windows NT4 domain will be authenticated by NTLM. The Kerberos authentication method is quicker and more secure than NTLM. In addition, as it is a standard, a UNIX host can be authenticated by a Windows 2000 domain controller by having an account in Active Directory. Kerberos is also used for authentication across inter-domain trust relationships.

◉ For more information, see RFC 1510, which describes the Kerberos protocol.

Minimal configuration

The minimal configuration for Windows 2000 Professional is as follows:
- 166 MHz processor
- 32 MB of RAM (64 MB is recommended).
- 685 MB of disk space. You should provide 1 GB in order to allow for future system development.

It is very important to know the hardware items that make up your computer. These hardware items must be included in the Hardware Compatibility List (HCL), so as to ensure the correct functioning of your system.

If you intend to upgrade your old system (Windows 95/98 or NT Workstation), you can use the command **winnt32.exe /check-upgradeonly**, to list the hardware items on your workstation that will not be supported by Windows 2000.

2. Windows 2000 Server

The Windows 2000 Server version offers all the features of Windows 2000 Professional. It uses the strong points of Windows NT 4.0 Server, and it provides numerous additional features, all of which makes it a formidable enterprise server.

a. Characteristics

Adapting to large networks

Windows 2000 was originally designed to manage very big networks. It meets all administration needs by organizing domains into administrative units. Even for very big networks, a single domain is sufficient. This is because the Windows 2000 directory database allows you to store several million objects (such as user accounts and computer accounts).

Active Directory Service

One of the major new features of Windows 2000 Server is that it manages network objects using a directory. Previously, user accounts, computer accounts and groups were stored in a database called SAM *(Security Account Manager)*. This database resided on the primary domain controller and a copy was kept on the backup domain controllers. When the primary domain controller was unavailable, users could still open a session on the domain, but the SAM could not be modified without promoting one of the backup domain controllers. In addition, administration was limited by the number of objects, which could not exceed 40 000.

The Active Directory database is duplicated on all the Windows 2000 domain controllers, each of which has a read/write copy. This feature enhances fault tolerance. This approach simplifies administration and ensures the development capacity of the system. The total cost of ownership (TCO) is very competitive. This is because the group strategies belong to Active Directory, which limits the time that is required in order to configure each client machine, particularly during the distribution of applications and the setting up of user working environments. An additional strong point of active directory is that it uses a set of standard protocols. This makes it compatible with any other system. These protocols include the Domain Name System (DNS) and the LDAP protocol (*Lightweight Directory Access Protocol*) for database access.

Administrative tools

In addition to a number of administration tools that are provided as standard, Windows 2000 offers Microsoft Management Console (MMC), which allows you to customize and to create several consoles to meet your administration needs. This gives you all the tools that you require.

Enhancing network services

Apart from the supplementary services that are available with Windows 2000, such as the index service, the certificate service, the Remote Installation Service (RIS) and the remote storage service, many existing services have been markedly improved. For example the DDNS (*Dynamic DNS*) that authorizes DNS and DHCP clients to register with a DNS server automatically. Again the TCO is reduced in this case. This is because the administrator no longer need be concerned by the update of the DNS database, as this item develops according to the clients. Integrating DNS zones into Active Directory provides fault tolerance and load sharing.

The DHCP service is also optimized so as to help clients to register with the DNS server. The class scopes allow you to attribute configurations according to criteria for belonging to a class. You can also create super-scopes and multicast scopes.

Internet services have also been improved thanks to the Windows 2000 kernel, which supports processor quotas and the different supplementary features such as IPP (*Internet Printing Protocol*), which allows you to print via the Internet, and the reservation of bandwidth for Web sites.

Remote network access

Increasingly, companies need to access remote networks via telephone lines, the Internet, X25 networks, Frame Relay networks, ATM or ISDN. These requirements are met by standard versions of Windows 2000. These versions provide a very effective, remote access service that allows you to act as remote access server and VPN *(Virtual Private Network)* server. The security is ensured on the IP transit level, in the tunnel that is created by PPTP (Point to Point Tunneling Protocol) or L2TP (Layer 2 Tunneling Protocol), and at authentication level by RADIUS (Remote Authentication Dial In User Service).

Backup

The backup utility that is supplied with Windows 2000 is now comparable to tools that are supplied by specialists in this field. Using a graphic calendar, you can schedule all types of backup.

A major advantage of this utility is that it allows you to make a full backup of your system and to restore a server without losing information. Active Directory objects can also be restored.

Network monitor

The network monitor is derived from the one delivered with SMS *(System Management Server)*. It allows you to capture frames that are being transmitted on the network. You can do this by filtering them, either according to specific protocols, or according to specific machines, or according to specific contents. This is an essential tool that allows you to understand and to analyze your network. It will help you to solve problems in many situations.

Windows 2000, a veritable router

In addition to the implementation of RIP v2 *(Routing Information Protocol)*, the routing features of Windows 2000 have been enhanced by the use of OSPF *(Open Shortest Path First)*, which is a widely used, link state routing protocol. RIP is used with smaller networks. whilst OSPF is more suitable for large networks.

Terminal Services

The features of Windows NT 4 Terminal Edition are offered by the Windows 2000 Server versions in the form of a service. This service provides a Windows 2000 desktop to users who have machines that are not powerful, and that do not support 32-bit applications. The desktop along with the applications that are run by the user in the terminal server session, are run entirely on the server. In addition, administrators can install Terminal Server services with the sole objective of remotely administering servers.

b. Minimal configuration

Here is the minimal configuration for Windows 2000 Server:
- 166 MHz processor
- 64 MB of RAM (128 MB is recommended).
- 685 MB of disk space. You should provide 1 GB in order to allow for future system development.

It is very important to know the hardware items that make up your computer. These hardware items must be included in the Hardware Compatibility List (HCL), so as to ensure the correct functioning of your system.

3. Windows 2000 Advanced Server

The Windows 2000 Advanced Server version offers the same features as the Windows 2000 Server version. In addition, Advanced Server allows you to organize several servers into a cluster configuration. The advantage of this feature is that users can access services 24 hours a day, as, if one server fails, the other server in the cluster will take over automatically. Similarly, if an application fails, you can start it on the other server. In addition to fault tolerance features, organizing machines into a cluster configuration allows you to spread the workload for network services and for Web services.

This Windows 2000 version is more suitable than the Server version for processing large volumes of information (for example, databases, transactions or decision aids). This capacity is provided by the EMA (*Enterprise Memory Architecture*), which allows Windows 2000 to manage up to 8 GB of RAM on Intel systems.

SMP features allow Windows 2000 Advanced Server to run on up to 8 processors.

4. Windows 2000 Datacenter Server

Windows 2000 Datacenter Server is characterized by the SMP, which can be configured so as to allow a Windows 2000 server to manage up to 32 processors. This version can manage up to 64 GB of RAM on Intel systems.

Of course, the Datacenter Server version offers all the features that are supported by Windows 2000 Server, along with the cluster configuration and the workload distribution.

Chapter 2: Installing Windows 2000 Professional

A. System requirements

1. Minimal hardware requirements

You can install Microsoft Windows 2000 Professional in different ways. Whichever method you choose, you must carry out a series of tasks that is called the "**pre-installation**". If you carry out these tasks you will save a lot of time later.

First you must check that the hardware that will be used is referenced in the hardware compatibility list (HCL) that is supplied by Microsoft. In fact, a hardware item that is not included in this list could make the operating system malfunction, and cause you to spend time in diagnosing the problem. You can find a copy of this HCL (**HCL.txt**) on the Windows 2000 CD-ROM, in the **support** directory.
Alternatively, it is available on the Internet at the address **http://www.microsoft.com/hcl**.

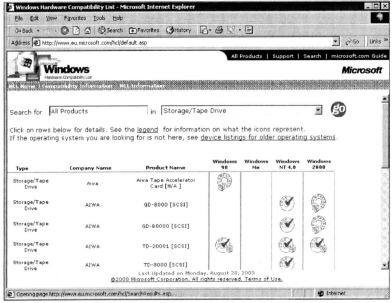

Minimal configuration required for the installation of Microsoft Windows 2000 Professional

- Processor: Pentium 166 MHZ.
- 32 MB of RAM (64 MB is preferable).
- 685 MB of disk space for the system partition (1 GB is preferable so as to accommodate future system evolution).
- Standard VGA graphic card
- Keyboard, mouse or other pointer peripheral.
- and, according to your computing environment, CD-ROM drive, floppy disk drive, sound card and network adapter.

2. Knowledge of hardware components

Although Windows 2000 automatically detects and configures your peripherals when it is installed, it is useful to know about these components.

Type of card	Required Information
Video	reference and bus width (at least VGA)
Network	IRQ I/O address, Type of connector (BNC, TP, AUI for example), DMA (if used)
SCSI controller	model, bus width, IRQ
Mouse	Type, port (COM1, COM2, bus or PS/2)
Sound	IRQ, I/O address, DMA
External modem	port used (e.g. COM1 or COM2.)
Internal modem	model, port used or IRQ and I/O address (for non-standard configurations)

IRQ occupation table (hardware IRQs):

IRQ	0	System clock
IRQ	1	Keyboard
IRQ	2	Redirected towards IRQ 8 to IRQ 15, sometimes available
IRQ	3	Serial port COM2
IRQ	4	Serial port COM1
IRQ	5	Parallel port LPT2: often available
IRQ	6	Floppy disk controller
IRQ	7	Parallel port LPT1:
IRQ	8	Real-time clock
IRQ	9	Available
IRQ	10	Available
IRQ	11	Available, unless SCSI
IRQ	12	Available
IRQ	13	Math coprocessor; available if the processor is a 486 SX
IRQ	14	IDE disk controller
IRQ	15	Second E-IDE disk controller; sometimes available

3. Memory address configuration

It is also important to be well aware of the input/output addresses that are available when you install a PC device. This is because an address conflict with another hardware item would prevent the system from running correctly.

Here is the list of input/output ports that are most commonly used:

I/O Addresses	Devices that generally use this address interval
1F0-1F8	Hard disk controller
2F8-2FF	Second serial port
278-27F	Second parallel port
378-37F	First parallel port
3B0-3DF	VGA, SVGA
3F0-3F7	Floppy-disk controller
3F8-3FF	First serial port
280-340	Useable for a new device (e.g. a network interface card at 300-31F)

Troubleshooting

In order to view the settings of the complete set of devices, along with any conflict pro-blems, you can use the **Computer Management** utility, after you have installed Win-dows 2000. To start this utility, right-click the **My Computer** icon and then select **Ma-nage**.

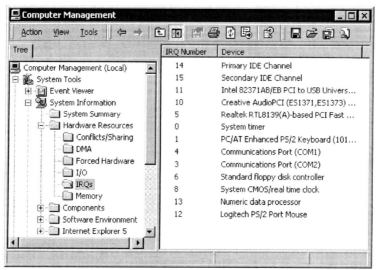

By expanding **System Information**, and then **Hardware Resources**, you will find all the necessary information such as the list of IRQs that are used, and the memory addresses that are used. It must be noted that the **Conflicts/Sharing** sub-directory indicates any conflicts between devices.

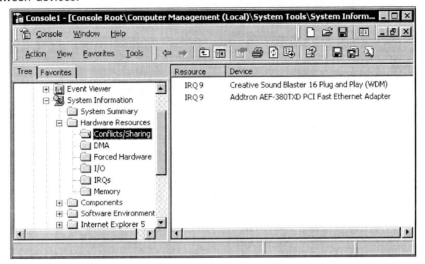

B. Preparing your installation

During the installation phase, you can modify your partitioning scheme and carry out certain operations on your disks (delete and create partitions). Use this feature simply to configure the partition on which you want to install the system. Subsequently, you can use the **Disk Manager** utility that is supplied with Windows 2000 in order to configure your other partitions or disks.

It is strongly recommended that you install your system on a 2-GB partition in order to allow for the future development of your system. If you do not allow enough space for the system partition, you might have to re-install your workstation because you lack space (possible causes include evolution of the swap file and the installation of applications that store information on the system partition).

1. Disk partitioning scheme

During the installation phase, you can modify your partitioning scheme and carry out certain operations on your hard disks. This is necessary in order to specify the partitions on which Windows 2000 must be installed.

You can install the preloader, (Windows 2000 boot sector) and the loader, **NTLDR**, on the first partition (the **system partition**), and you can install the rest of the files on a separate partition (the **boot partition**).

On an Intel platform, the system partition is the primary (active) partition. The boot partition, which contains the Windows 2000 kernel (**NTOSKRNL.EXE**), can be a logical drive on an extended partition.

The system partition does not need a great deal of space. In most cases, 10 MB is ample. This partition can remain in FAT, so that it will support a multiple boot and simplify troubleshooting in the event of any startup problems.

The essential files that are contained on this partition can be duplicated onto a boot diskette. Not only will this provide a copy of these files, but it will also produce a backup diskette that you can use in the event of a simple system-boot problem.

In the most critical cases, the full set of four backup diskettes provide access to the Windows 2000 system, and allow you to carry out repair work.

> You can create these diskettes using the **makeboot** tool that is located in the **bootdisk** folder on the Windows 2000 Installation CD-ROM.

The boot partition, which contains system files such as the Windows 2000 kernel, must have at least 1.2 GB of space. This will allow for future system developments such as the inclusion of numerous high-volume DLLs into the **system32** subdirectory of the installation directory. In addition, you must not forget to allow space for the swap file, and possibly for a spool file.
This partition will be converted to NTFS for security reasons.
Alternatively, you can install Windows 2000 entirely on a single partition. In this case the system partition and the boot partition will be the same.

2. Choosing a file system

Windows 2000 supports FAT (or FAT16), FAT32 and NTFS file systems.

a. NTFS file system

NTFS (*NT File system*) 5.0 is the recommended file system for Windows 2000. It enhances security by allowing security control at directory and file level. It manages disk and file compression. In addition, it allows users to control the disks by applying quotas and providing data encryption.

b. FAT/FAT32 file system

If you want still to be able to start up your old operating system, such as MS-DOS, Windows 95 or Windows 98, then you must keep a file system that is recognized by the systems that make up the multiple boot. FAT and FAT32 do not provide security control at file and directory level. **The FAT file system does not support partitions larger than 2 GB**. FAT32 is a development of FAT that overcomes this limitation.

⊙ You can convert a disk from FAT/FAT32 format to NTFS format without losing data. However, you must note that this operation is irreversible. You can carry out this conversion using the following command:
CONVERT 'drive' : /FS:NTFS

⊙ If you wish to convert from NTFS to another file system, then you must first back up your data and format the partition for the desired file system. You can then restore your data.

With Windows 2000 you must choose NTFS in the following circumstances:
- Windows 2000 will be the only operating system that is installed.
- You would like to have local security control (this is strongly recommended!).
- You would like to be able to manage large partitions (of over 500 MB) efficiently.
- An audit of the file system is required.
- You wish to manage compression individually.
- You wish to manage disk quotas.
- You wish to encrypt your data (EFS).
- You wish to mount volumes in empty directories.
- You wish to implement remote storage.

If you decide to use NTFS 5.0, it is advisable to convert your file system during the installation process. This is because permissions are applied for certain specific groups in specific directories in the file system tree. If you convert later using the **convert** command, then irreversible, local **Full Control** permissions will be granted to the **Everyone** group.

3. Workgroup or domain

You can work either in a workgroup environment, or in a Windows 2000 domain. In a workgroup environment, each computer runs with local security. On the other hand, in a Windows 2000 domain, the user information is centralized in the Active Directory, and the workstations in the network are also managed and administrated centrally.

C. Installing Windows 2000 Professional

1. Choosing an installation method

You can install Windows 2000 Professional in several ways. You can use the same types of installation methods as Windows NT 4 offers, or alternatively, you can use new methods. In addition, Windows 2000 offers vast improvements in terms of **simplicity of installation, and reduction of costs associated with the deployment and update of software applications**.

You can upgrade to Windows 2000 Professional from Windows 95, Windows 98, Windows NT Workstation 3.51, or Windows NT Workstation 4.

◎ In particular, upgrading from Windows NT Workstation to Windows 2000 Professional is very simple and requires very little preparation.

You can install Windows 2000 Professional locally, either using a bootable CD-ROM, or you can upgrade from a previous version of Windows, or you can use the four Windows 2000 Setup floppy disks (for a new installation, or for an upgrade, or to repair an existing system).

System preparation tools for auto install

With Windows 2000, the automatic installation tools have been greatly improved. Notably, you can create installation images that you can duplicate, once the system preparation tool **SysPrep** has removed from the image all the unique identifiers that must not be duplicated on the network. You can then deploy the resulting image, byte by byte, using a tool provided by a third party vendor.

◎ Such duplication tools include **Drive Image Pro** from **PowerQuest**, **Norton Ghost** from **Symantec, Rapideploy** from **Altiris,** and **Imagecast** from **Storagesoft.**

When you have done this, all you have to do to complete the installation is to restart each of these workstations and enter the specific identifiers.

Remote installation service

An alternative way of deploying installation images is to use the **Remote Installation Service** (RIS). You can use the RIS from a bootable diskette, using a network interface card that is equipped with a bootable PROM, or using a BIOS that allows you to start-up the machine concerned via the network.

Setup manager

With Windows 2000, it is easy to create scripts that allow you to carry out fully automated installations on several workstations simultaneously. The setup manager (**SetupMge.exe**) has been enhanced for this purpose.

2. Upgrading from an existing version of Windows

a. Preparing a computer for upgrade

You can upgrade a Windows 95/98 system, or a Windows NT 3.51/4 system, to Windows 2000 Professional. You can fully automate this procedure using scripts. Here are the steps that you must follow in order to carry out this upgrade:

Hardware and software compatibility

The first step is to check both hardware and software compatibility. The **Readiness Analyzer** carries out this check automatically before each upgrade.

This tool is very useful. It generates a clear and informative upgrade report.

In all cases, you must check each hardware component that you are using before you attempt to upgrade.

Hardware compatibility list

To check the hardware components you can consult the Windows 2000 Hardware Compatibility List (HCL).

The HCL is available in the **support** folder on the installation CD-ROM for Windows 2000 Professional.

Another, preferable, alternative is to access the very latest version of the HCL on the Internet at the following URL address:
http://www.microsoft.com/hcl/:

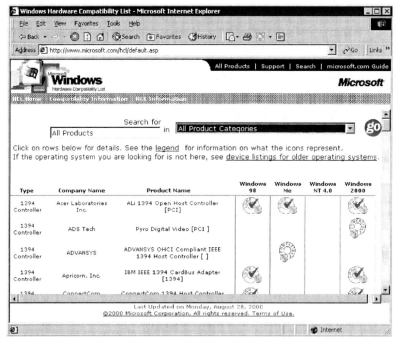

Readiness Analyzer

You can call the **Readiness Analyzer** explicitly using the following command:

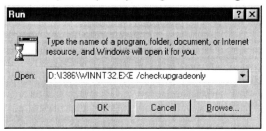

○ The programs **winnt.exe** and **winnt32.exe** are contained in the **I386** folder on the installation CD-ROM for Windows 2000 Professional.

The **Readiness Analyzer** produces a report as follows:

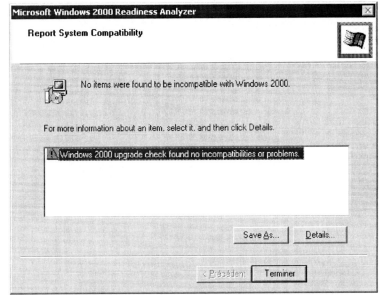

You can also obtain this report when you upgrade a system to Windows 2000 Professional.

Of course, you can print this report, or save it as a file. Here is an example of an upgrade report that Windows 2000 **Readiness Analyzer** produced on a Windows 98 computer.

```
Upgrade Report
--------------

Reliability and quality are key design goals of Windows 2000.

Microsoft realizes that compatibility issues with devices and programs
can compromise these goals if you are not given the best information
available. During Windows 2000 testing of certain devices and programs,
Microsoft found some compatibility problems you might encounter after
you upgrade to Windows 2000. This report describes those problems. In
most cases, new software updates from the hardware or software vendor
can correct these problems. If you are concerned about the results of
this report, you should not upgrade to Windows 2000 until these pro-
blems are corrected.
For more information about product compatibility with Windows 2000, you
should contact your hardware or software manufacturer. You can also
visit http://www.microsoft.com/windows2000/compatible for additional in-
formation.
```

```
Contents:
        Hardware
        Software Incompatible with Windows 2000
        Software to Reinstall
        Program Notes
        General Information
```

```
Hardware
--------
This section of the report describes hardware compatibility issues.
Incompatible Hardware
The following hardware may not support Windows 2000 without additional
files. Please see the Microsoft Windows 2000 Hardware Compatibility
List at http://www.microsoft.com/windows2000/compatible/ for a list of
compatible hardware. (Some of the following entries might be software
that is registered as hardware.)
    Display adapters
    S3 Inc. Trio3D/2X V1.00.19
You can continue with the upgrade, but the hardware may not work -until
you supply the additional files.
Unknown Devices (Scanners or Digital Cameras)
Setup did not recognize the following scanners or digital cameras.
Before upgrading, check the packaging that came with the device to see
if it supports Windows 2000, or contact the device manufacturer. Reins-
tall each device when Setup is complete, using the software that came
with the device.
    ScanWise 1.0
Software Incompatible with Windows 2000
----------------------------------------
This section lists information about programs that are incompatible
with Windows 2000. Before upgrading, evaluate how important these pro-
grams are to you.
Software That Does Not Support Windows 2000
Setup has found programs on your computer that do not support Win-
dows 2000. Contact your software vendors to obtain updates or Win-
dows 2000-compatible versions. If you donÆt update these programs be-
fore you upgrade, the programs will not work.
    Client WSP (in Control Panel)
Before you upgrade to Windows 2000, you should remove any incompatible
programs. After the upgrade, uninstall might not work. Add/Remove Pro-
grams in Control Panel can help you uninstall most programs. Click
Start, point to Settings, click Control Panel, and then click Add/Remo-
ve Programs.
Software to Reinstall
---------------------
The following programs need to be reinstalled after the upgrade, be-
cause they use different files and settings in Windows 2000.
    Microsoft Proxy Client
```

You should remove the program before upgrading. (Many programs can be removed using Add/Remove Programs in the Control Panel). After upgrading to Windows 2000, you can then reinstall the program.

```
Program Notes
-------------
```

This section describes issues that might affect some of the programs you use. Be sure to read this section before you begin the upgrade to Windows 2000.

Microsoft Outlook 2000

> After Windows 2000 Setup is complete, you have to reinstall Microsoft Outlook 2000. To do this, start Outlook. If Outlook 2000 is part of your Startup folder, reinstallation will automatically begin the first time you log on to Windows 2000. Reinstallation takes a while, and the progress bar restarts several times.

```
General Information
-------------------
```

This section provides important information that you need to be aware of before you upgrade.

Backup Files Found

Setup found files on your computer that appear to be a backup of part of Windows 98. During the upgrade to Windows 2000, Setup removes Windows 98 from your computer, including any backups you may have on your hard disk. Some files in the following folders will be removed:

```
    c:\ie5
```

Protect your backup files by copying them to floppy disks, a network server, a compressed archive file, or other backup mechanism.

Time Zone

The current time zone for your computer ((GMT+01:00) Brussels, Copenhagen, Madrid, Paris, Vilnius) matches more than one Windows 2000 time zone. After Setup completes, you should use the Regional Settings icon in Control Panel to check your time zone settings.

It is important to identify devices and applications that may cause problems so that you can replace them. In particular, other drivers may be required during the unattended installation phase.

b. Upgrading from Windows NT Workstation 3.51/4

As Windows NT Workstation has many features in common with Windows 2000 Professional, this is the simplest system to upgrade.

These common features include the following:
− Registry structure
− File and folder hierarchy
− Architecture of the system kernel

- Device drivers
- Security environment.

Upgrade procedure

However, in order to ensure that the upgrade runs smoothly, you must check the software components. In particular, you must check the compatibility of the software applications and that of the device drivers you will use.

> Some applications, such as anti-virus software for example, will run only with a specific system version.

You may well need to replace some applications by others that will run in Windows 2000 Professional.

You may also need to upgrade other applications so that they will run in this environment.

c. Upgrading from Windows 95/98

Upgrading from Windows 95/98 may be more difficult than upgrading from Windows NT. In particular, you may have problems with applications that were not designed to run on Windows 2000.

You can carry out this upgrade in several ways.

Re-installing software applications after upgrade

This method consists of uninstalling each software application, upgrading your system, and then re-installing each software application. This approach can be very effective, and is particularly useful if your applications support automatic installation using scripts.

Re-installing operating system and software applications

Alternatively, you can cleanly install a standard configuration on a machine, and then install your software applications. Subsequently, you can deploy this standard installation in the form of an image. This technique is very useful if the computing hardware in your network is truly homogeneous.

Upgrading your software applications

Another approach is to obtain from your vendors the necessary upgrades that will allow your applications to run on Windows 2000. Upgrade DLL files are available that convert registry keys so that they will be suitable for Windows 2000.

The Windows 2000 CD-ROM provides many upgrade DLL files for applications for third-party applications:

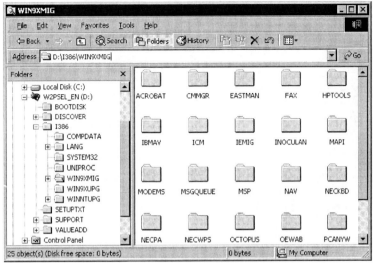

You can copy these DLL files using automatic installation scripts.

Alternatively, you can upgrade your software applications from the Microsoft Internet site at the following address:
http://windowsupdate.Microsoft.com.

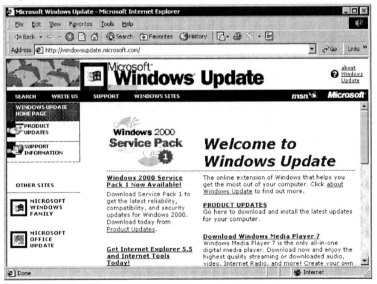

In all cases, when you upgrade, the **Setup Wizard** will ask you to specify upgrade programs.

Support of file systems

Windows 2000 Professional supports the file systems FAT16 and FAT32. You can specify that the setup wizard must convert from FAT to NTFS v.5 during the system upgrade, provided that you have not implemented a multiple boot on the machine concerned.

> You cannot upgrade drives that you have compressed on Windows 95/98. You must decompress such drives before you launch the upgrade.

3. Clean install

a. Installing from a local CD-ROM

You can run the Windows 2000 installation program on a CD-ROM in several ways:

- Either, you have a Microsoft operating system; in which case you need only insert the CD-ROM in the CD-ROM drive and then run the installation program, **setup.exe** .
- Or, your BIOS will start up on the CD-ROM, which will start the Windows 2000 installation program, automatically.
- Or, you can create a set of installation diskettes. You can do this by running the **makeboot.exe** program using the command **makeboot a**. This command is situated in the **bootdisk** directory of the CD-ROM. Then, start up the computer using these diskettes.

If you run the **setup.exe** program using an operating system, here are the steps that you must follow:

First phase of the installation

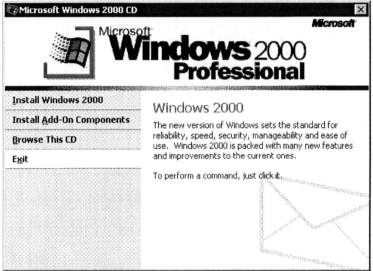

→) Once you have selected **Install Windows 2000**, the following screen appears:

After you have chosen the type of installation, the License Agreement appears:

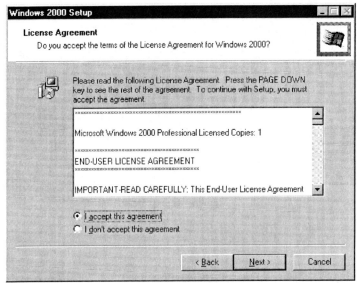

→) When you have accepted this agreement, click **Next**.

According to the distribution of your Windows 2000 system, you may need to enter the product key at this point. If your distribution requires it then, you must enter the product key, and then press **Next**.

The following screen allows you to specify any special options that you may require.

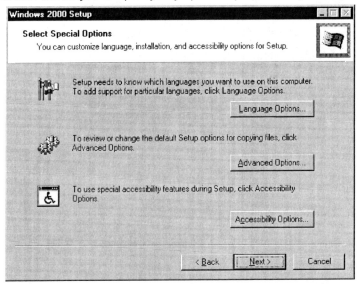

The **Language Options** button allows you to configure your system so that it will support several languages using UNICODE:

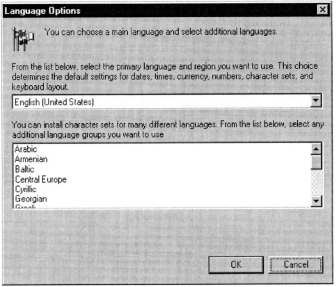

→) Validate these settings by clicking **OK**. The wizard then returns to the **Select Special Options** screen.

→) The **Advanced Options** button allows you to specify the source of the installation files and the folder into which you want to install them. You can even ask the wizard to copy all the setup files to your hard disk:

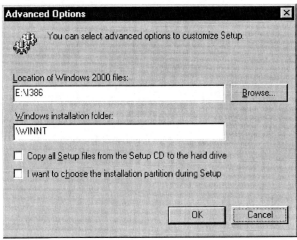

→) Validate by clicking **OK**. The wizard then returns again to the **Select Special Options** screen.

→) The **Accessibility Options** button allows you to request a **Magnifier** and/or a **Narrator** for visually impaired users:

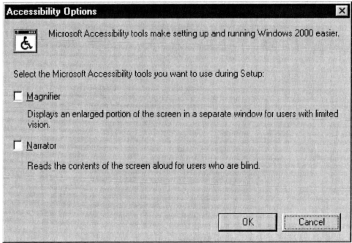

→) Validate by clicking **OK**, and click **Next** in order to close the **Select Special Options** screen.

Then, the wizard copies the installation files onto your hard disk:

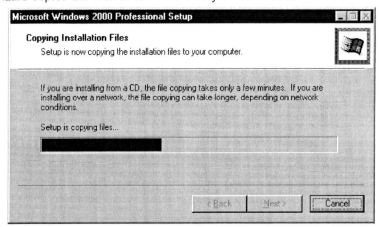

When the wizard has finished copying the installation files, it re-starts the computer.

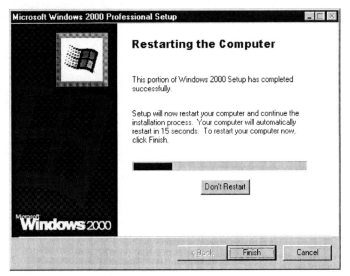

Second phase of the installation, in text mode

Here are the different steps in the text mode:

- The setup program copies a minimal version of Windows 2000 into memory.
- If you have **SCSI** *(Small Computer System Interface)* or **RAID** *(Redundant Array of Independent Disks)* peripherals that are not listed in the HCL, then press the F6 key at the beginning of text mode, in order to load their drivers.
- Then, either choose the installation partition, or create it.
- At this stage, you must select the file system onto which the operating system will be installed.
- Then, indicate the name of the installation directory (this is \winnt by default).

If you are installing by running the **setup.exe** program from the operating system, then the text mode phase will not ask you to select the file system and the installation directory. This is because these two steps will already have been carried out.

At this stage your computer will reboot for the second time.

Third phase of the installation, in graphic mode

The setup wizard restarts the machine again. At the beginning of this phase, the setup wizard detects the devices that are connected to your workstation and installs them.

Regional Settings

When you have clicked the **Next** button, you must specify all the regional characteristics of your workstation. You can specify the formats for numbers, times, dates and money for the keyboard that you will use on the workstation.

In order specify these characteristics, click the upper **Customize** button (**To change system or user locale settings...**).

The following dialog box appears:

You can also modify the system characteristics concerning the **Installed input locales** by selecting the corresponding tab.

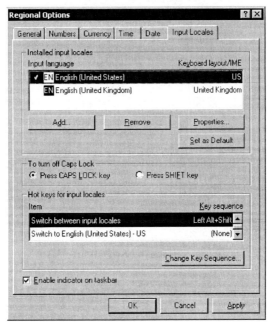

Personalizing Your Software

When you have closed the **Regional Options** dialog box, and clicked **Next** in order to move on from the **Regional Settings** page, the setup wizard asks you to enter your name along with that of your organization.

> Windows 2000 will use your name in order to create a user with permission to work on your workstation, and it will use the name of your organization as a prefix in order to generate a computer name that is unique in your network.

Computer Name and Administrator Password

The setup wizard generates a unique name for your computer, for example ENI-BA58DYBJMXI.

> The setup wizard uses as a prefix, the name of the organization that you entered in the previous screen (ENI in the above example).

> Alternatively, you can enter any name you like for your computer provided that is does not exceed 15 characters and that it is unique on your network.

In addition, you must enter a password for the local **Administrator**, and you must confirm this password.

Date and Time Settings

The next screen allows you to confirm or to adjust the local date and time, and the local time zone.

Networking Settings

At this point the setup wizard installs networking components. Then, it allows you to choose one of two options:

Typical settings

If you choose this default option, the setup wizard will install a client for Microsoft networks along with the Server service, and it will install and automatically configure the TCP/IP protocol (as a DHCP client).

> The **Dynamic Host Configuration Protocol** (DHCP) allows you to attribute IP configurations dynamically to clients that request them. A DHCP server must be present on your network in order to allow you to communicate with a suitable IP address.

> If your workstation is unable to obtain an IP address from a DHCP server, Windows 2000 will automatically assign an IP address from the address scope that is reserved for Microsoft. This scope is from 169.254.0.1 to 169.254.255.254, in class B. Your workstation will use this address until it finds a DHCP server.

Custom settings

If you choose this option, the setup wizard allows you to specify the following settings:

Client for Microsoft Networks
File and Printer Sharing for Microsoft Networks
Internet Protocol (TCP/IP)

You can specify an IP address manually by selecting **Internet Protocol (TCP/IP)** and then clicking **Properties**.

Workgroup or Computer Domain

You must specify whether your computer will belong to a workgroup, or whether it will belong to a domain. Then, you must enter the name of the workgroup or the domain concerned.

Installing Components

At this point the setup wizard copies and configures certain files.

Performing Final Tasks

The setup wizard then:
- Installs **Start** menu items,
- Registers components,

- Saves settings,
- Removes any temporary files used.

The setup wizard then invites you to close the installation by clicking the **Finish** button. When you have done this, the setup wizard automatically restarts the system.

Getting started with the system

Finally, the Network Identification Wizard asks you how you will be using your workstation. Click **Next** to begin.

Users of This Computer

You can choose one of two options:
- **Users must enter a user name and password to use this computer,** or
- **Windows always assumes the following user has logged on to this computer.**

If you take the second option, which is the default option, the wizard suggests as a user name the name that you entered during the third installation phase.

→) If you choose the second option, input a password for this user.

When you have clicked **Finish**, the following screen appears:

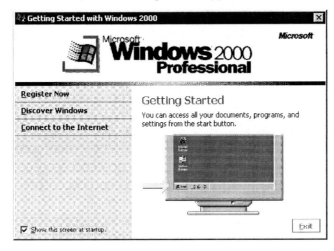

b. Installing from the network

This method is useful if you want to install Windows 2000 on several computers. In order to start this method you need to copy the contents of the i386 directory from the CD-ROM to a network share.

Then, you need install only a minimum network management version on the destination machine (for example, network client 3.0 on MS-DOS) so that you will be able to connect to this resource and start the installation using the **WINNT.EXE** command. In addition, you can use the **WINNT32.EXE** command if you are installing Windows 2000 from a 32-bit Microsoft operating system. These commands will create a temporary directory called **Win_nt.~ls** and will copy the Windows 2000 installation files into this temporary directory.

 If you are installing from an MS-DOS client, then you can speed up the installation by running the **smartdrv** program before you run the **winnt.exe** command.

c. Setup switches

The programs **winnt.exe** and **winnt32.exe** allow you to install Windows 2000, or to upgrade to Windows 2000:

Winnt

```
WINNT   [/s[:sourcepath]][/t[:temporary_drive]]
        [/u[:answer_file]] [/udf:id[,UDB_file]]
        [/r:folder] [/r[x]:folder] [/e:command][/a]
```

/s[:sourcepath]

Specifies the location of the Windows 2000 source files. This must be a full path in the format **x:\[path]** or **\\server\share[\path]**.

/t[:temporary_drive]

Specifies the drive that must contain the temporary installation files, and installs Windows 2000 on this drive. If you do not specify a drive, Setup will try to find a drive that has enough free-space.

/u[:answer_file]

Carries out an unattended installation using an answer file. This type of installation requires the switch **/s**. This answer file provides answers to some or all of the questions that the user would normally supply.

/udf:id[,UDB_file]

Indicates an identifier (id) that Setup must use in order to specify how a Uniqueness Database (UDB) file modifies an answer file (see /u). The **/udf** parameter replaces the values in the answer file, and the identifier (id) determines which values in the UDB file must be used. If you do not specify a UDB file, then you must insert a disk that contains the file **$Unique$.udb**.

/r:folder

Allows you to install an additional directory. This folder will remain after the installation is complete.

/rx:folder

Allows you to install an additional directory. This folder will be deleted at the end of the installation.

/e:command

Runs a command at the end of the GUI-mode setup.

/a

Enables accessibility options.

Winnt32

This program allows you either to install, or to upgrade to, Windows 2000 Server or Windows 2000 Professional. You can execute the **winnt32** command from a command prompt on Windows 95, Windows 98 or Windows NT.

```
WINNT32 [/s[:sourcepath]] [/tempdrive:drive_letter]
[/unattend[num]:[answer_file]]
[/copydir:folder_name] [/copysource:folder_name]
[/cmd:command_line]
[/debug[level][filename]]
[/udf:id[,UDB_file]]
[/syspart:drive_letter]
[/checkupgradeonly] [/cmdcons][/m:folder_name]
[/makelocalsource][/noreboot]
```

/s[:sourcepath]

Specifies the location of the Windows 2000 source files. To copy files simultaneously from several servers, you must specify several **/s** sources. If you use several **/s** switches, then the first server that you specify must be available, or else Setup will fail.

/tempdrive:drive_letter

Specifies the partition that must contain the temporary installation files, and installs Windows 2000 on this partition.

/unattend

Upgrades a previous version of Windows 2000, Windows NT 3.51/4.0 or Windows 95/98 in unattended Setup mode. All user settings from the previous installation are preserved. Consequently, the installation requires no user intervention. If you use the **/unattend** switch, then it is assumed that you have read and accepted the end-user license agreement for Windows 2000.

Before you use this switch to install Windows 2000 on behalf of an organization other than your own, you must ensure that the end user (whether it is an individual or the organization itself) has received, read and accepted the terms of the End-User License Agreement (EULA) for Windows 2000. Original Equipment Manufacturers (OEMs) are not allowed to specify this key on machines that they sell to end-users.

/unattend[num]:[answer_file]

Carries out a new installation in unattended Setup mode. The answer file contains the Setup program with your custom specifications. **Num** is the number of seconds that must elapse from the moment when Setup finishes copying the files and the moment when it restarts your computer. You can use the **num** parameter on any computer that is running Windows NT or Windows 2000.

/copydir:folder_name

Creates an additional folder, within the folder in which the Windows 2000 files are installed. For example, suppose that the source folder contains a folder called **local_ drivers** containing modifications that apply only to your site. In this case you can enter **/copydir:local_drivers** in order to indicate to Setup that it must copy this folder into the folder in which it must install Windows 2000. Thus, the folder location will be **c:\winnt\local_drivers**. You can use **/copydir** switches in order to create as many additional folders as you wish.

/copysource:folder_name

Creates an additional, temporary folder, within the folder in which the Windows 2000 files are installed. For example, suppose that the source folder contains a folder called **local_drivers** containing modifications that apply only to your site. In this case you can enter **/copysource:local_drivers** in order to indicate to Setup that it must copy this folder into the folder in which it must install Windows 2000. Thus, the folder location will be **c:\winnt\local_drivers**. Unlike the folders that you create using **/copydir** switches, Setup will delete the **/copysource** folders at the end of the installation.

/cmd:command_line

Allows you to specify that Setup must run a specific command before the final Setup phase. Setup will run this command after the second restart of your computer, after it has collected the configuration details that it needs, and before the end of the Setup.

/debug[level]:[filename]

Creates a debug log at the level that you specify. For example, you could enter: **/debug3:c:\Win2000.log**. By default, the debug log **c:\%windir%\winnt32.log** is created at level 2. The log levels are as follows: 0 severe errors, 1 errors, 2 warnings, 3 information, and 4 detailed debug information. Each level incorporates the levels below it.

/udf:id[,UDB_file]

Indicates that the identifier (id) that is used by Setup in order to specify a uniqueness database file (UDB) will modify an answer file (see the **/unattend** switch). The UDB file replaces values that are in the answer file with those that are contained in the UDB file. The identifier (id) determines the values of the UDB file that will be used.

For example, the switch **/udf:RAS_user, your_company.udb** replaces the parameters that are specified for the RAS_user in the file **your_company.udb**. If you do not specify a UDBfile then Setup asks the user to insert a disk that contains the **$Unique$.udb** file.

/syspart:drive_letter]

Specifies that Setup must copy the installation startup files to a hard disk, that it must mark this hard disk as active and that it must then install the disk on another computer. When you start this other computer, it will automatically start the next Setup phase. If you use the **/syspart** switch, then you must also use the **/tempdrive** switch.

The **winnt32.exe /syspart** switch will run only on a computer that is running Windows NT 3.51/4.0 or Windows 2000. It will not run on Windows 95/98.

/checkupgradeonly

Checks the compatibility of your computer with upgrade to Windows 2000. For upgrades from Windows 95/98, Setup creates a report called **Upgrade.txt** in the Windows installation folder. For upgrades from Windows NT 3.51/4.0, Setup writes the report to the **Winnt32.log** file, in the Windows installation folder.

/cmdcons

This switch adds a **Recovery Console** option to the operating system selection screen. This option allows you to repair an installation that has failed. You can use this command only after Setup has run.

/m:folder_name

This switch specifies that Setup must copy replacement files from an alternative location. Setup searches for the files in this alternative location and, if it finds them, it uses them instead of the files that the default location contains.

/makelocalsource

This switch specifies that Setup must copy all the installation source files to your local hard disk. You can use this switch when you are installing from the CD-ROM so that the installation files will be available when the CD-ROM is no longer available in a later phase of the Setup.

/noreboot

This switch specifies that Setup must not restart the computer when it has completed the phase in which it copies the **winnt32** files. This technique allows you to run another command at this point.

4. Resolving installation problems

You may encounter problems when you are installing. Here are the problems that are the most commonly met:

- Hardware not recognized: check that your components are present in the HCL.
- Antivirus is activated in the BIOS: deactivate virus detection by the BIOS.
- No network interface card is installed: install a virtual network interface card, in order to have connections and a good configuration.
- Cannot join a domain: check the network adapter settings, the name of the domain, the protocol that is used and possibly its addressing. Also, check that a computer account has been created in the domain.
- Not enough disk space: use the installation program to delete the partition and then to recreate it with a suitable size.
- CD-ROM is not supported: change the CD-ROM drive or install via the network.

Windows 2000 Professional

Chapter 3: Deploying installations and applications

A. Deploying installations

1. Setup Manager

a. Introduction

You can automate the installation of Windows 2000 so that you will not have to respond to all the steps of the installation sequences that are in text and in graphic mode. In order to do this, you must create an answer file (or unattended file), which is a file that provides responses to the installation program.

Setup Manager is a graphic utility that allows you to create answer files and UDF files. This utility is part of the Windows 2000 Resource Kit.

b. Creating an answer file

When you have installed the Resource Kit, start the Setup Manager Wizard.

→) Click **Next**.

You must then indicate whether you want to create a **New or Existing Answer File**.

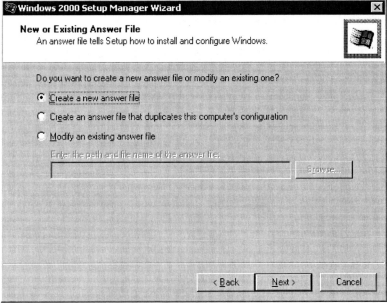

The **Modify an existing answer file** option allows you to develop your deployment by trial and error before you carry it out.

The next dialog box allows you to create a typical answer file for RIS installations (to install Windows 2000 remotely) and for the system preparation tool, **Sysprep**.

These types of installation will be covered later in this chapter.

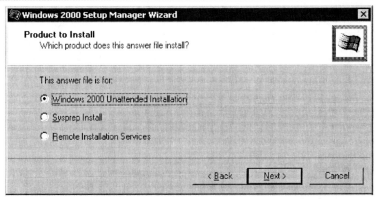

➜) You must then choose the operating system that you want to deploy.

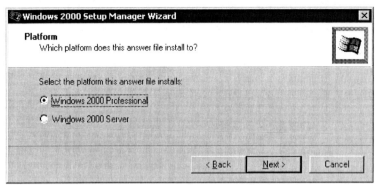

The wizard then asks you to specify how much you want to interact with the installation program.

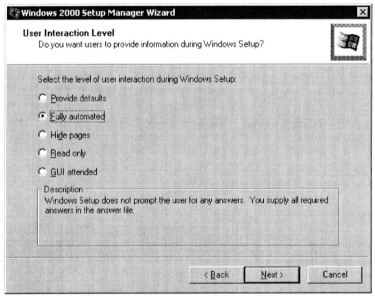

Provide defaults

The wizard systematically suggests the options by default to the user who can correct these options at each stage of the installation.

This method is often useful when the machines in your network are equipped with heterogeneous hardware. It allows the administrator to run the installation automatically, whilst monitoring each step.

Fully automated

This is the most automatic option, as it requires no user intervention. With this method, you must have defined all the installation options in the answer file.

Hide pages

This option allows you to hide the wizard pages from the user during the setup.

Read only

If you do not wish to hide the wizard pages during the setup, this option prevents the user from modifying the options that appear on the screen as the setup runs.

GUI attended

This option allows you to create an answer file for the text-mode sequence.

You must then accept the terms of the **End User License Agreement**.

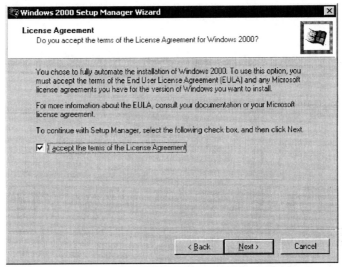

Finally, you must indicate your name and that of your organization.

This new version of **Setupmgr** allows you to generate a UDF *(Uniqueness Database File)*. This is a new feature that the Windows NT Resources Kit did not offer.

To customize the installation of each computer, you can specify the name of each of the destination computers.

Windows 2000 Professional

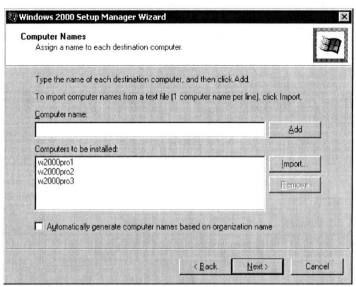

You must also indicate the **Administrator Password** and whether or not the system must automatically log on the administrator, once or more times, when the system starts.

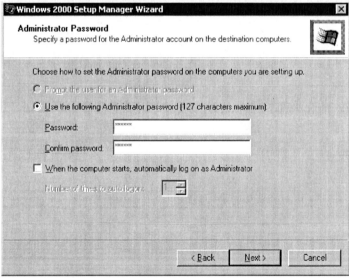

You must indicate the **Display Settings** that you require.

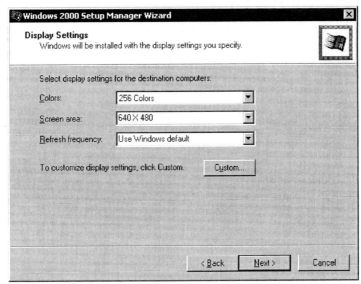

You must then indicate the **Network Settings** that you require.

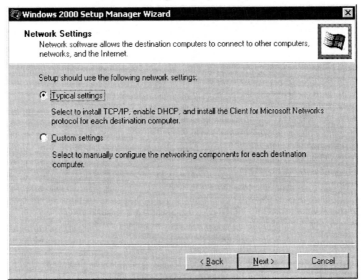

In the next step, you must indicate whether the destination computers must operate in a workgroup, or in a domain (with centralized security). If you choose the latter option then you must indicate the name and the password of a user who is allowed to create a computer object in an Active Directory domain (the right to **Add workstations to domain**).

⊙ You can also choose to add computer objects before the automatic installation phase.

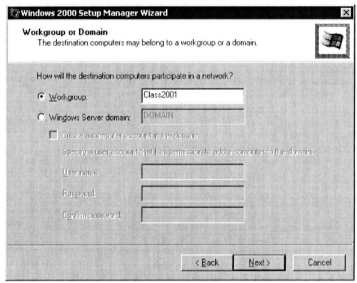

You can then indicate any **Additional Settings** that you require.

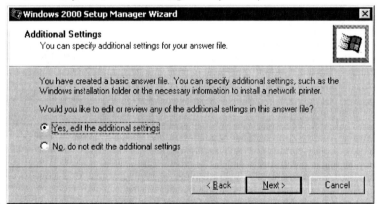

These include telephony settings, regional options, language options, Internet browser configuration and settings to access a Proxy server.

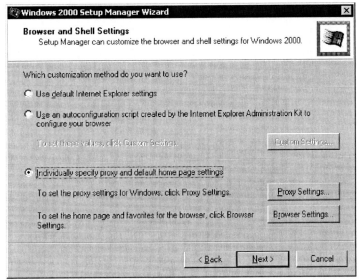

You can then set up the **Installation Folder**.

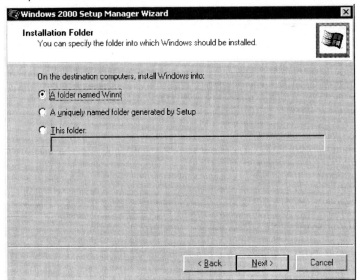

In the next step, you can indicate the path to the location where you want to install a network printer,

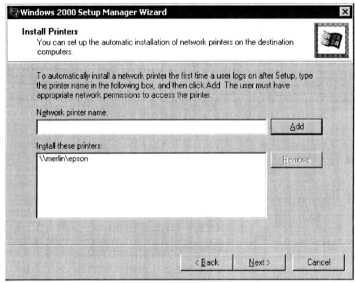

along with the name of a program that Windows will **Run Once** automatically when a user logs on for the first time.

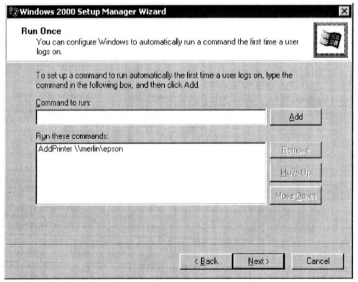

You can also modify the folder that contains distribution files and installation scripts. This file will be shared automatically.

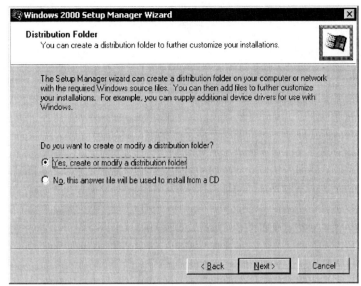

If you choose the **Yes, create or modify a distribution folder** option, then the following screen appears.

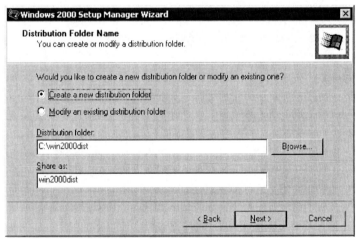

In this case, you can also specify that your automatic set up must:

- add one or more mass storage drivers,
- replace the HAL *(Hardware Abstraction Layer)* which improves system portability by isolating hardware differences,
- run a command at the end of the installation, without waiting for the command to terminate,
- change the logos the installation programs adds,

- copy additional files and folders to the destination computers,
- copy the distribution files from the CD-ROM or from another source (if you chose to create a new distribution folder).

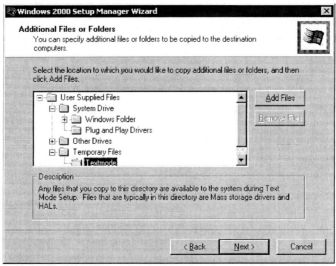

Here is an example of the folder hierarchy that the wizard creates:

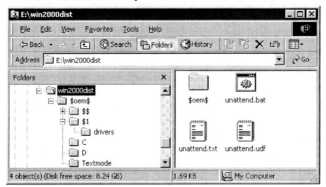

c. The OEM file hierarchy

If the [Unattended] section of the answer file includes the **OemPreinstall=Yes** key, the installation program will examine the **OEM** folder and the **Cmdlines.txt** file. If you specify the **Winnt32 /unattend** switch without an answer file then the installation program will ignore this file hierarchy.

The **OEM** hierarchy allows you to install additional applications and to replace Windows 2000 components.

To create this file hierarchy, you can use the **Setup Manager**. Alternatively, you can create the folders and subfolders manually. The **OEM** root is a subfolder of the **i386** folder.

You can use the **OemFilesPath** key in the [Unattended] section of the answer file to change the location of the **OEM** hierarchy.

OEM

Windows 2000 creates this **OEM** as a subfolder of **i386**. **OEM** contains all the obligatory additional files.

IP can include the optional **Cmdlines.txt** file. This file contains the list of commands that the installation program must run in its graphic phase (GUI-mode setup).

 This approach allows you to install an application, or to run a program such as **sysdiff.exe**, or any other executable program.

OEM\Textmode

This folder contains essential SCSI device drivers or specific HALs.

OEM\$$

This folder is the equivalent of **%Windir%**, for example: **C:\Winnt**.

 This approach allows you to specify additional files in a subfolder, for example **OEM\$$\System32.**

OEM\Drive_letter

This folder contains the folders and files that the installation program will copy into the root of the corresponding drive.

For example, **OEM\D\Dir1** will create the **Dir1** folder into the root of the **D:** disk.

OEM\$1

This folder is equivalent to the drive letter of the partition that contains the operating system. This folder is the equivalent of **%Systemdrive%**.

OEM\$1\Drivers

This folder contains additional device drivers that Windows 2000 does not provide.

d. Examples of generated files

This section contains examples of files that **Setupmgr.exe** generates.

To use these files, you must log on to the remote share and enter the following command:

Unattend W2000Pro1
in which, W2000Pro1 is the name of the first computer that you want to install.

The system will then run the following command:

```
\\MERLIN\win2000dist\winnt32 /s:%SetupFiles%
/unattend:%AnswerFile% /udf:%ComputerName%,
%UdfFile% /makelocalsource
```

for example:

```
winnt32 /s:\\MERLIN/win2000dist /unattend:.
\unattend.txt /udf:W2000PRO1,unattend.udf
/makelocalsource
```

 The server name used here **(MERLIN)** is the name of the server on which you ran **setupmgr.**

Unattend.bat file

```
@rem SetupMgrTag
@echo off
rem
rem This is a SAMPLE batch script generated by the Setup Manager
Wizard.
rem If this script is moved from the location where it was generated,
it may have to be modified.
rem
set AnswerFile=.\unattend.txt
set UdfFile=.\unattend.udf
set ComputerName=%1
set SetupFiles=\\MERLIN\win2000dist
if "%ComputerName%" == "" goto USAGE
\\MERLIN\win2000dist\winnt32    /s:%SetupFiles%    /unattend:%AnswerFile%
/udf:%ComputerName%,%UdfFile% /makelocalsource
goto DONE
:USAGE
echo.
echo Usage: unattend ^<computername^
echo.
:DONE
```

Unattend.txt file

```
;SetupMgrTag

[Data]
    AutoPartition=1
    MsDosInitiated="0"
    UnattendedInstall="Yes"
```

```
[Unattended]
    UnattendMode=FullUnattended
    OemSkipEula=Yes
    OemPreinstall=Yes
    TargetPath=\WINNT

[GuiUnattended]
    AdminPassword=*
    OEMSkipRegional=1
    TimeZone=85
    OemSkipWelcome=1

[UserData]
    FullName=ENI
    OrgName=ENI
    ComputerName=*

[Display]
    BitsPerPel=8
    Xresolution=640
    YResolution=480

[SetupMgr]
    ComputerName0=w2000pro1
    ComputerName1=w2000pro2
    ComputerName2=w2000pro3
    DistFolder=C:\win2000dist
    DistShare=win2000dist

[Branding]
    BrandIEUsingUnattended=Yes

[Proxy]
    Proxy_Enable=0
    Use_Same_Proxy=1

[GuiRunOnce]
    Command0="rundll32 printui.dll,PrintUIEntry /in /n \\merlin\epson"

[Identification]
    JoinWorkgroup=Class2001

[Networking]
    InstallDefaultComponents=Yes
```

⊙ Note that this file contains the administrator's password in clear text!

Unattend.udf file

```
;SetupMgrTag

[UniqueIds]
    w2000pro1=UserData
    w2000pro2=UserData
    w2000pro3=UserData

[w2000pro1:UserData]
    ComputerName=w2000pro1

[w2000pro2:UserData]
    ComputerName=w2000pro2

[w2000pro3:UserData]
    ComputerName=w2000pro3
```

Each section of the UDB file (**unattend.udf** in this case) will replace the equivalent section in the **unattend.txt** file.

2. Using Sysprep and duplicating disks

a. Introduction

In order to install Windows 2000 on a large number of machines, the most efficient technique is disk duplication. This method consists of creating a disk image of a computer on which Windows 2000 has been installed and configured and then restoring it onto the destination machines. The utility that is used to implement this disk duplication is called **sysprep.exe**.

b. Implementing the Windows 2000 deployment

The following sequence must be followed:

- Install and configure Windows 2000 on a computer that is called the reference computer.
- Install the applications on this computer. Do not forget to copy the custom user parameters in the default user profile. In order to do this, right-click **My Computer** and then select **Properties**. Under the **User Profiles** tab, select the profile that you want to use for the software installation and then click the **Copy To** button.

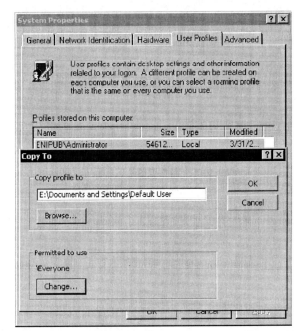

Under **Copy profile to**, enter **%systemdrive%\Documents and Settings\Default User**.

Under **Permitted to use**, select the **Everyone** group.

Run the **sysprep.exe** utility in order to delete all the configuration settings that are specific to a given computer (computer name that must be unique on the network and SID, the unique security identifier). In addition, **sysprep.exe** will install the part of the installation program that asks the user to enter a new computer name. This will be done after the image has been restored on the destination computer, once this computer has been restarted. So that this will be carried out automatically without user intervention, you can create an answer file **sysprep.inf** using the Setup Manager Wizard. This file must be located in the **sysprep** directory, on the system partition along with the files **sysprep.exe** and **se-tupcl.exe**.

Sysprep will run after your computer has restarted. Log on as administrator and then run the following command: **Drive:\sysprep\sysprep.exe** switches.

The switches are as follows:

-quiet	Runs **sysprep.exe** without displaying messages on the screen.
-pnp	Forces plug-and-play to detect and install on the destination computers, hardware items that may be different from those on the reference computer.
-reboot	Forces the destination computers to reboot after installation of the image.

-nosidgen   Runs **sysprep.exe** without generating a unique security identifier. Use this switch if you are not duplicating the hard disk on which you are running **sysprep.exe**.

❱ Important note: **sysprep.exe** does not support Windows 2000 Professional or Windows 2000 Server as a stand-alone server.

❱ Important note: you can install the images only on computers that have the same mass storage device driver and the same hardware abstraction layer (HCL) as the reference computer.

Once the disk has been prepared, the image is ready to be created using a disk duplication utility of a third-party vendor.

❱ For example Norton Ghost. by Symantec, or PowerQuest, by DriveImage.

❱ Important note: You can deploy only Windows 2000 Professional using the Microsoft Remote Installation Service. The tools that other manufacturers offer provide a multicast deployment feature in their latest versions. This means that several machines can receive the installation image simultaneously, rather than each machine receiving a separate copy of the image. This technique reduces network traffic considerably.

3. Using the RIS service of Windows 2000 Server

a. Introduction

The objective of the Microsoft Remote Installation Service (RIS) is to allow users to **deploy an operating system throughout a company without having to install each computer physically**.

b. RIS components

The RIS features simplify remote installation tasks. Client computers can connect to a server, which supplies them with a version of Windows 2000 Professional.

In order to provide this feature, the RIS uses a number of components. This chapter will describe each of these components and explain how these components interact with each other.

Here are the essential components that the RIS requires:
− Active Directory and group policies
− Dynamic Domain Name Service (DDNS)
− Dynamic Host Configuration Protocol (DHCP) Service
− Remote Information Service (RIS)
− services and tools associated with the RIS.

Active Directory, group policies and DDNS

Windows 2000 manages the distributed domain database using Active Directory. Advanced group policy management and inheritance management ensure Active Directory security.

This directory database runs on the DDNS service. DDNS stores the IP addresses of network hosts. It acts as a veritable server that registers the services available on the network (for example, the catalog server and the domain controllers).

DHCP service

A DHCP server must be available on the network. The DHCP server allows a client to obtain an IP address and to download its configuration from the RIS server, via the network.

Services associated with the RIS

When you install Remote Installation Services, you add the following items automatically:
- **Boot Information Negotiation Layer** (BINL)

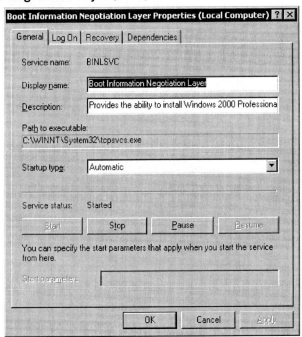

This service answers client requests. It consults the Active Directory in order to check whether or not the client has sufficient rights. In addition, it allows you to assign settings that are suitable for the client during the installation phase.
- **Trivial File Transfer Protocol Daemon** (TFTPD)

This is a fast service that runs in connectionless mode. It allows clients to download specific files. In particular it allows clients to download the **Client Installation Wizard** (CIW) along with all its dialog boxes.

- **Single Instance Store** (SIS)

The SIS reduces the amount of disk space that the RIS volume requires for its installation images. When you install RIS as an optional component, you must specify an installation drive-letter and directory. This is the RIS volume. An SIS agent tracks the RIS volume automatically in order to check for duplicate images. When it finds a duplicate file it copies the file to the SIS and replaces the file by a link, saving disk space.

Tools associated with the RIS

RIS installation program (RISetup.exe)

RIS is an optional Windows 2000 Server component. You must set up this service in two steps.

First, you must install this optional component. Then, after you have restarted your machine you must configure your RIS server using the **RISetup** program (by indicating storage volume and image settings, for example).

- **Setup and administration options**

By default, a RIS server is not operational immediately after you have installed it. To configure a RIS server, you must follow four steps.

You must:
- authorize the RIS server in the **DHCP** snap-in,
- authorize each server individually in the Active Directory Users and Computers snap-in,
- define the global policies in the **Group Policy** tool, in order to specify the installation options that the **Client Installation Wizard (CIW)** will offer to particular user groups,
- use Security Descriptors, or Discretionary Access Control Lists (DACLs) in order to specify which users will be able to access the images that the RIS server offers. In addition, you can assign specific rights to particular groups in the unattended installation setup answer files (.sif files). This technique allows you to force the client's choice, or at least to restrict it.

Client Installation Wizard

Once your client machine has connected to the RIS server, the system invites you to press the F12 function key. Then, you must follow the Active Directory authentication procedure (by supplying your username, password and domain name). The **Client Installation Wizard** starts up and displays a menu, the options of which will depend on your user rights.

```
┌─────────────────────────────────────────────────────────────┐
│ Client Installation Wizard                        Main Menu  │
│                                                              │
│  Use the arrow keys to select one of the following options:  │
│                                                              │
│     ▌Automatic Setup                                         │
│      Custom Setup                                            │
│      Restart a previous Setup attempt                        │
│      Maintenance and Troubleshooting                         │
│                                                              │
│                                                              │
│                                                              │
│                                                              │
│  Description:  This is the easiest way to install an operating system │
│  on your computer. Most installation options are already configured by│
│  your network administrator.                                 │
│                                                              │
│  [ENTER] continue          [F1] help        [F3] restart computer │
└─────────────────────────────────────────────────────────────┘
```

Remote Installation Preparation Wizard (RIPrep.exe)

When you install Windows 2000 using the RIS, you can work either with images from the installation CD-ROM or with Sysprep images for RIS (using the **RIPrep.exe** program).

You can access this tool in the share that you set up when you installed the RIS server.

🔘 This program requires the **imirror.dll** dynamic link library.

As with Sysprep, the RIPrep tool allows you to produce an installation image that does not contain any unique identifiers. Unlike Sysprep images, the system writes the RIPrep image directly on the RIS server. A RIPrep image can be only that of a Windows 2000 Professional operating system.

🔘 You can run **RIPrep** only on a Windows 2000 Professional system.

Creating a RIS boot diskette (rbfg.exe)

You can boot two types of computer remotely:

– computers that are equipped with **PXE** (**Pre-boot eXecution Environment**) Remote Boot ROM

- computers that are equipped with a network interface card that the remote boot diskette supports

The **rbfg.exe** program allows you to generate a remote boot diskette.

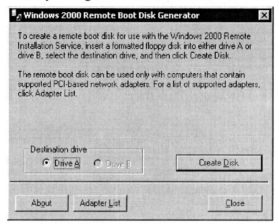

c. Overview of PXE and remote booting

When a PXE client starts up, it must follow two steps:
- it must obtain an IP address from a DHCP server,
- it must locate the PXE boot server (the RIS server in this case), which must return the files that the client needs in order to boot.

The client/server dialog will differ according to the following two server configurations:
- the RIS service and the DHCP service are configured on the same server,
- the RIS service and the DHCP service are configured on different servers.

RIS and DHCP run on the same server

The client/server dialog is more concise when the RIS and DHCP services are on the same server. This is because DHCP calls a local RIS server. The RIS then uses the BINL (*Boot Information Negotiation Layer*) in order to negotiate with remote boot clients.

The DHCP server asks the RIS server if it would like to add its own information to the **DHCP Offer** (DHCP transmits **DHCP Offers** to client that request them using a **DHCP Discover** query).

This technique allows the server to send to the client an IP address and a PXE server reference. In this way, when the server asks for an IP address it receives the address of a PXE server as well.

The client/server dialog takes place as follows:

DHCP Discover

The client looks for a DHCP server in order to obtain a complete IP configuration and other settings such as the address of a PXE boot server.

DHCP Offer

The DHCP/RIS server offers the client an IP address and the address of a PXE boot server (its own address).

DHCP Request

The client responds to the offer from the DHCP/RIS server.

DHCP Ack

The DHCP server confirms its offer. This packet contains the assigned IP address, the IP address of the RIS server, the name of the RIS server and the first download file.

RIS and DHCP are on different servers

The RIS and DHCP servers are assumed to be on the same subnet.
In this case, the client/server dialog takes place as follows:

DHCP Discover

The client looks for a DHCP server in order to obtain a complete IP configuration and other settings such as the address of a PXE boot server.

DHCP Offer (1)

The DHCP server offers an IP address to the client.

DHCP Offer (2)

The RIS server offers the client the address of the PXE boot server.

DHCP Request

The client responds to the IP address offer of the DHCP server.

DHCP Ack

The DHCP server confirms the IP address offer.

Note that the client does not respond to the offer from the RIS server (DHCP Offer) with the expected query (DHCP Request) in either case. The client gives priority to the DHCP query that offers an IP address rather than the DHCP query that contains the address of a PXE server. Ideally, the client receives both pieces of information at the same time (in the case where the RIS server is the same as the DHCP server).

Once the client has received an IP address, it tries to localize the RIS server with a further **DHCP Discover** query.

DHCP Discover

Although the client now has an IP address, it still has to obtain the address of a PXE boot server.

DHCP Offer (1)

The DHCP server offers the same IP address to the client.

DHCP Offer (2)

The RIS server offers the client the address of the PXE boot server.

DHCP Request

This time, the client responds to the offer from the RIS server.

DHCP Ack

The RIS server confirms its offer. It sends to the client its RIS IP address, its name and the first file that the client must request with a TFTP (Trivial File Transfer Protocol) query.

> ◐ This is normally the **startrom.com** file.

The PXE client now has an IP address, it has located the boot server and it can download the file that it needs in order to boot remotely. When it has downloaded the file, a message appears that invites the user to press the F12 key to boot from the network.

4. Hardware requirements for clients and servers

This section describes the hardware configuration that clients and servers require in order to implement Remote Installation Services.

Server configuration

- 166 MHz, Pentium II processor (200 MHz, Pentium is recommended).
- At least 64 MB of RAM (if you configure DNS, DHCP and Active Directory, then you will need 96 MB, or even 128 MB of RAM).
- Allow 2 GB of disk space for the RIS Server hierarchy on a separate partition from that which contains the system files.
- Network Interface Card of at least 10 Mbps (100 Mbps are recommended).

> ◐ You are recommended to use a dedicated fast disk subsystem (SCSI).

Client configuration

- 166 MHz, Pentium II processor, or greater.
- At least 32 MB of RAM.
- A hard disk of at least 1.2 GB.

- A DHCP, PXE-based bootable ROM, version .99c, or greater, or a network interface card that the RIS boot diskette supports.

The next section lists the network interface cards that the RIS boot disk supports. This list contains only PCI Ethernet network interface cards. You can generate a boot diskette using the **rbfg.exe** tool. This tool is available in the RIS server in the **\remoteinstall\admin\i386** subfolder. The **\remoteinstall** folder is shared on the RIS server under the name of **REMINST**.

List of network interface cards that the boot diskette supports

3Com: 3c900 (Combo and TP0), 3c900B (Combo, FL, TPC, TP0), 3c905 (T4 and TX), 3c905B (Combo, TX, FX)

AMD: AMD PCNet and Fast PC Net

Compaq: Netflex 100 (NetIntelligent II), Netflex 110 (NetIntelligent III)

Digital Equipment Corporation: DE 450, DE 500

Hewlett Packard: HP Deskdirect 10/100 TX

Intel: Intel Pro 10+, Intel Pro 100+, Intel Pro 100B (including the E100 series)

SMC: SMC 8432, SMC 9332, SMC 9432

> At the time of publication, the RIS boot diskette supported neither ISA cards, nor EISA cards, nor Token Ring cards.

a. Setting up the Remote Installation Service

This section describes the procedure for installing RIS in a Windows 2000 Server domain environment. In order to run correctly, your RIS server will need the presence of a Dynamic DNS (DDNS).

> For example, you could install the Windows 2000 server as a stand-alone server, add the DNS service, set up the Active Directory using the **dcpromo** tool and assign the domain controller role to the server.

Overview of the RIS setup procedure

Here are the steps that you must follow to implement the Remote Installation Service.

1 - Check that your client and server configurations meet the hardware and software requirements.

2 - Install and configure a DHCP server on the network with an active scope. The Active Directory must authorize this server to distribute IP addresses.

3 - Install the Remote Installation Service on the server.

4 - Configure the Remote Installation Service: indicate an OS image, either from a Windows 2000 Professional CD-ROM or using the **RIPrep** tool. The Active Directory must also authorize this server.

5 - Define the authorizations of client computers and the users that the RIS must recognize.

Installing the RIS (Remote Installation Service)

RIS is an optional Windows 2000 component. To set up this service you must follow two steps.

First, you must install this optional component. To do this, open the **Control Panel - Add/Remote Programs - Add/Remove Windows Components**. In the **Components** box, select **Remote Installation Services**.

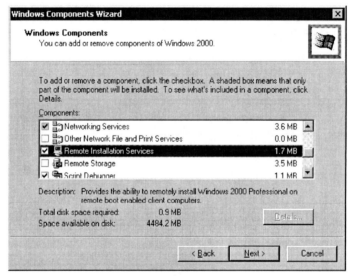

Configuring the RIS (Remote Installation Service)

Upon restart, your server may prompt you to carry out the next step directly with the **Windows 2000 Configure Your Server** tool. Alternatively, you can start this **RISetup.exe** program by entering this name in the **Start - Run** dialog box.

By default however, the **Windows 2000 Configure Your Server** dialog box will appear upon restart. This dialog box will tell you that you have installed certain components, but that you have not yet configured them.

If you click the **Finish setup** link, then the **Add/Remote Programs** dialog box re-appears.

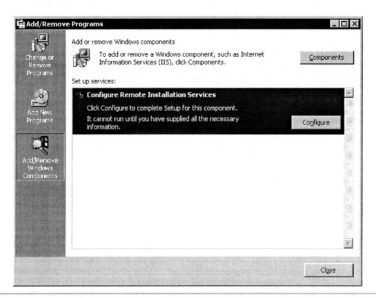

⊙ If your RIS server is not a domain controller, then you must first include it in a domain and configure it as a DNS client. Finally, you must log on to the domain before continuing to set up your RIS server.

In the next step, the **Remote Installation Services Setup Wizard** asks you to indicate the path to the folder that must contain the installation images and the RIS tools.

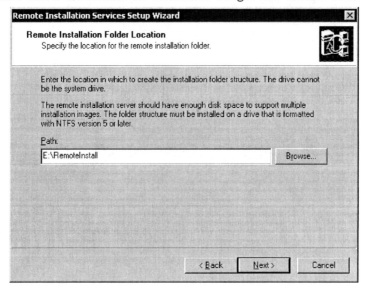

⏺ Important note: You cannot designate the Windows 2000 Server system drive as your RIS drive.

Then, you must indicate the level of **Client support** that you require.

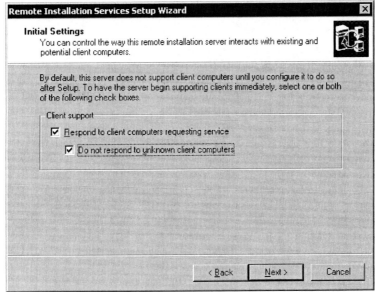

The first option in this dialog box allows you to indicate whether or not the RIS server must respond to client requests immediately after you have finished configuring it.

Changing the RIS server configuration

You can change the configuration of your RIS server later, by accessing its **Properties** in the Active Directory Users and Computers snap-in.

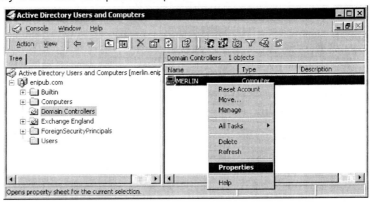

The **Remote Install** page allows you to specify that the RIS must **Respond to client compu-ters requesting service**.

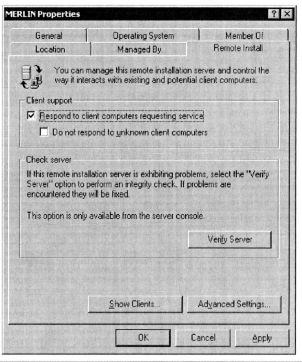

⊙ Important note: This setting is not sufficient to allow client computers to access the RIS. In addition, the client machines must be authorized in the Active Directory.

The **Do not respond to unknown client computers** option allows you to prevent the RIS server from responding to clients that do not have an Active Directory account.

Windows 2000 will create a computer account using the naming format that you specify on the **New Clients** page of the computer's **Remote-Installation-Services Properties** dialog box. To access this page, click the **Advanced Settings** button under the **Remote Install** tab.

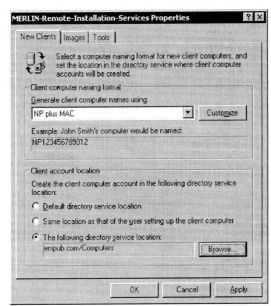

The above example specifies that Windows 2000 must generate a computer account using the MAC address of the network interface card (the network interface card that the RIS boot diskette uses).

The following example shows a computer account, whose name is based on the MAC address of its network adapter (which the RIS remote boot disk will use). This account name is **NP0050DA84CB6E**, for example, where 0050DA84CB6E is the MAC address of the 3Com PCI network adapter.

In addition, the Global Unique Identifier / Universal Unique Identifier (**GUID/UUID**) is also based on the MAC address of the network adapter.

You must code this identifier on 16 bytes (32 hexadecimal symbols from 0 to F). This identifier relates either to the PXE client (BIOS) or to the MAC address of the network adapter. In the latter case, to form the GUID, you must add leading zeros to the MAC address (20 zeros in this case) to make up the 32 characters of this identifier. The "Creating a computer account for a RIS client" section later on in this chapter describes how to create this account.

RIS configuration buttons

The **Remote Install** page provides three configuration buttons. The **Advanced Settings** button allows you to configure the properties of the server. The **Show Clients** button allows you to view the current clients. The **Verify Server** button allows you to check your RIS server.

Verify Server

This button allows you to start up the **Check Server Wizard** in order to carry out elementary checks. If the wizard finds any problems, it writes them to the **Event Viewer**.

After the welcome screen, you can start the tests.

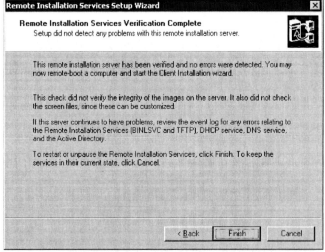

When it has finished testing, you can close the wizard.

Show Clients

This button allows you to view clients that are associated with your RIS server.

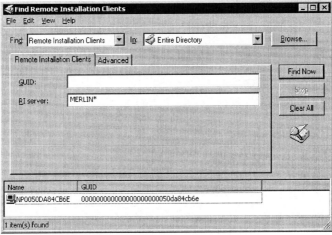

Advanced Settings

This button opens the server's **Remote-Installation-Services Properties** dialog box, which has three tabs: **New Clients**, **Images** and **Tools**.

The **New Clients** page allows you to specify the name of the Active Directory account that the RIS will user for its clients. You can indicate if the system must create the account in the default container (**Windows**) or in another container.

You must check that the user account that you specified at the beginning of the RIS installation has sufficient rights in the Active Directory in order to create the computer account.

The **Images** page shows the list of available installation images and allows you to add new images to this list.

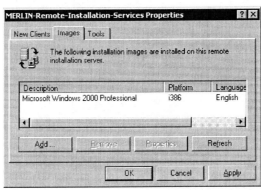

In addition, you can add a new answer file to an existing image.

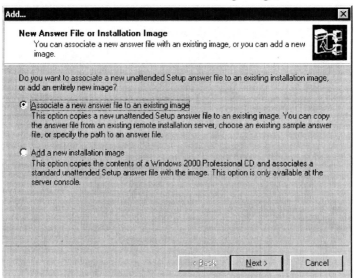

The following screen appears when you choose this first option:

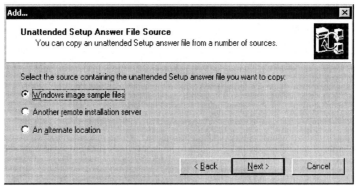

If you choose the second option, then the system will display the **RISetup.exe** screens.

When you have set up the image(s), you can add a certain number of tools that will help you to deploy and install the operating system.

This feature is useful for ISVs *(Independent Software Vendors)* or OEMs *(Original Equipment Manufacturers)* who want to provide their own maintenance and trouble-shooting tools for administrators, technical support personnel or the users of the client machines during the installation phase.

As the hard disks of the destination machines must be empty when you start installing the operating system, these tools can be very useful.

This tools provide a simple means of updating client machines before starting the installation (for BIOS updates in Flash memory, for example).

The **Tools** page of the server's **Remote-Installation-Services Properties** dialog box shows the list of any OEM tools that are currently installed.

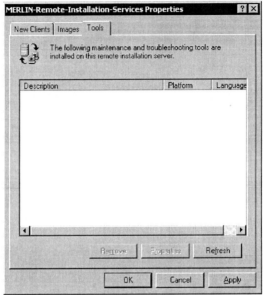

This page offers three actions that allow you to work on this list.

Remove

This button allows you to delete the Template Setup Information (SIF) file that is associated with the selected tool. This file contains a description of the tool for the user.

If you select a tool and then press this button, Windows 2000 will delete the tool's SIF file and the client installation wizard will no longer offer this tool.

Properties

This button displays information on the features of the selected tool.

Refresh

This button refreshes the contents of this page.

The **Tools** page of the server's Remote-Installation-Services Properties dialog box does not allow you to add tools. ISVs and the OEMs provide external installation programs that add their own tools into the **\RemoteInstall** hierarchy. When these programs add tools, they appear on the **Tools** page and the client installation wizard will offer them to the user.

Authorizing the RIS server in the Active Directory

In the Active Directory, you must authorize the computer(s) that run the DHCP and RIS services.

⊙ If your RIS and DHCP services run on the same machine, then you do not need to authorize the machine twice. In fact, you authorize at server level using the **DHCP** snap-in (for both DHCP and RIS).

1 - Firstly, check that you are the **Administrator** of the domain in which you configured the RIS server.

2 - Then, open the **DHCP** snap-in in order to authorize the server concerned.

⊙ Initially, the server is not authorized to provide IP addresses as a DHCP server, or to respond to clients with DHCP Offers as a RIS server.

You must authorize each of the computers concerned. If the server is not authorized, it appears in the console with a red down-arrow.

To authorize the server in the Active Directory, right-click the server concerned and choose the **Authorize** option.

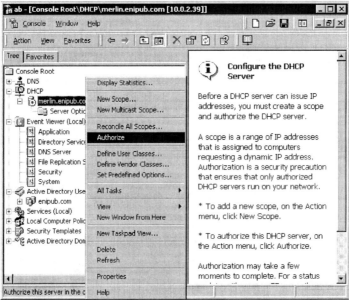

To check that Windows 2000 has authorized the server correctly, right-click **DHCP** and choose the **Manage authorized servers** option.

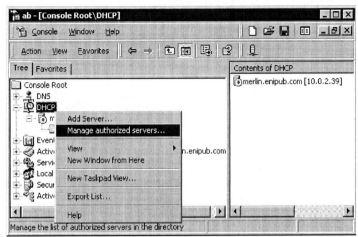

The **Manage Authorized Servers** dialog box appears.

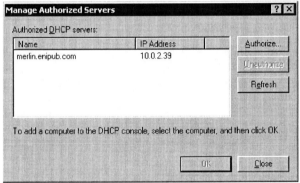

Check that your server appears in the **Authorized DHCP servers** list (the green up-arrow on the server in the DHCP snap-in may take a few minutes to appear).

If the RIS service and the DHCP service run on separate computers, then you must carry out this operation for both machines.

b. Configuring installation images with RIPrep

You can use RIPrep to duplicate an installation image of a Windows 2000 Professional client computer on a remote Windows 2000 RIS server. This image can contain specific settings and applications. This technique can help you to deploy Windows 2000 Professional workstations in a company.

This approach allows you to create a different image for each user group (for Accountants, Secretaries and Design Office groups, for example). You can define specific application programs for each group.

When you deploy your workstations (to make clean installs) the clients will download these images, using either a PXE Remote Boot Rom, or a diskette that you generated with the **rbfg.exe** program.

Prerequisites

As the client starts the download in the text mode installation phase, RIPrep allows the clients to have different hardware configurations (such as the boot devices that they contain).

❯ RIPrep is merely a Sysprep tool that duplicates Windows 2000 Professional installation images.

However, RIPrep has a certain number of usage constraints. You can use RIPrep to create an image only if you respect the following conditions:
- you must have created the first client using the RIS.

❯ This means that you must have created the first installation image from a CD-ROM using RISetup.

Once you have installed the first workstation with RIS, you can implement any application on this workstation. You can take into account any company policies. You can define specific screen colors, you can display a specific background image (such as the company's logo) and you can configure a proxy server in order to access the Internet.
- The RIS server must contain at least one image that you have created from a CD-ROM, so that clients can obtain system files later.
- Only one partition is allowed (the **C:** drive). This means that a single partition must contain the operating system and all the applications.
- The source computer and the destination computers must run on the same Hardware Abstraction Layer (HAL). In addition, either they must all be equipped with the ACPI (*Advanced Configuration and Power Interface*) or none of them must be equipped with this interface.
- On each of the destination client computers the size of the local disk must be at least that of the installation image that the RIS server stores.
- When you create the image, the reference client must not contain any encrypted (*Encrypted File System*) files.

Preparing your remote installation with RIPrep

1 - First, you must install Windows 2000 Professional using a version that your RIS server contains: from a PXE client, connect to the RIS server and deploy your first machine. This will be your reference machine.

❯ You must have copied the first shared version on the RIS server from a CD-ROM, using RISetup.

2 - On this reference machine, install and configure locally all the applications to associate with the profile that you want to create. For example, you may want your *Accountants* profile to include the Office pack, Internet access via a proxy server and a specific screen background.

3 - Start the RIPrep program. Firstly, the RIPrep program will delete all the unique identifiers of the workstation. Then RIPrep will start creating a duplicate installation image on the RIS server.

When you install the Remote Installation Service, the system shares the necessary tools along with a first installation image from the Windows 2000 Professional CD-ROM.

Access the RIS server and run the RIPrep.exe program, for an x86 platform, for example: **\\RIS_Server_Name\Reminst\i386\RIPrep.exe.**

4 - Next, you must indicate the name of your RIS server. The server on which you are running **RIPrep** appears as the server name by default.

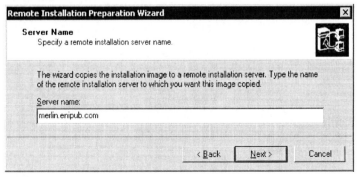

5 - Enter the name of the folder into which the wizard must copy the installation image. By default, this folder will be a subfolder of the **\\RISservername\ REMINST\Setup***SystemLanguage***\Images** network path.

> Note that the subfolder under **Setup** corresponds to your system language: **English** for example.

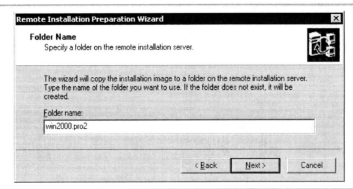

> The Windows 2000 Professional machine image that the **RIPrep** program uses must have been created using the RIS. Consequently, if you are using only one RIS server then this server must contain this reference image. In the example above, **win2000.pro2** was chosen as the folder name, as the **win2000.pro** image already exists.

6 - Next, enter a **Friendly description** along with a **Help text** in order to assist users to choose an installation image.

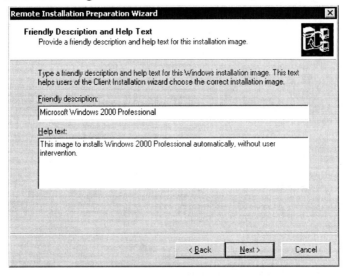

You may use only standard OEM ASCII characters in these text boxes. If you attempt to use extended ASCII characters, the following message appears:

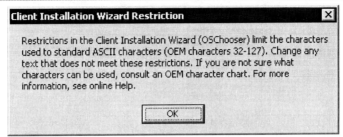

Client Installation Wizard Restriction

Restrictions in the Client Installation Wizard (OSChooser) limit the characters used to standard ASCII characters (OEM characters 32-127). Change any text that does not meet these restrictions. If you are not sure what characters can be used, consult an OEM character chart. For more information, see online Help.

OK

7 - The **Review Settings** dialog box allows you to check your entries.

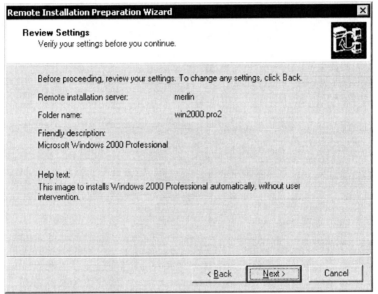

Remote Installation Preparation Wizard

Review Settings
Verify your settings before you continue.

Before proceeding, review your settings. To change any settings, click Back.

Remote installation server: merlin

Folder name: win2000.pro2

Friendly description:
Microsoft Windows 2000 Professional

Help text:
This image to installs Windows 2000 Professional automatically, without user intervention.

< Back   Next >   Cancel

8 - Click **Next** twice in order to begin the image preparation.

The wizard implements the new installation image on the RIS server and then shuts down the computer.

c. Installing the remote operating system on the client computers

Defining client authorizations

To allow the clients to receive a remote installation you must define their rights.

You must assign to these clients the right to **Log on as a batch job**.

→) Access the **Active Directory Users and Computers** snap-in, right-click the **Domain Controllers** container, select the **Properties** option and access the **Group Policy** tab.

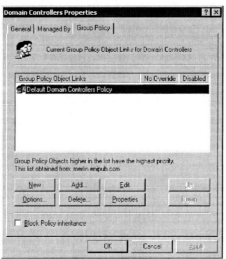

→) Click the **Edit** button to access the **Default Domain Controllers Policy**.

→) In the **Group Policy** console, expand the Tree to display the **Users Rights Assignments**, right-click the **Log on as a batch job** policy and choose the **Security** option.

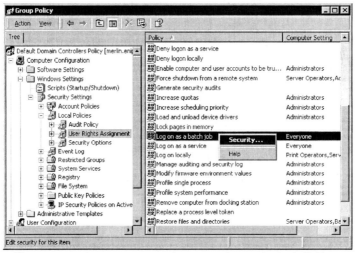

→) Add any specific groups whose users must carry out remote installations.

→) Close the **Group Policy** console.

To ensure that Windows 2000 will apply these settings rapidly, open a command prompt and enter the following command:
Secedit/**refreshpolicy machine_policy**

The system may display a message to tell you that it may take a few minutes to apply these settings.

The security settings that you define on a domain controller using the **Group Policy** console may not take effect immediately. The **secedit** command allows you to speed up the application of your settings.

The system writes a message to the **Application** log of the **Event Viewer** when it has applied your modifications.

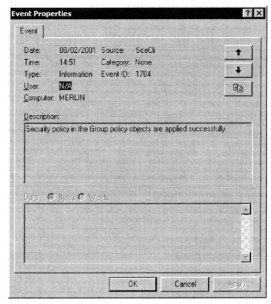

Customizing the client

Even when you have authorized the users to use the RIS, as administrator, you must also ensure that they have the right to create computers in the container that is specified in the RIS server properties.

For this specific container, you must grant users the right to add computers to the domain.

In the **Active Directory Users and Computers** console, right-click the new client computers and select the **Delegate Control** option.

A wizard appears that allows you to select the users who must be able to install their computers using the RIS.

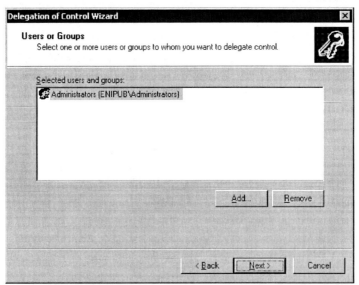

→) Next, you must authorize the user group(s) concerned to **Create, delete, and manage user accounts** in this container.

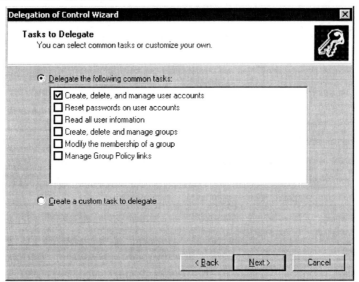

→) Finally, you must confirm your settings.

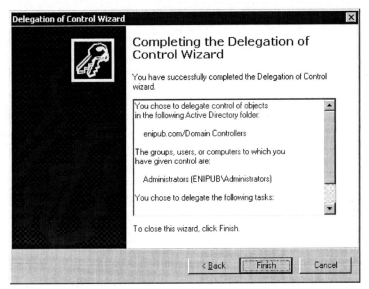

Customizing the Welcome screen

You can configure the operating system of the RIS server so that it will offer you a choice of several languages. In addition, you can customize the Welcome screen during the client installation phase. For this purpose, you can use the Multilanguage Welcome screen that the remote server provides at the following path:
\\RISservername\REMINST\OSChooser\multilng.osc.

```
<OSCML>
<META KEY=ENTER HREF="LOGIN"
<META KEY=F3 ACTION="REBOOT"
<TITLE> Client Installation Wizard
Multilanguage Welcome Example </TITLE>
<FOOTER> Select a language and press [ENTER] to continue </FOOTER>
<BODY left=5 right=75>
<BR>
<BR>
Select a language from the list below. The language you select determi-
nes which language-specific operating system choices and tools are
offered for installation.
<BR>
<FORM ACTION="WELCOME">
<SELECT NAME="LANGUAGE"> SIZE=4>
<OPOTION VALUE="ENGLISH"> English
<OPTION VALUE="GERMAN"> Deutsch
<OPTION VALUE="SPANISH"> Espanol
<OPTION VALUE="FRENCH"> Francais
</SELECT>
```

```
</FORM>
<BR>
NOTE TO ADMINISTRATORS:   This file is an example of a multilanguage
Welcome screen. By using a multilanguage Welcome screen, you can host
multiple languages of an operating system (OS) on a remote installation
server, yet present only the language-specific OS options. When a user
selects a language, the remote installation service presents a list of
operating systems that match the chosen language. You need to ensure
that the languages listed above are available as images on the remote
installation servers on your network.
</BODY>
</OSCML>
```

Moreover, you can modify the text of the Welcome screen, in the **welcome.osc** file that the RIS server provides in the same folder:

```
<OSML>
<META KEY=ENTER HREF="LOGIN">
<META KEY=F3 ACTION="REBOOT">
<META KEY=ESC HREF="LOGIN">
<META KEY=F1 HREF="LOGIN">
<TITLE> Client Installation Wizard
Welcome</TITLE>
<FOOTER> [ENTER] continue </FOOTER>
<BODY left=5 right=75>
<BR>
<BR>
<BR>
Welcome  to  the  Client  Installation  wizard.  This  wizard  helps  you
quickly and easily set up a new operating system on your computer. You
can  also  use  this  wizard  to  keep  your  computer  up-to-date  and  to
troubleshoot computer hardware problems.
<BR>
<BR>
In  the  wizard,  you  are  asked  to  use  a  valid  user  name,  password,  and
domain  name  to  log  on  to  the  network.  If  you  do  not  have  this
information, contact your network administrator before continuing.
</BODY>
</OSCML>
```

Restricting access to the installation images

You can restrict user access to the RIS installation images in two ways:

- either using the **Group Policy**
- or by defining the access rights in the RIS server file hierarchy, notably in the **\templates** folders of the images concerned.

Using the Group Policy

→) Access the **Active Directory Users and Computers** console, right-click the **Domain Controllers** container, select the **Properties** option and access the **Group Policy** tab.

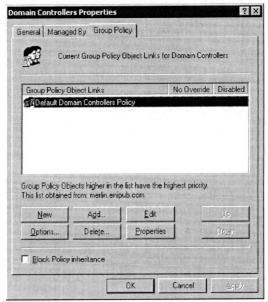

→) Click the **Edit** button to access the **Default Domain Controllers Policy**.

→) The **Group Policy** console appears.

→) Expand the Tree to access **User Configuration - Windows Settings - Security Settings - Remote Installation Services**.

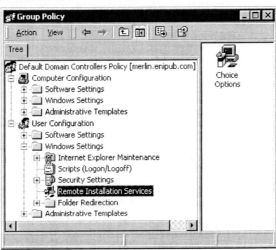

➜ In the right-hand pane, double click **Choice Options** to define your configuration.

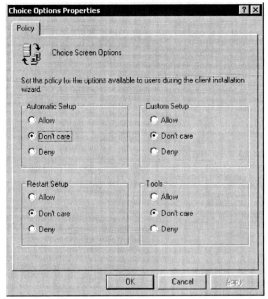

For each of the installation options, you must select one of three choices:

Allow

    The client installation wizard will offer this option to the users to whom this policy applies.

Don't care

    In this case, the policy settings of the parent container will apply. For example, if the domain administrator has defined a specific Group Policy for the RIS, then this option will apply the domain policy to all the users that this policy affects.

Deny

    The client installation wizard will not offer this option.

Defining access rights on installation files and folders

You can also assign specific permissions to users and groups in the RIS server file hierarchy.

For example, if you set explicit permissions on the **SIF** files of a specific installation image, then the client installation wizard will allow only the access that these permissions define.

🌓 Each Windows 2000 Professional CD-ROM image is associated with a **\templates** folder that contains the unattended installation data (SIF) files. By adjusting the permissions on these folders, you can authorize or prohibit certain types of installation.

If you did not specify any unattended setup answer file, then the **\templates** folder will contain only the standard answer file: **ristndrd.sif**.

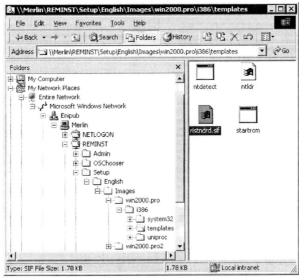

➔) To define specific permissions, right-click the file concerned, select the **Properties** option and access the **Security** tab.

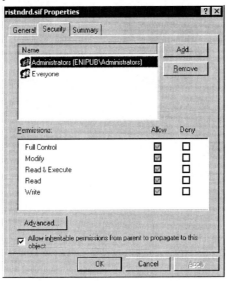

Generating remote boot disks

The Remote Boot Disk Generator tool allows you to generate a remote boot disk that will act as a PXE client.

When you boot the remote computer on this diskette, it first becomes a DHCP client, then it becomes a RIS client and finally it downloads the installation startup program, **startrom.com** from the RIS server via TFTP.

This installation startup program then starts the **Client Installation Wizard** (CIW).

Creating a remote boot disk

Connect to the RIS server share (in the example below this is **\\merlin**). Then, access the subfolder that contains the RIS administration tools, including **rbfg.exe**, the **Remote Boot Disk Generator**.

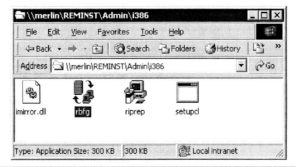

⊙ You can start this tool from any computer.

→) Start this program.

It provides the list of Ethernet PCI network adapters that it supports.

Windows 2000 Professional

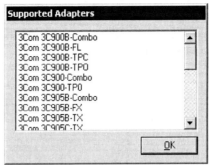

➜) Insert a formatted diskette into the floppy disk drive and click the **Create Disk** button.

The procedure takes only a few seconds to run.

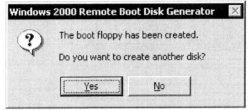

It produces a bootable diskette that contains a small binary file.

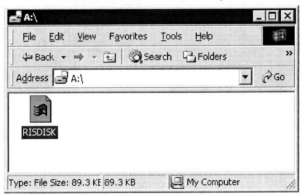

Client Installation Wizard

Once your client machine has connected to the RIS server, the system invites the user to press the F12 function key.

The system then loads the **Client Installation Wizard** onto the client machine.

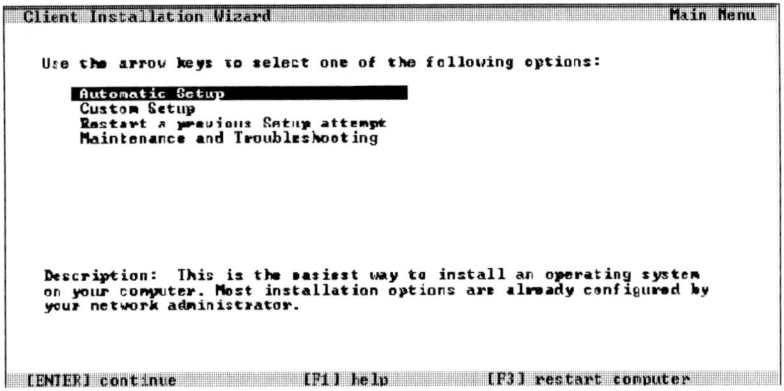

```
┌─────────────────────────────────────────────────────────────────┐
│ Client Installation Wizard                          Main Menu     │
│                                                                    │
│   Use the arrow keys to select one of the following options:      │
│                                                                    │
│      Automatic Setup                                               │
│      Custom Setup                                                  │
│      Restart a previous Setup attempt                              │
│      Maintenance and Troubleshooting                               │
│                                                                    │
│                                                                    │
│                                                                    │
│                                                                    │
│   Description: This is the easiest way to install an operating system │
│   on your computer. Most installation options are already configured by │
│   your network administrator.                                      │
│                                                                    │
│                                                                    │
│ [ENTER] continue          [F1] help          [F3] restart computer │
└─────────────────────────────────────────────────────────────────┘
```

The user must supply username and password and specify the domain name. Once Windows 2000 has authenticated the user's logon request in the Active Directory, the **Client Installation Wizard** allows the user to choose from the available images and menus, according to the level of permissions that you defined, as administrator.

If you authorized the user to carry out only an automatic setup for a given image, then the wizard will display only the confirmation menu and the summary screens.

The different options that the Client Installation Wizard provides are described below.

🔵 By default, the Client Installation Wizard offers automatic setup.

The RIS authorizes or refuses access to the different options according to the Group Policy that you defined.

In the example that the _Restricting access to the installation images" section described above, the administrator configured the remote installation restrictions in the **Default Domain Controllers Policy**.

→) In the **Active Directory Users and Computers** console, access the **Properties** of the **Domain Controllers** container, activate the **Group Policy** tab and click the **Edit** button to access the **Default Domain Controllers Policy**.

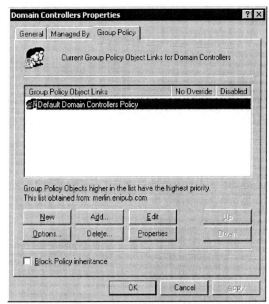

→) Expand the Tree to access the **Remote Installation Services**.

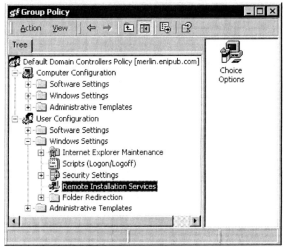

Then, double click **Choice Options** to define your own configuration.

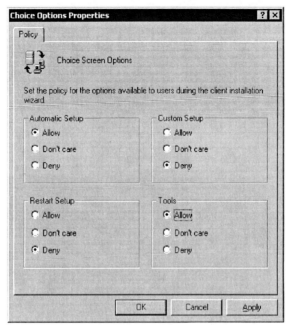

This dialog box allows you to choose the items that the CIW menus will offer to the user during the installation phase.

Automatic Setup

This is the most flexible installation option. It allows the user to choose an operating system to install but it does not allow the user to choose any configuration options. If only one operating system is available, then the CIW starts the automatic setup automatically without requesting any user intervention.

Custom Setup

This option allows the user to choose an alternative name for the computer that will be created in the Active Directory. It also allows the user to choose an alternative directory service location from that which the RIS Server **Properties** dialog box specifies in the **Advanced Settings** of its **Remote Install** page.

As administrator, this option allows you to pre-install a computer for another user within their organization.

Restart Setup

This option restarts a setup attempt that has failed, using the same installation image.

Tools

This option allows the user to access the maintenance and troubleshooting tools that you configured on the RIS server.

Windows 2000 Professional

⊙ Remember that you can direct the system to speed up the application of a new policy using the **Secedit /refreshpolicy machine_policy** command.

→⊃ Check that the system has applied your new policy in the **SceCli** source by consulting the **Application** log in the **Event Viewer**.

Creating a computer account for a RIS client

For security reasons, you may wish to predefine the computer accounts that the RIS will install. This section explains how you can add an account for a computer that you will set up using a remote boot disk and a PCI adapter on an Ethernet network.

→⊃ Open the **Active Directory Users and Computers** snap-in.

The following example creates in the **Computers** container, a computer account called **NP0050DA84CB6E**, where 0050DA84CB6E is the MAC address of a PCI network adapter.

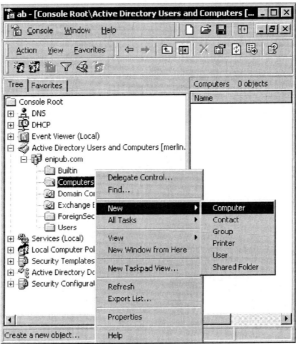

→⊃ Enter the name of the computer that you want to create.

→) In the next screen, activate the **This is a managed computer** option and specify the Global Unique Identifier / Universal Unique Identifier (GUID/UUID).

This identifier is based on the MAC address of the network adapter for a computer that you will set up using a remote boot disk. You must add leading zeros to this MAC address in order to code the identifier on 16 bytes (32 hexadecimal symbols).

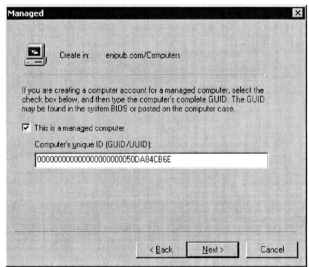

→) Enter the Fully Qualified Domain Name (FQDN) of the RIS server.

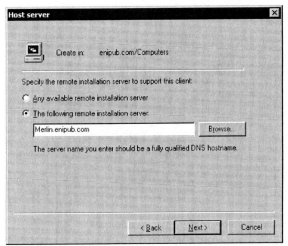

Finally, a summary screen appears and asks you to confirm your settings.

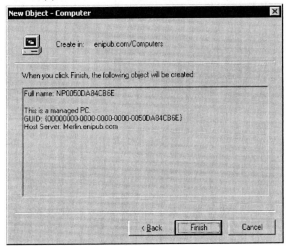

5. Troubleshooting RIS setup problems

a. Troubleshooting according to the remote boot load sequence

Step 1

The PXE client or the remote boot disk stops at the BOOTP message.

This message indicates that the client has requested an IP address from a DHCP server.

If the client does not continue beyond this stage, then you should check the following points:
- Is the DHCP service started?
- Have you defined a scope in the DHCP server?
- Have you activated the DHCP scope?
- Have you authorized the DHCP and the RIS services in the Active Directory?
- Is a router preventing broadcasts between the RIS client and the RIS server?
- Does the **System** log contain errors for the **DHCPServer** source?
- Are other non-RIS clients able to receive IP addresses from this server?
- Is the BIOS antivirus activated? If so, deactivate it.

Step 2

The PXE client or the remote boot disk stops at the DHCP message.

When the client receives an IP address, the setup message changes to **DHCP**.

This message means that the client has received an IP address and is now trying to contact the RIS server.

If the client does not continue beyond this stage, then the client will not have received any response from the RIS server.

In this case you should check the following points:
- Is the RIS service started on the server (this is the boot information negotiation layer, BINLSVC)?
- Is the RIS server authorized in the Active Directory?
- Are other clients able to receive the Client Installation Wizard? If so you must check that your client computer is supported.
- Is there a router between the RIS client and the RIS server? The RIS server communicates by broadcasting DHCP packets on the network.
- Does the **Event Viewer** contain any error messages that concern BINLSVC, DHCPServer, DNS or Active Directory?

Step 3

The client then displays **BINL** and invites the user to press the F12 function key. The client has successfully contacted the RIS server and is now waiting for the server to send the first installation image using TFTP.

If the RIS server does not respond, then the client will time-out and display an error message. In this case, you can try stopping and restarting the BINLSVC service. When you have done this, if no error message appears on the client machine, then you must check the RIS configuration. Check again to see if the **Event Viewer** contains any error messages concerning BINLSVC, DHCPServer or DNS.

b. Monitoring the RIS client startup phase

This section describes an example of the log that the BINL (*Boot Information Negotiation Layer*) service writes when it starts up and when the RIS client starts up.

BINLSVC is the principal RIS service. You can stop and restart this service by opening a command prompt and entering the following commands:

net stop binlsvc

net start binlsvc

To activate a first debug level on your server, add the **Debug** value with a **REG_WORD** data type, set to **0x80FFFFFF**, in the following registry key:
HKEY_LOCAL_MACHINE\System\CurrentControlSet\Services\Binlsvc\Parameters

Stop and restart the BINLSVC service in order to apply the modifications. The service then writes precise information to the **binlsvc.log** file in the **%SystemRoot%\Debug** folder.

Here is an example of this file, in which some of the important elements have been highlighted in bold format.

After net start binlsvc

```
[BinlServer] 03/11 13:50:51 [INIT] Initializing ..
[BinlServer] 03/11 13:50:51 [INIT] DS startup completed.
[BinlServer] 03/11 13:50:52 [OPTIONS] Client Timeout = 900 seconds
[BinlServer] 03/11 13:50:52 [OPTIONS] Port Number = 4011
[BinlServer] 03/11 13:50:52 [OPTIONS] Scavenger Timeout = 60000 milliseconds
[BinlServer] 03/11 13:50:52 [OPTIONS] Update from DS Timeout = 14400000 milliseconds
[BinlServer] 03/11 13:50:52 [OPTIONS] DS Error log timeout = 600000 milliseconds
[BinlServer] 03/11 13:50:52 [OPTIONS] New Client Timeout Minimum = 0 seconds
[BinlServer] 03/11 13:50:52 [OPTIONS] LDAP Search Timeout = 30 seconds
[BinlServer] 03/11 13:50:52 [OPTIONS] Cache Entry Expire Time = 25000 milliseconds
[BinlServer] 03/11 13:50:52 [OPTIONS] Maximum Cache Count = 250 entries
[BinlServer] 03/11 13:50:52 [OPTIONS] Assign new clients to this server = 0
[BinlServer] 03/11 13:50:52 [OPTIONS] ServerDN = 'CN=MERLIN,OU=Domain Controllers,
DC=enipub,DC=com'
[BinlServer] 03/11 13:50:52 [OPTIONS] SCPDN = 'CN=MERLIN-Services-d'installation-à-distance,
CN=MERLIN,OU=Domain Controllers,DC=enipub,DC=com'
[BinlServer] 03/11 13:50:52 [OPTIONS] NewMachineNamingPolicy = 'NP%MAC'
[BinlServer] 03/11 13:50:52 [OPTIONS] DefaultContainer = CN=Computers,DC=enipub,DC=com
[BinlServer] 03/11 13:50:52 [OPTIONS] BinlMaxClients = 100
[BinlServer] 03/11 13:50:52 [OPTIONS] (Last) CurrentClientCount = 0
[BinlServer] 03/11 13:50:52 [OPTIONS] AnswerRequests = True
[BinlServer] 03/11 13:50:52 [OPTIONS] AnswerOnlyValidClients = False
[BinlServer] 03/11 13:50:52 [OPTIONS] AllowNewClients = True
[BinlServer] 03/11 13:50:52 [OPTIONS] LimitClients = False
[BinlServer] 03/11 13:50:54 [MISC] Service is interrogated.
[BinlServer] 03/11 13:50:54 [OPTIONS] Client Timeout = 900 seconds
[BinlServer] 03/11 13:50:54 [OPTIONS] Port Number = 4011
[BinlServer] 03/11 13:50:54 [OPTIONS] Scavenger Timeout = 60000 milliseconds
[BinlServer] 03/11 13:50:54 [OPTIONS] Update from DS Timeout = 14400000 milliseconds
[BinlServer] 03/11 13:50:54 [OPTIONS] DS Error log timeout = 600000 milliseconds
[BinlServer] 03/11 13:50:54 [OPTIONS] New Client Timeout Minimum = 0 seconds
[BinlServer] 03/11 13:50:54 [OPTIONS] LDAP Search Timeout = 30 seconds
[BinlServer] 03/11 13:50:54 [OPTIONS] Cache Entry Expire Time = 25000 milliseconds
```

[BinlServer] 03/11 13:50:54 [OPTIONS] Maximum Cache Count = 250 entries
[BinlServer] 03/11 13:50:54 [OPTIONS] Assign new clients to this server = 0
[BinlServer] 03/11 13:50:54 [OPTIONS] ServerDN = 'CN=MERLIN,OU=Domain Controllers,
DC=enipub,DC=com'
[BinlServer] 03/11 13:50:54 [OPTIONS] SCPDN   = 'CN=MERLIN-Services-d'installation-à-distance,
CN=MERLIN,OU=Domain Controllers,DC=enipub,DC=com'
[BinlServer] 03/11 13:50:54 [OPTIONS] NewMachineNamingPolicy = 'NP%MAC'
[BinlServer] 03/11 13:50:54 [OPTIONS] DefaultContainer = CN=Computers,DC=enipub,DC=com
[BinlServer] 03/11 13:50:54 [OPTIONS] BinlMaxClients = 100
[BinlServer] 03/11 13:50:54 [OPTIONS] (Last) CurrentClientCount = 0
[BinlServer] 03/11 13:50:54 [OPTIONS] AnswerRequests = True
[BinlServer] 03/11 13:50:54 [OPTIONS] AnswerOnlyValidClients = False
[BinlServer] 03/11 13:50:54 [OPTIONS] AllowNewClients = True
[BinlServer] 03/11 13:50:54 [OPTIONS] LimitClients = False

Starting the RIS client

[BinlServer] 03/11 13:51:21 [MISC] Client Guid: {00000000-0000-0000-0000-**0050da84cb6e**}
[BinlServer] 03/11 13:51:21 [MISC] MachineDN = CN=**NP0050da84cb6e**,CN=Computers,
DC=enipub,DC=com
[BinlServer] 03/11 13:51:21 [MISC] HostName = **merlin.enipub.com**
[BinlServer] 03/11 13:51:21 [OPTIONS] Server allows new clients and the Server is generating
the OS Chooser path response.
[BinlServer] 03/11 13:51:21 [MISC] SamName = NP0050da84cb6e$
 [BinlServer] 03/11 13:51:21 [MISC] Name = NP0050da84cb6e
[BinlServer] 03/11 13:51:21 [OPTIONS] **Recognizing client**.
[BinlServer] 03/11 13:51:25 [MISC] Client Guid: {00000000-0000-0000-0000-0050da84cb6e}
[BinlServer] 03/11 13:51:25 [OPTIONS] Recognizing client.
[BinlServer] 03/11 13:51:26 [MISC] Client Guid: {00000000-0000-0000-0000-0050da84cb6e}
[BinlServer] 03/11 13:51:26 [OPTIONS] Recognizing client.
[BinlServer] 03/11 13:51:26 [STOC] Sending response to = 172.16.98.1, XID = 6370d9ac.
[BinlServer] 03/11 13:51:33 NULL screen name so we are retrieving the Welcome Screen.
[BinlServer] 03/11 13:51:33 **Retrieving screen file: 'C:\RemoteInstall\OSChooser\welcome.osc'**
[BinlServer] 03/11 13:51:42 **Retrieving screen file: 'C:\RemoteInstall\OSChooser\English\LOGIN.OSC'**
[BinlServer] 03/11 13:51:58 **Retrieving screen file: 'C:\RemoteInstall\OSChooser\English\CHOICE.OSC'**
[BinlServer] 03/11 13:52:00 **Retrieving screen file: 'C:\RemoteInstall\OSChooser\English\OSAUTO.OSC'**
[BinlServer] 03/11 13:52:00 [MISC] Client Guid: {00000000-0000-0000-0000-0050da84cb6e}
[BinlServer] 03/11 13:52:00 [MISC] MachineDN = CN=NP0050da84cb6e,CN=Computers,
DC=enipub,DC=com
[BinlServer] 03/11 13:52:00 [MISC] HostName = merlin.enipub.com
[BinlServer] 03/11 13:52:00 [OPTIONS] Server allows new clients and the Server
is generating the OS Chooser path response.
[BinlServer] 03/11 13:52:00 [MISC] SamName = NP0050da84cb6e$
[BinlServer] 03/11 13:52:00 [MISC] Name = NP0050da84cb6e
[BinlServer] 03/11 13:52:00 **Retrieving screen file: 'C:\RemoteInstall\OSChooser\English\OSCHOICE.OSC'**
[BinlServer] 03/11 13:52:05 **Retrieving screen file: 'C:\RemoteInstall\OSChooser\English\WARNING.OSC'**
[BinlServer] 03/11 13:52:10 **Successfully created account for**   a84cb6e
[BinlServer] 03/11 13:52:10 Retrieving screen file: 'C:\RemoteInstall\OSChooser\English\INSTALL.OSC'

DHCP/RIS network activity

Here is an example of DHCP network activity between the RIS client and the RIS and
DHCP servers.

This example shows the following exchanges:

DHCP DISCOVER

DHCP OFFER

DHCP REQUEST

DHCP ACK

Notice that the server acknowledgement includes the server's TFTP server host name along with the name and the path of the first file that the client must download.

RIS client

MAC address   0050DA84CB6E

Serveur DHCP et RIS

IP address   172.16.3.1
Name   MERLIN

Network Monitor trace Fri 02/09/01 15:30:52 client RIS final.txt

****

Frame Time Src MAC Addr Dst MAC Addr Protocol Description Src Other Addr Dst Other Addr Type Other Addr
19 34.609766 **0050DA84CB6E** *BROADCAST **DHCP Discover** (xid=6370D9AB) 0.0.0.0 255.255.255.255

+ Frame: Base frame properties
+ ETHERNET: ETYPE = 0x0800 : Protocol = IP: DOD Internet Protocol
+ IP: ID = 0x1; Proto = UDP; Len: 328
+ UDP: IP Multicast: Src Port: BOOTP Client, (68); Dst Port: **BOOTP Server** (67); Length = 308 (0x134)
+ DHCP: Discover   (xid=6370D9AB)

****

Frame Time Src MAC Addr Dst MAC Addr Protocol Description Src Other Addr Dst Other Addr Type Other Addr
21 34.699896 **MERLIN**   *BROADCAST **DHCP Offer**. (xid=6370D9AB) MERLIN 255.255.255.255

+ Frame: Base frame properties
+ ETHERNET: ETYPE = 0x0800 : Protocol = IP: DOD Internet Protocol
+ IP: ID = 0x1628; Proto = UDP; Len: 328
+ UDP: IP Multicast: Src Port: BOOTP Server, (67); Dst Port: BOOTP Client (68); Length = 308 (0x134)
  DHCP: Offer   (xid=6370D9AB)
     DHCP: Op Code   (op)   = 2 (0x2)
     DHCP: Hardware Type   (htype) = 1 (0x1) 10Mb Ethernet
     DHCP: Hardware Address Length (hlen) = 6 (0x6)
     DHCP: Hops   (hops) = 0 (0x0)
     DHCP: Transaction ID   (xid)   = 1668340139 (0x6370D9AB)
     DHCP: Seconds   (secs) = 0 (0x0)
   + DHCP: Flags   (flags) = 0 (0x0)
     DHCP: Client IP Address (ciaddr) = 0.0.0.0
     DHCP: Your IP Address (yiaddr) = 172.16.98.1
     DHCP: Server IP Address (siaddr) = 172.16.3.1
     DHCP: Relay IP Address (giaddr) = 0.0.0.0
     DHCP: Client Ethernet Address (chaddr) = 0050DA84CB6E
     DHCP: Server Host Name (sname) = **ank**

```
        DHCP: Boot File Name    (file)   = ank
        DHCP: Magic Cookie = 99.130.83.99
      + DHCP: Option Field      (options)
```

```
*******************************************************************************
```

Frame Time Src MAC Addr Dst MAC Addr Protocol Description Src Other Addr Dst Other Addr Type Other Addr
27 38.585483 **0050DA84CB6E** *BROADCAST **DHCP Request**. (xid=6370D9AB) 0.0.0.0 255.255.255.255

+ Frame: Base frame properties
+ ETHERNET: ETYPE = 0x0800 : Protocol = IP: DOD Internet Protocol
+ IP: ID = 0x2; Proto = UDP; Len: 328

+ UDP: IP Multicast: Src Port: BOOTP Client, (68); Dst Port: BOOTP Server (67); Length = 308 (0x134)
+ DHCP: Request   (xid=6370D9AB)

```
*******************************************************************************
```

Frame Time Src MAC Addr Dst MAC Addr Protocol Description Src Other Addr Dst Other Addr Type Other Addr
28 38.615526 **MERLIN**   *BROADCAST **DHCP ACK**   xid=6370D9AB) MERLIN 255.255.255.255

```
+ Frame: Base frame properties
+ ETHERNET: ETYPE = 0x0800 : Protocol = IP:  DOD Internet Protocol
+ IP: ID = 0x162C; Proto = UDP; Len: 332
+ UDP: IP Multicast: Src Port: BOOTP Server, (67); Dst Port: BOOTP Client (68); Length = 312 (0x138)
  DHCP: ACK             (xid=6370D9AB)
      DHCP: Op Code         (op)    = 2 (0x2)
      DHCP: Hardware Type     (htype)  = 1 (0x1) 10Mb Ethernet
      DHCP: Hardware Address Length (hlen) = 6 (0x6)
      DHCP: Hops             (hops)   = 0 (0x0)
      DHCP: Transaction ID    (xid)   = 1668340139 (0x6370D9AB)
      DHCP: Seconds          (secs)   = 0 (0x0)
    + DHCP: Flags           (flags)  = 0 (0x0)
      DHCP: Client IP Address (ciaddr) = 0.0.0.0
      DHCP: Your   IP Address (yiaddr) = 172.16.98.1    future IP address of the RIS client
      DHCP: Server IP Address (siaddr) = 172.16.3.1     IP address of MERLIN (DHCP server)
      DHCP: Relay  IP Address (giaddr) = 0.0.0.0
      DHCP: Client Ethernet Address (chaddr) = 0050DA84CB6E
      DHCP: Server Host Name  (sname)  = merlin.eni.com    the RIS server send its name
   DHCP: Boot File Name    (file)   = OSChooser\i386\startrom.com    along with first file for TFTP
      DHCP: Magic Cookie = 99.130.83.99
    + DHCP: Option Field      (options)
```

B. Deploying applications

1. Publishing and assigning

Group policies allow you to distribute applications and service packs to users and to computers. **Intellimirror** provides this feature.

Applications deployment runs on Windows Installer technology. This service runs on each Windows 2000 computer (it can also run on other operating systems such as Windows NT). It allows you to install and to maintain applications. You can use this service in order to install new application components, as and when your users need them. This service can also replace missing files or repair corrupt files. It can do this automatically without user intervention by taking the required files from the installation sources.

Before an application can be deployed, it must be in the form of a **package** that can be interpreted by **Windows Installer**. Such a package is made up of an installation file that has an **.MSI** filename extension, together with other files that are required in order to install the product.

This installation method will become increasingly common. Some application development products already offer such packages. For example, the Windows 2000 CD-ROM provides the VERITAS WinINSTALL LE tool, as an MSI package called SWIADMLE.MSI. The \VALUEADD\3RDPARTY\MGMT\WINSTLE directory of this CD-ROM contains this package.

Using group policies, you can deploy applications as follows:

→) Create a share that can be accessed by the users concerned. This share must contain the source of the product in MSI format.

→) Create a new policy, either at site level, or at domain level, or at OU level.

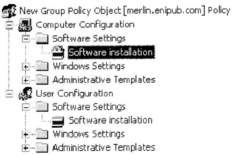

→) If you want to deploy the programs to computers irrespective of the people that will use them, right-click **Software installation**, under **Computer Configuration**. Alternatively, If you want to deploy the programs to users irrespective of the computers that they will use, right-click **Software installation**, under **User Configuration**.

→⟩ Select **New**, followed by **Package**.

→⟩ Select the MSI file of the package that you wish to deploy.

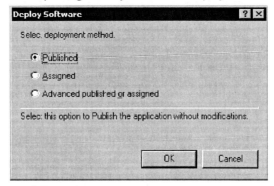

→⟩ You must choose one of three options:

Published

> When you publish an application, the users will be able to install the program with the **Add/Remove Programs** icon from the **Control Panel**. Alternatively, a user can double-click the file with a name extension that is associated with the published program to install the program automatically without using the **Add/Remove Programs** icon. This option is available only in the group policies for user settings.

Assigned

> When an application is assigned, a shortcut is added in the **Start** menu. To install this application automatically, the user must either select this shortcut, or double-click the document with a name extension that is associated with the published program. If you assign an application to computers, rather than to users, the application will automatically be installed on the computers concerned.

Advanced published or assigned

> This option allows you to customize the installation of the products concerned.
>
> Published applications appear with the 🖳 icon, whereas assigned applications appear with the 🖳 icon.

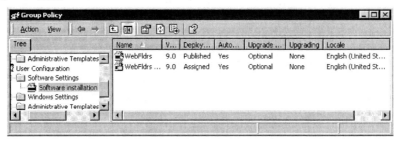

You can modify the application settings by double-clicking the package concerned in the **Group Policy** window.

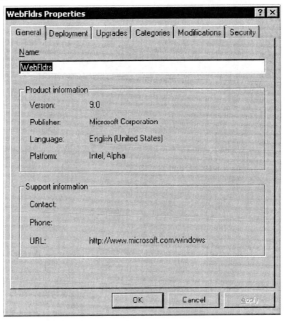

You can set up the deployment using six tabs:

General

This tab shows product information, along with the deployment name.

Deployment

This tab allows you to define how the application must be deployed (either published or assigned). In addition, you can specify, whether or not the application must be installed when the user double-clicks a file with the name extension that is associated with the program, whether or not a published application package must be displayed in the **Add/Remove Programs** and whether or not the application must be uninstalled if the user is no longer associated with the container in which the policy has been placed.

Upgrades

This tab allows you to create application upgrade packages (for new versions or for service packs).

Categories

This tab allows you to organize published applications in the **Add/Remove Programs** applet in categories that you create.

Modifications

This tab allows you to customize your packages.

Security

This tab allows you to apply permissions.

Before you can organize published applications in categories, you must first create the categories concerned. You can do this by right-clicking **Software Installation**, selecting **Properties** and then selecting the **Categories** tab.

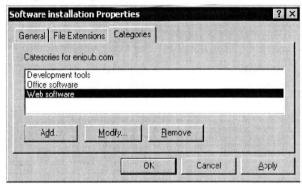

Click the **Add** button to define the name of a new category.

2. Installing applications using packages

Here is the **Add/Remove Programs** screen that the users will see before the applications are published:

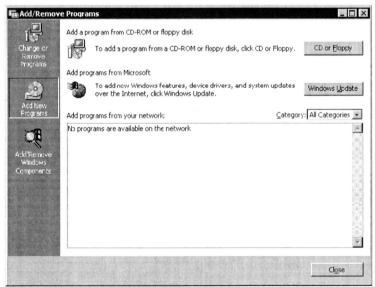

Here is the **Add/Remove Programs** screen that the users will see after the applications have been published:

Windows 2000 Professional

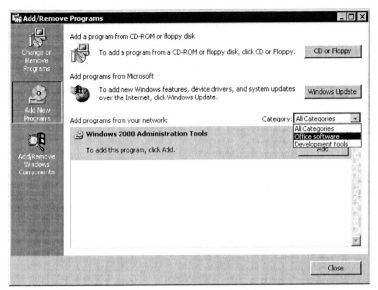

To install the application, a user need only click the **Add** button.

3. Upgrades and service packs

Once your application has been published or assigned, you can upgrade it (with the latest version of the product), or you can apply any service packs concerned.

You can upgrade the version of a program as follows:

➨ Add the new version of the program to the group policy as a new package.

➨ Right-click your new package and select **Properties**. Select the **Upgrades** tab then click the **Add** button.

➨ Select the package that must be upgraded, then indicate whether you want to uninstall the existing package and then install the upgrade package, or whether you wish to upgrade over the existing package.

➨ If you want to force the upgrade when the user next uses the application, then enable the **Required upgrade for existing packages** option. Alternatively, you must disable this option if you prefer to allow the user to choose when the upgrade must be carried out.

You can add a service pack to a program as follows:

➨ Place the service pack files in MSI format in the directory that contains the software distribution files.

➨ Right-click the package for which you want to apply the service pack.

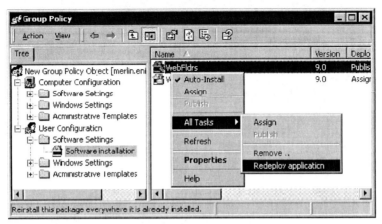

→) Select **All Tasks**, followed by **Redeploy application**.

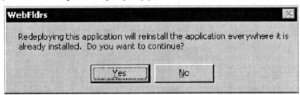

→) Click **Yes** in order to confirm the redeployment.

You can remove a program as follows:

→) Right-click the package that you wish to remove.

→) Select **All Tasks**, followed by **Remove**.

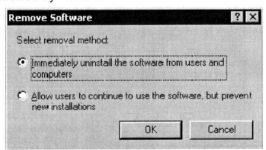

You then have two options:

- You can force the program removal. In this case, the application will be uninstalled at the next computer startup, or the next user logon.
- Alternatively, you can prevent any fresh installations of the software, but allow users who have installed the program to continue to work with it.

Chapter 4: Configuring the system

First, this chapter will cover the installation, the configuration and the troubleshooting of hardware devices. Then, the chapter will describe how to set up the user working environment.

A. Configuring devices

1. Introduction

The main tool that allows you to configure hardware devices is the **Control Panel**.

Windows 2000 provides a number of shortcuts that allow you to access some of these icons more rapidly. For example:

- You can access **Control Panel - Administrative Tools - Computer Management** by selecting the **Manage** option from the **My Computer** shortcut menu.
- You can access **Control Panel - Date/Time** by double-clicking the time display in the bottom left hand corner of your screen.
- You can access **Control Panel - Display** by selecting the **Properties** option from the desktop shortcut menu.
- You can access **Control Panel - Network and Dial-up Connections** by selecting the **Properties option** from the **My Network Places** shortcut menu.
- You can access **Control Panel - System** by selecting the **Properties** option from the **My Computer** shortcut menu.

In addition the on-line **Help** feature provides a very rich source of information. Also, you can use the **Windows 2000 Hardware Troubleshooter**, which you can access directly from the on-line **Help** utility.

The following sections of this chapter will describe the different tools that the **Control Panel** provides, and will describe how you can configure your hardware devices in order to transform your Windows 2000 Professional machine into a veritable multimedia workstation.

2. Display

Display

Several tabs are provided:

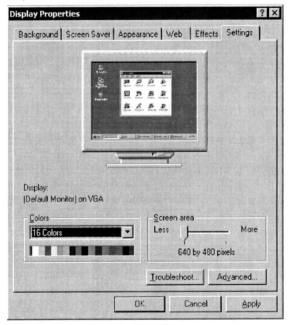

Background

This tab offers images and wallpapers that you can use as a screen background. By clicking the **Browse** button, you can add your own pictures for use as wallpaper.

Screen Saver

This tab offers a variety of screen savers. These programs move an image around the screen in order to protect the phosphorous layer from being damaged by prolonged display of a fixed image. You can parameter most of the screen savers and you can protect them with passwords. This tab also allows you to manage the power supply.

Appearance

This tab allows you to customize the colors of such items as menu fonts, title bars and dialog boxes.

Web

This tab allows you to display images or HTML files as wallpapers.

Effects

This tab allows you to modify the icons that are on your desktop and to apply visual effects to them (such as smoothing the edges of fonts).

Settings

This tab allows you to adjust the number of colors and the resolution of the screen.

Connecting several monitors

Windows 2000 allows you to connect up to ten monitors on the same computer in order to extend its display capabilities. This feature allows a user to work on several applications at the same time, by moving from screen to screen. In order to use this feature, you must use PCI (*Peripheral Component Interconnect*) or AGP (*Accelerated Graphics Port*) type graphic cards. Consult the HCL so as to find out the list of graphic cards that support this feature. Then add the AGP or PCI graphic cards in free slots, connect up your additional screen monitors and restart your computer. Windows 2000 automatically detects the new peripherals and installs the drivers. Next go into the **Display Properties**, select the **Settings** tab and, for each additional monitor, activate the **Extend my desktop onto this monitor** check box.

Troubleshooting a video adapter

Here are two video adapter problems that are commonly met:

Graphics card is not recognized other than in VGA mode

- Check that your card appears in the HCL.
- Obtain the driver that is suitable for Windows 2000.

Screen goes blank after system startup

- Your video card is not resetting itself, or the video interrupt is being shared by another device.
- If your workstation will not restart, then press F8 during the first startup phase and choose the **Enable VGA mode** option.
- If your workstation does not restart after you have reconfigured the video driver, then press F8 during the first startup phase and choose the **Last Known Good Configuration** option.

Otherwise, you can consult the **Display Troubleshooter:**

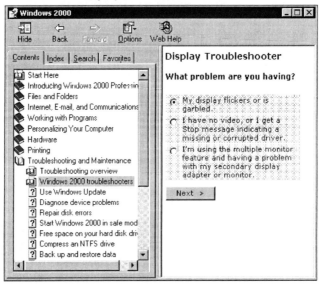

3. Add/remove hardware

Add/Remove
Hardware   Windows 2000 supports the Plug-and-Play feature by automatically installing the drivers of devices that offer Plug-and-Play. This feature means that you can physically connect a new device and then let Windows automatically sort out its configuration (IRQ...). The advantage of this feature is that you no longer have to worry about this set up, which allows you to avoid all sorts of conflict problems.

If you have devices that are not Plug-and-Play, you can use the **Add/Remove Hardware** program to install, remove, disconnect or troubleshoot them.

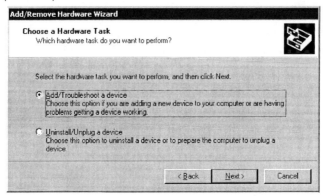

If you select **Add/Troubleshoot a device**, Windows 2000 looks for new Plug-and-Play devices. If Windows 2000 does not detect your device, then you can install it by selecting **Add a new device:**

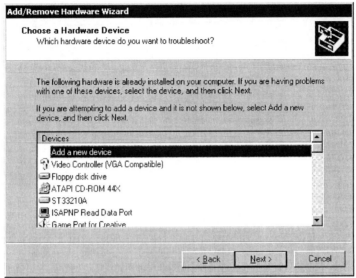

If you select a device that is listed under **Devices**, and then click **Next**, Windows 2000 will indicate the status of this device.

Chapter 4

Required privileges

In order to add new devices, you must have administrator privileges on the Windows 2000 workstation.

In addition, if your computer is configured so that it can open sessions on a Windows 2000 domain, then the network policy that has been defined may not grant you the necessary permissions.

On the other hand, if an administrator loads the drivers for you, then you can install the device even if the system does not recognize you as an administrator.

4. Keyboard

Keyboard   This module allows you to configure the settings of your keyboard, such as the character repeat delay and rate, the input language and the driver that is used.

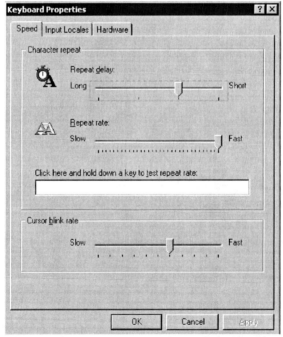

In addition to this graphic interface, you can use the registry in order to specify whether or not the numeric keyboard must be active during the logon phase. By default, the numeric keyboard is deactivated before logon and activated during logon. In order to change these settings, go into the registry editor and modify the **InitialKeyboardIndicators** value.
InitialKeyboardIndicators=0: numeric keyboard deactivated
InitialKeyboardIndicators=2: numeric keyboard activated

Windows 2000 Professional

In order to change the keyboard status after logon, modify this value in **HKEY_CURRENT_USER\Control Panel\Keyboard**. In order to change the keyboard status before logon, modify this value in **HKEY_USER\DEFAULT\Control Panel\Keyboard**.

You can also define another type of keyboard, and you can configure the switch between keyboards using a key sequence:

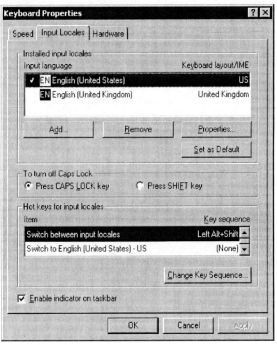

5. Game Controllers

Game
Controllers   In order to install the required device, you must first connect it to your computer, physically. You must follow the instructions that the vendor supplies. You may need to restart your computer.

 You must switch off your computer before you attempt any physical installation of an internal device card.

Normally, Windows 2000 will detect the new device when you start-up, and will automatically launch the **Add/Remove Hardware** wizard.

Non Plug-and-Play devices

For devices that do not offer the Plug-and-Play feature, you must run the **Add/Remove Hardware** module from the **Control Panel**. Click the **Next** button on the opening screen and then choose the **Add/Troubleshoot a device** option.

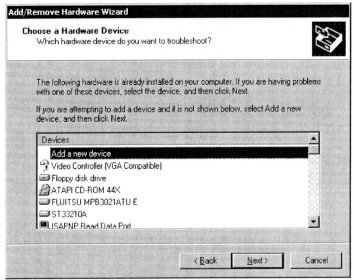

Under **Devices,** select **Add a new device**, click **Next**, and in the next screen select the **No, I want to select the hardware from a list** option.

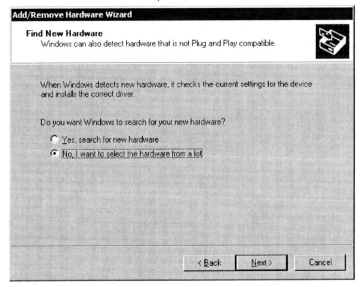

Click **Next** then select the type of hardware concerned from the **Hardware types** list.

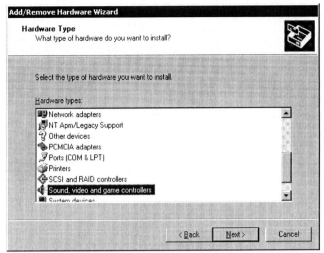

Finally, you must configure the options that are specific to your device.

USB device or IEEE 1394 device

Connect your device to the correct port. You do not need to stop your computer to do this.

⊚ Be careful: although USB and IEEE connections look very similar, you cannot connect a USB device to an IEEE port, or vice-versa.

Troubleshooting

If you have any difficulties in installing a joystick controller, you may find the following information useful:

Your device is connected to a USB port

- Check that your BIOS supports USB devices, and that it is activated for this purpose (you may need to upgrade your BIOS with a more recent version, in which case you must contact your supplier).
- Check that the USB controller is configured correctly. In order to do this, go into the **Device Manager**, access the **Properties** of the controller, and then check its configuration in the **Device status** frame of the dialog box that appears (you can access the **Device Manager**, by selecting **Control Panel - Administrative Tools - Computer Management - Device Manager**).
- Also in the **Device Manager**, check the separate entry that is associated with the USB port itself (using the **Properties** option).

Your device is connected to a serial port or to a joystick port

- Go into the **Device Manager**, and then check the status of the controller.

– If necessary, use the hardware troubleshooter.

The game does not recognize the controller

– Some games, recognize only one controller, even when several contollers are installed (in particular, this may be the case for games that have been designed for MS-DOS and for Windows 3.x).
– If the game does not recognize the controller that you want to use, then check that your contoller is assigned to controller ID number 1.

The controller is not connected to the port that the system expects

– Check that the controller has not been moved since it was installed. If it has, then it will not function correctly until you update the new configuration settings in the **Sound, video and game controllers** module of the **Device Manager**.

You are unable to reserve the IRQ for the ISA device

– Check that the IRQ for a non PCI (Peripheral Component Interconnect) device has not been reserved for a PCI device in the BIOS.

Troubleshooter

Otherwise, you can use the **Multimedia and Games Troubleshooter** in order to solve your problem.

6. Printers

Printers This module allows you to add and remove printers.
Chapter 8 of this book describes this feature in more detail.

7. Phone and modem options

a. Configuring a modem

➨) To add a modem on your workstation, connect it physically and then start the **Add/Re-move Hardware** module of the **Control Panel**. Click **Next**, select the **Add/Troubleshoot a device** option, and click **Next** again:

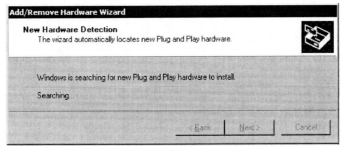

➨) Windows 2000 detects any new Plug-and-Play hardware:

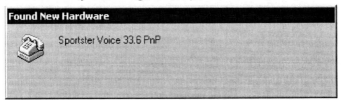

➨) Windows 2000 may detect your modem several times.

➨) The **Add/Remove Hardware Wizard** then displays the list of Plug-and-Play devices that it has found:

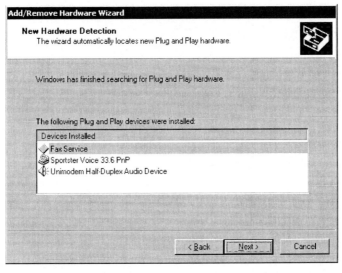

→) You can test your modem by starting the **Phone and Modem Options** module of the **Control Panel**, and activating the **Modems** tab of the dialog box that appears:

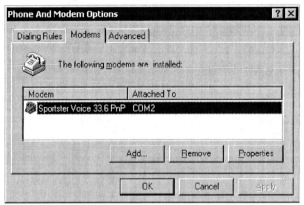

→) Click the **Properties** button. The modem **Properties** dialog box appears with three new tabs:

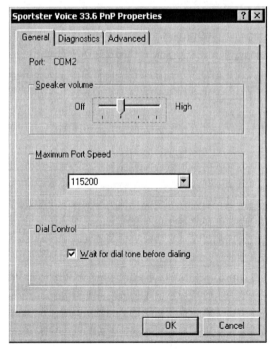

The **Diagnostics** tab is particularly useful as it allows you to query the modem using elementary HAYES commands and to check that the modem responds correctly:

To test the modem in this way, click the **Query Modem** button.

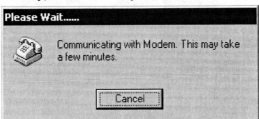

These tests are added to the **Diagnostics** page:

→) You can also access the modem log by clicking the **View log** button:

The **Advanced** tab of the modem **Properties** dialog box provides a **Change Default Preferences** button that allows you, in particular, to specify the idle time period after which a call will be automatically disconnected, the type of flow control, and whether the modem compression must be enabled or disabled:

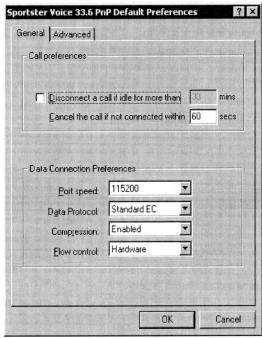

The **Advanced** tab of the modem **Default Properties** dialog box allows you to specify hardware settings including the number of data bits, the number of stop bits, and the parity.

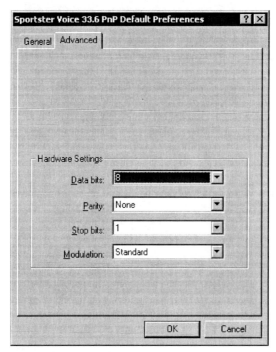

b. Troubleshooting a modem

You can troubleshoot modem installation problems in several ways:

You can use the **Device Manager**, by selecting **Control Panel - Administrative Tools - Computer Management - Device Manager**.

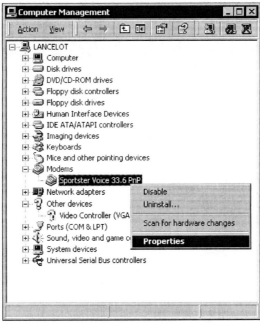

→) Access the **Properties** of your modem:

Windows 2000 Professional

→) Then, you can launch the **Hardware Troubleshooter**, by clicking the **Troubleshooter** button:

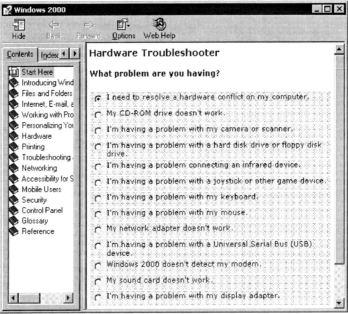

You can also start the **HyperTerminal** program (**Start - Programs - Accessories - Communications - HyperTerminal**) and test the modem using HAYES commands (such as **ATI3** and **ATI4**, for example), to see if your modem responds:

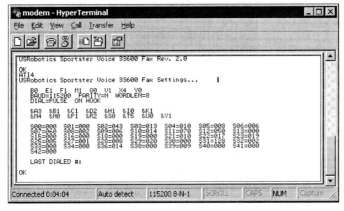

In addition, the on-line **Help** utility provides a rich source of information:

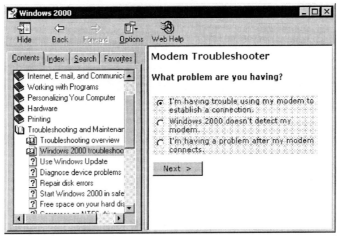

Here are a number of typical problems, together with actions that you can follow in order to solve them:

The modem tests indicate that the modem is not receiving commands
- Check the modem cable.
- Check the physical connection of the modem.
- Check that the modem is covered by the HCL.
- Search for a compatible modem in the modem documentation.

Although the modem diagnostics indicate that the modem works, you cannot set up a connection
- Check the physical connection of the modem to the telephone line.
- Check the dialing mode (pulse or tone dialing).

Although the telephone line works, you cannot connect to a remote modem
- Check that the both modems have identical connection settings (the usual configuration is 8 data bits, no parity and one stop bit).

An RS-232 serial device runs very slowly or very badly
- Adjust the device speed (to a maximum speed of 115 Kbps, which is the maximum speed that a PC serial port supports).

The port is already being used, or the port has not been configured for remote access connections
- Switch on your modem before you start up Windows, in order to ensure that the system detects Plug-and-Play devices correctly.
- Check that no other program is using the port (for example a fax emission program).
- Check that the characteristics of the port and the modem have been updated correctly.

8. Scanners and cameras

a. Introduction

In order to install a scanner, a digital camera, or another still image device, go into **Control Panel** and double-click the **Scanners and Cameras** icon:

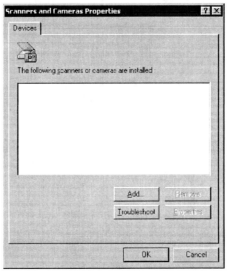

When you click the **Add** button, the **Scanner and Camera Installation Wizard** offers to detect your device.

Either the wizard will detect your device, or you must specify the characteristics of your device manually:

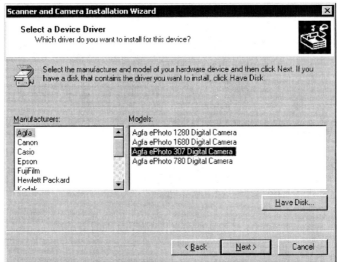

Windows 2000 Professional

b. Managing colors

Windows 2000 provides a color programing interface called **Image Color Management (ICM) 2.0**.

This interface allows you to obtain a precise and coherent presentation on all publication devices.

In the absence of a standard on the subject, each vendor used to provide its own color management and the results would vary according to the harware and software that you used. Thus, for a given program, you used to have to configure a specific color profile by successive approximations.

Nowadays, the ICM technique provides a flexible, universal solution to this problem. Windows 2000 installs a **Color Profile** for each new device that you add onto your operating system. This profile defines the color palette for each scan, print or display.

By default, Windows 2000 stores the color profiles in:
%SystemRoot%\System32\Spool\drivers\Color.
The files concerned have the name extensions **.icm** or **.icc**.

For simple publication programs you can configure the color management so that the system will set up color profiles automatically. On the other hand, users with specific needs, for example those working in graphic creation and desktop publishing fields, can set up their own complete color profiles manually. By this means, users can adjust their color profiles to suit specific scanners, screens or printers.

c. Troubleshooting

You can troubleshoot most devices by right-clicking **My Computer** and selecting **Manage**, followed by **Device Manager**. Then, display the shortcut menu of the device concerned, select **Properties** and then click the **Troubleshooter** button.

→) Alternatively, you can go into the **Control Panel**, double-click the **Scanners and Cameras** icon, and click the **Troubleshoot** button.

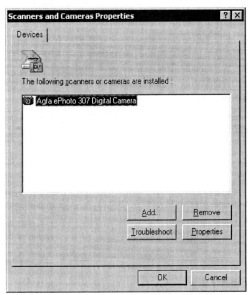

Either of these techniques will display the **Hardware Troubleshooter** relating to cameras and scanners:

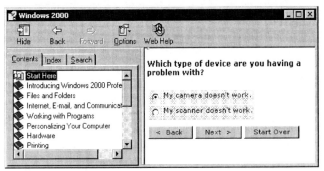

9. Mouse

Mouse   You can customize the use of the mouse. For example, you can adjust the double-click speed, modify the mouse pointer, or specify whether it must be right-handed or left-handed (this allows you to inverse the button roles). You can even configure your mouse so that you can open a document by a single click.

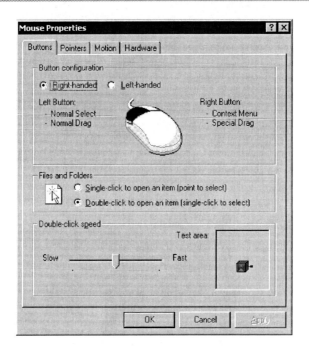

10. Fax

a. Introduction

Fax   This tool allows you to fax a text document or a graphic image, just as easily as if you were using a printer. When you transmit an image, the system digitalizes it automatically and converts it to TIFF (*Tagged Image File Format*).

Using a mail program, you can send an e-mail and a fax simultaneously.

In order to send and receive faxes, you need a device that is suitable for the purpose: either a fax or a modem/fax.

The basic functioning of this Windows 2000 tool does not allow you to share the fax on the network.

As with Windows print queues, you can create several copies of the fax printer. This approach allows you to define specific print options, such as the paper format or orientation, or the document dispatch time.

b. Configuring a Fax Printer

Firstly, your operating system must recognize the device. As Windows 2000 should detect most modem/faxes automatically, in order to complete this step, normally you would need only physically to connect your device to your computer.

The next step is to add a fax printer to your system environment.

→) In order to do this, activate **Control Panel - Fax - Advanced Options**, and then select the **Add a Fax Printer** option.

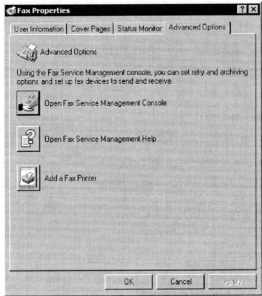

→) Then, Windows 2000 should display a message telling you that your fax printer was created sucessfully.

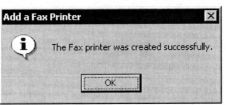

→) Define your user profile: it is important that you enter this information correctly, as the system will use it by default in your fax cover pages.

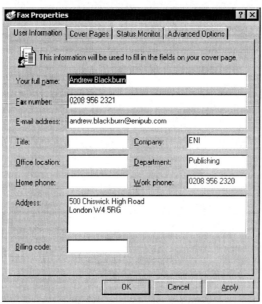

→) Define cover pages for your faxes: you can choose standard models, and/or you can choose or customize personal cover pages in order to suit your requirements.

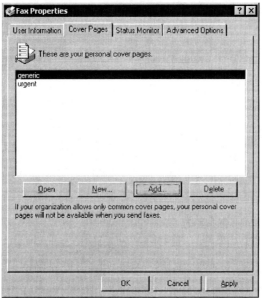

The standard, or common cover pages are stored in **\Documents and Settings\All Users\Documents\My Faxes\Common Coverpages**.

Your personal cover pages are stored in **\Documents and Settings**_Username_**\My Documents\Fax\Personal Coverpages**.

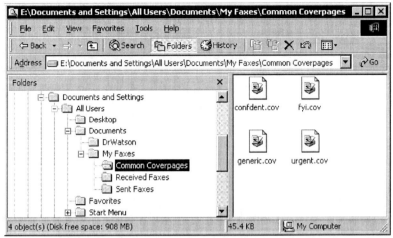

→) You can also customize a cover page to your needs using the **Fax Cover Page Editor**:

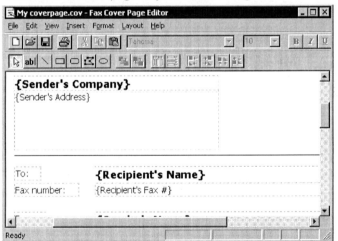

➔ Finally, you can specify how you want the system to notify you when it sends or receives a fax:

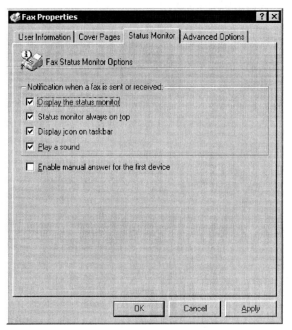

c. Fax management tools

You can access the following tools by selecting **Start - Programs - Accessories - Communications - Fax**:

Fax Queue

This tool allows you to display, to cancel, to pause or to resume a fax that you are sending.

Fax Service Management

This tool allows you to configure your fax device so that it will receive faxes, and to define security authorization settings, the number of rings before answering a fax, and the number of send retries.

My Faxes

This tool allows you to display, to print or to delete faxes that you have sent or received. In addition, the folder that corresponds to this tool contains all the common cover pages.

🗘 This folder has the following path: **\Documents and Settings\All Users\Documents\My Faxes.**

Send Cover Page fax

This tool allows you to fax only the cover page. When you activate this tool you launch the **Send Fax Wizard.**

d. Sending a fax

With Windows 2000, the user sees the fax or the modem/fax as a printer. By this approach, when you print from any application, you can choose to use the fax.

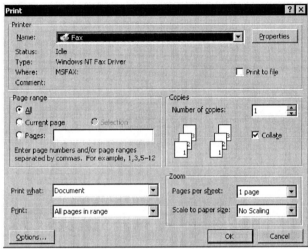

→) When you do this, the **Send Fax Wizard** starts up and invites you to fill in the various important fields: in particular you must specify the fax number of the recipient:

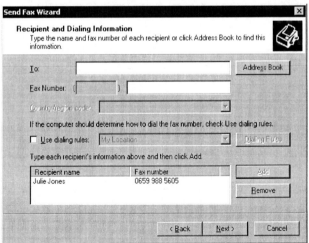

◐ You are strongly advised to use an address book for the fax numbers of your correspondents.

Next, you can specify the subject of your fax, together with a personal note:

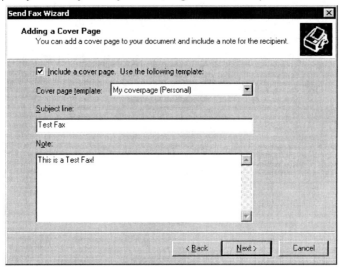

◐ The cover page generally uses these pieces of information.

→) Then you must specify when you want to send your fax:

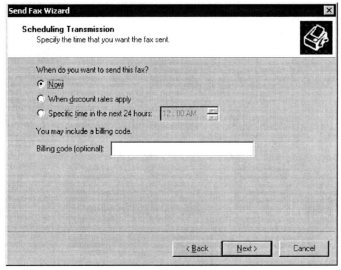

→) Finally you must confirm your action:

The **Fax Queue** receives your fax:

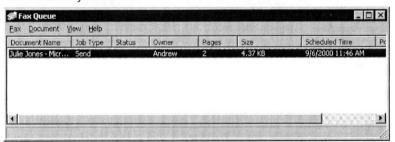

The **Fax Monitor** starts up, and the system starts sending your fax:

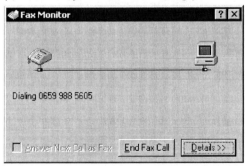

The **Fax Monitor** allows you to view the log of recent fax events:

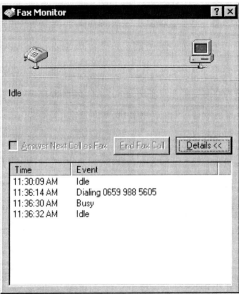

→) When the system has sent your fax, you can view your document as the system sent it, by selecting: **Start - Programs - Accessories - Communications - Fax - My Faxes - Sent Faxes**.

→) Just double click a document in this folder to launch the Kodak **Imaging Preview**:

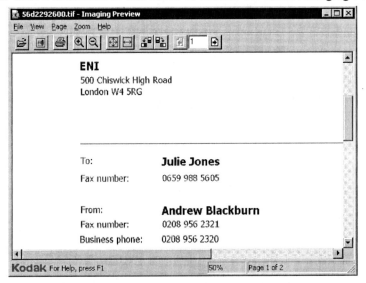

→) You can alter the settings of your fax printer by selecting: **Start** - **Programs** - **Printers**:

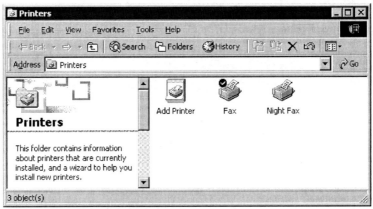

→) You can access the properties of your fax printer, and you can specify a certain number of settings. However, you cannot share the fax queue.

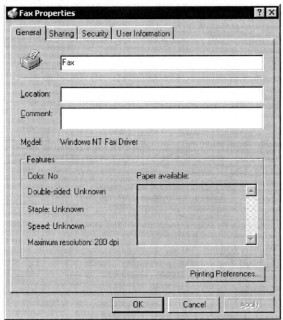

The **General** page of the **Fax Properties** dialog box allows you to specify your **Printing Preferences**:

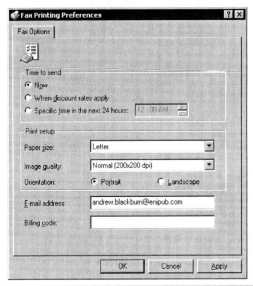

⚙ You can add a new fax printer queue by selecting **Control Panel - Fax**, then selecting the **Advanced Options** tab and clicking the **Add a Fax Printer button**.

The **Security** page of the **Fax Properties** dialog box allows you to specify permissions for the users of the queue:

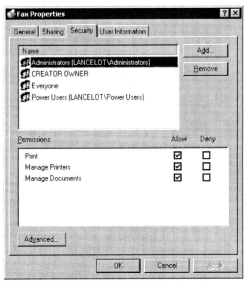

Windows 2000 Professional

The **User Information** page of the **Fax Properties** dialog box contains information concerning the fax user.

⊙ The **Sharing** page of the **Fax Properties** dialog box displays the message: **Sharing is not supported**.

e. Troubleshooting a fax

If you have difficulties in sending a fax using a modem/fax, try the following:

Check that Windows recognizes your modem and/or your fax
- Consult the HCL,
- Launch the hardware detection and check that Windows is able to detect your fax or modem/fax.

Check that Windows is able to communicate with your modem
- Consult the configuration of your modem, by going into **Control Panel - Phone and Modem Options**, then clicking the **Modems** tab, selecting your modem, clicking the **Properties** button followed by the **Diagnostics** tab, and clicking the **Query Modem** button.
- Check that your modem is associated with the correct serial port.
- Check that your modem is connected properly.
- Check the IRQ that is associated with the port.
- Check that no other program is using the port or the modem.
- Check that there is free space on the partition that contains the fax temporary folder.

⊙ If the problem concerns the configuration of the modem, consult the "Phone and modem options" section in this chapter.

Check that your fax can send documents
- Go into Microsoft Word, or another text editor.
- Try printing a simple document, choose the queue that is associated with the fax, specify a valid fax number, indicate that you do not want to include a cover page, and specify that you want to send the fax **Now**.

Check that another program is not answering the call
- (especially if the model/fax responds but fails during the negocation phase). For example, check that a remote access is not configured as a (dial-in) server: in this case, you can either disable its automatic answering feature, or specify a high number of rings before it responds, to ensure that the modem/fax will answer first.

11. CD-ROM drives and DVD-ROM players

a. Introduction

Digital Video Disk (DVD) technology concerns data storage on optical disks. A DVD is similar to a CD-ROM, except that it has a much greater storage capacity. DVDs are used to store bulky multimedia data such as cinema films.

A DVD player can read DVDs and CDs. However, you need a DVD decoder in order to be able to view films on your computer.

A DVD decoder can be either hardware or software. The installation of a hardware decoder is completely automatic, provided that Windows 2000 provides the corresponding drivers.

To find out whether or not Windows 2000 provides the necessary drivers for your DVD, consult the Internet site **http://www.hardware-update.com**. If Windows 2000 does not provide the necessary drivers for your DVD, then consult your vendor's Web site to see if your vendor offers software decoders together with the necessary drivers.

b. Installing

Provided that your device is included in the Windows 2000 HCL, it is very simple to install.

In this case, Windows 2000 will automatically detect and recognise your device and it will include it in the **Computer Management** console:

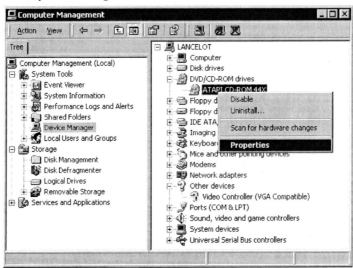

As with any other device, you can access its properties:

As with any other multimedia device, you can also access this information by going into **Control Panel - Sounds and Multimedia**, and then selecting the **Hardware** tab.

c. Tools associated with CD-ROM and DVD players

Once the installation is complete, you can access the corresponding players by selecting: **Start - Programs - Accessories - Entertainment**:

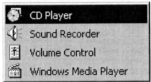

→ You can then use the CD player (**cdplayer.exe**), or the DVD player (**dvdplayer.exe**).

d. Troubleshooting CD-ROM and DVD players

Problem with a CD device (you are unable to listen to an audio CD)

- Check that the CD-ROM player is installed correctly.
- Check that you can read a data CD using **Windows Explorer**.
- Check that the disk drivers are installed.
- Check that the audio volume is high enough by selecting: **Start - Programs - Accessories - Entertainment - Volume Control**.
- Check that your CD-ROM player has been enabled so that it will accept audio digital CDs: **Control Panel - Sounds and Multimedia**, select the **Hardware** tab, select your player, and click the **Properties** button followed by the **Properties** tab. Then, under **Digital CD Playback**, activate the **Enable digital CD audio for this CD-ROM device** check box.
- Check that the audio MCI driver has been installed properly: Select **Control Panel - Sounds and Multimedia**, and select the **Hardware** tab. Then, under **Devices**, select **Media Control Devices**, and click the **Properties** button.
- Check that the CD-ROM is connected to the sound card: if no sound comes from the speakers when you play a sound, try connecting a set of headphones directly, using the socket under the CD-ROM player.

Problem with a DVD device

- Check that the DVD player is marked as working properly in the **Device Manager**.
- Check that Windows 2000 can read the data on a DVD using **Windows Explorer**: you must see at least two folders: **Video_TS** and **Audio_TS**.
- Check that the **ActiveMovie component** is working correctly by running an **AVI file**.

12. Smart card readers

a. Introduction

A smart card is a device that is the same size as a credit card. You can insert it into a smart card reader that is connected to the computer. The smart card reader may be integrated into the computer or it may be connected externally.

Microsoft strongly recommends that you install only smart card readers that the WHQL (*Windows Hardware Quality Lab*) has tested and that have obtained the **Windows compatible logo**.

In addition, you must note that Windows 2000 supports only plug-and-play readers.

When Windows 2000 detects a smart card reader, it installs it automatically.

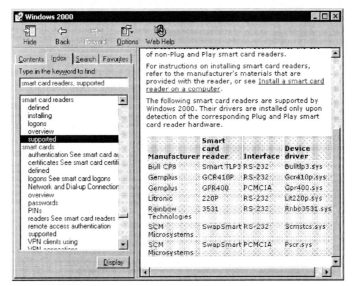

b. Smart cards and authentication

The advantage of a smart card with respect to a password is that a PIN (Personal Identification Number) code accompanies a smart card.

> This PIN code can be a sequence of digits, or it may contain other alphabetical or non-alphabetical characters.

With this technique, even if you know the PIN code, you still need to have the smart card physically in your possession in order to log on.

In addition, if someone enters an incorrect code several times in succession, then the smart card will lock out. This makes the card very difficult to violate.

Smart Card certificates

A smart card can provide an encrypted set of authentication credentials: this is a **certificate** that contains the digital signature of the certificate authority that issued it. Windows 2000 uses this certificate when it authenticates your network logon request. In fact, certificates ensure mutual authentication between your client machine and the server. Both client and server have their certificates and each presents its certificate to the other.

Certificates can reside either in your computer's certificate store or on a smart card.

c. Installing a smart card reader

Shut down your computer and switch off the power. Then, connect your smart card reader either to the serial port or into an available PCMCIA Type II slot.

Start up your computer and log on as administrator.

According to the type of smart card reader, Windows may or may not automatically detect this device.

> You may have to wait several minutes before the system detects your smart card reader. Windows 2000 will detect this device if its driver is available in the **%SystemRoot%\Driver cache\i386\driver.cab file** (for an x86 platform).

If Windows 2000 does not detect your smart card reader automatically, then you must install the appropriate driver using the **Add/Remove Hardware Wizard**, which should start up automatically.

d. Logging on with a smart card

1 - When the Windows logon screen appears, insert your smart card into the smart card reader.

2 - When your computer prompts you, enter the confidential PIN code that is associated with the card (instead of entering your domain username and password).

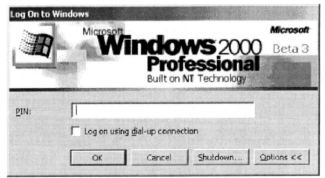

3 - If the system recognizes your PIN code as being correct, then it will log you on to the domain. Otherwise you can try again. However if you enter an incorrect PIN code several times in succession then your card will lock out. The number of unsuccessful attempts that the system will allow will depend on the smart card manufacturer.

e. Troubleshooting.

You are unable to log on to the domain

- Check that the domain controller is available. Even if you were able to log on previously you may not be able to log on when you try again. This is because the password caching mechanism does not operate when you use a smart card.
- Check that the domain controller's Certificate Revocation List for the certificate authority concerned is up to date.

13. Infrared devices

a. Introduction

These devices are equipped with infrared tranceivers. An infrared tranceiver is a small red window, such as the one that appears on a portable computer, or on devices such as printers, cameras, or dongles (a dongle is a hardware component that allows you to access a program when you connect it onto a serial port).

In order to enable two devices to communicate with each other via an infrared link, the infrared tranceivers must point to each other, and generally, they must not be spaced more than one meter apart.

b. Data transmission protocols

Infrared devices use **IrDA (Infrared Data Association) protocols**. Notably, these protocols support network connections, file transfers and printing.

These standards allow you to set up connections using infrared devices, which are inexpensive and have low power consumption.

Nowadays, most portable computers are equipped with an infrared (IrDA) port. Alternatively, you can install an IrDA tranceiver directly on a serial port.

The Infrared Data Association protocols describe a certain number of procedures:
- initializing links
- addressing devices, and resolving address conflicts
- setting up connections
- negociating transmission speeds
- exchanging data
- disconnecting.

Different protocols cover different types of link:
- IrLPT manages printing via an infrared port
- IrTran-P manages image transfers.

In addition, the IrDA application programming interface allows vendors to provide infrared connections that support different types of equipment, including the following:
- printers

- modems
- digital radio message receivers
- pocket computers
- digital cameras
- schedulers
- cellular telephones
- portable computers.

c. Components of the IrDA architecture

To understand how the IrDA protocols work, it is useful to examine the IrDA architecture:

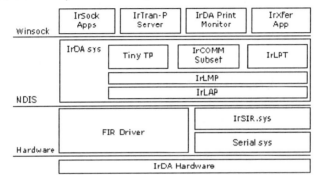

Winsock

Winsock is an Application Programming Interface (API) layer. It allows applications to access the IrDA protocols.

IrTran-P

IrTran-P is an image transfer protocol that functions in full-duplex mode (this means that it transmits data in both directions simultaneously).

❂ Windows 2000 receives only the data. It works with cameras that use infrared technology to transfer the data and automatically saves the data in a specific directory.

IrDA Print monitor

The IrDA Print monitor allows you to work with an infrared printer via an infrared port, as you would work with any other printer.

IrXfer

IrXfer is full-duplex file transfer application that allows you to drag files onto another computer using your mouse.

Tiny TP

Tiny TP is a transport protocol that provides flow control for the IrDA protocols.

IrDA.sys

The IrDA.sys module allows the system to treat Winsock applications as transport protocols.

IrCOMM

IrCOMM is a software component that manages IrTran-P.

IrLPT

The print monitor uses the IrLPT protocol to authorize printing directly to infrared devices.

IrLMP

The Infrared Link Management Protocol (IrLMP) allows a single connection to handle several links.

IrLAP

The Infrared Link Access Protocol (IrLAP) is a software layer that allows you to access the physical hardware. This protocol allows a specific component to use the infrared link for a certain time period.

d. IrDA standards

The two most common transfer rates are 115 Kbps (this is the maximum transfer rate of a serial port) and 4 Mbps.

Windows 2000 supports both of these transfer rates.

Infrared Data Association - Serial InfraRed (IrDA-SIR)

IrDA-SIR is an inexpensive solution that allows you to use existing infrared hardware. It allows short-range, asynchronous (1 start bit, 8 data bit and 1 stop bit) flow rates of up to 115 200 bps in half-duplex mode (alternate bi-directional communication).

It provides a low rate of transmission errors. In addition, it offers high interference protection in sunlight and in brightly lit office environments.

Infrared Data Association - Fast InfraRed (IrDA-FIR)

IrDA-FIR is a high-speed extension to IrDA-SIR. It allows transfer rates of up to 4 Mbps, in half-duplex mode. Portable computers now offer IrDA-FIR transceivers. In addition, IrDA-FIR hardware can communicate with IrDA-SIR hardware.

Infrared Line Printer

If your computer is equipped with an infrared device and you install an infrared transceiver with Windows 2000, then an infrared port will appear as a local port in the **Add Printer Wizard**. When you print to an infrared printer that you have associated with this port, Windows 2000 will use the IrLPT protocol in order to transfer the data.

Infrared Transmission Protocol

Windows 2000 supports the IrTran-P image transfer protocol used by digital cameras and other digital image capture devices. You can use this feature to transfer digital images from a digital camera, or from any other device that supports the IrTran-P protocol, to your computer via an IrDA connection. On Windows 2000, the IrTran-P feature is a listen-only service that never initiates an IrTran-P connection.

e. Installing an infrared device

→) To install an infrared device, go into the **Control Panel**, launch the **Add/Remove Hardware Wizard**, select **Add/Troubleshoot a device**, and then click **Next**.

Wait a short time in order to allow Windows 2000 to detect Plug-and-Play hardware.

→) Then, under **Devices**, select **Add a new device** and click **Next**.
On the next screen, you can select **Yes, search for new hardware**. Alternatively, you can choose your device manually by selecting **No, I want to select the hardware from a list**, and specifying the type of hardware:

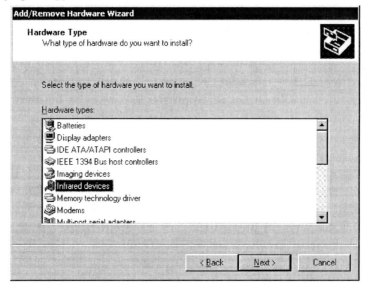

→) Then, select the device concerned:

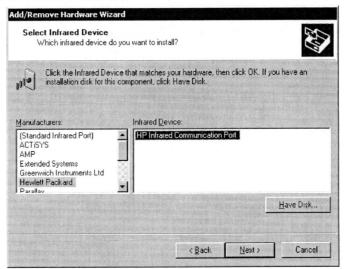

Windows 2000 then sets up your device. Whilst it is doing this, the wizard may indicate that it has detected a conflict with another device:

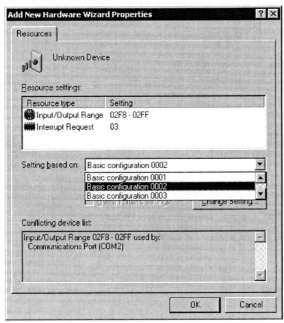

Otherwise, if the wizard does not detect any conflict it will install your device using default settings:

After you have installed an infrared link, the **Wireless Link** icon appears in the **Control Panel** :

Wireless Link

You can then adjust the settings of this link by double-clicking the icon:

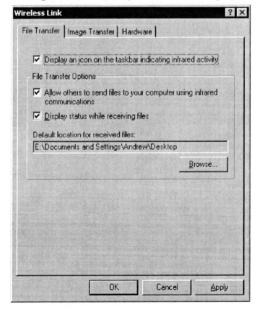

f. Setting up an infrared connection

This section will describe how to set up an infrared connection between two workstations.

Go into **Control Panel - Network and Dial-up Connections**.

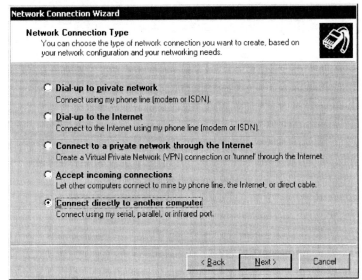

→⟩ Select **Make New Connection**. The **Network Connection Wizard** starts up, and invites you to choose a **Connection Type**:

→) Next you must specify the role that you want your computer to play:

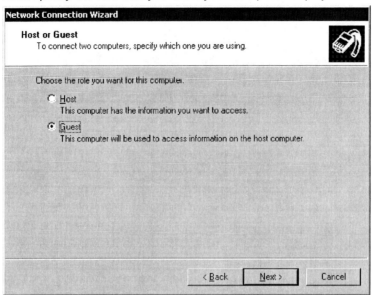

→) Then you must specify the infrared port that you want to use:

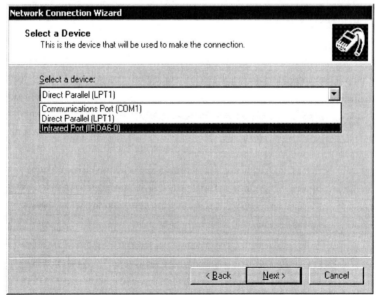

You can choose, either to customize your connection, or to leave it available for all users:

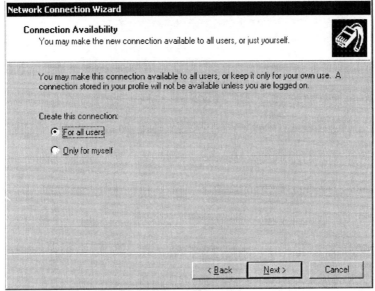

→) Finally, you can give your connection a name:

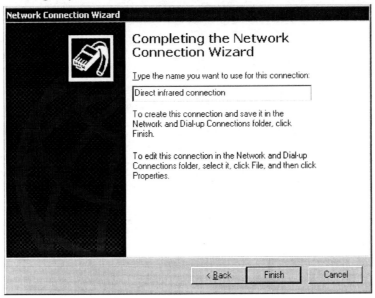

➜) Then, you must specify the name and password of the user who is allowed to use this connection:

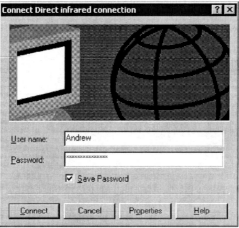

In the **Network and Dial-up Connections** console, you can now view the properties of this connection, and access the same information as you would for a remote access connection.

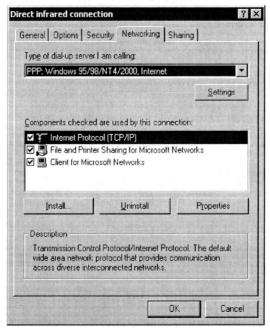

For further information on remote network access, see Chapter 5 of this book, "Configuring the network".

To view the properties of an infrared device:

→) Go into the **Control Panel** and start up the **Wireless Link** module. Select the **Hardware** tab:

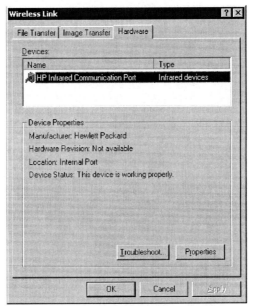

→) Select the device concerned and click the **Properties** button.
This dialog box offers four tabs that provide information on the status, the usage, the maximum connect rate, the communication port and the device settings.

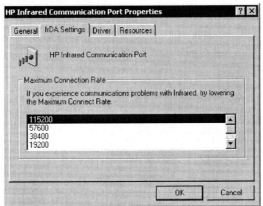

If you have communication problems with infrared devices, you could try lowering the maximum connect rate in the page of the dialog box that is shown above.

14. Wireless devices

As an example of installing a wireless device, this section will describe how to install an infrared printer then describe how to send files to another computer.

a. Installing an infrared printer

It is very easy to make Windows 2000 detect an infrared printer.

Provided that your computer is equipped with an infrared port, and is switched on, all you have to do is to place the print device within a meter of your computer and, after a few seconds, Windows 2000 will automatically detect the printer and will install the necessary drivers.

Windows 2000 adds the icon of your printer to the **Printers** folder.

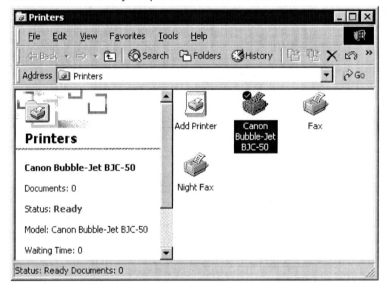

Windows 2000 Professional

The printer device uses the **IR (Infra Red) port**.

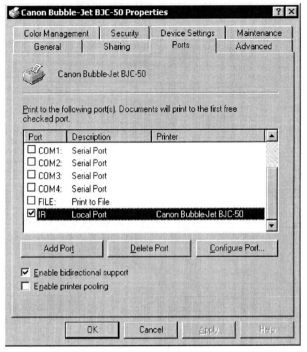

b. Printing on an infrared printer

Set up the connection by positioning the red windows opposite one another until the **Infra-red** icon appears on your taskbar. You can then print as you would with any other printer.

c. Sending files over a wireless connection

First, this section will describe how to configure file and image transfer. Then, it will describe how to send files over a wireless connection.

→) Access the configuration settings for this connection by going into the **Control Panel** and double-clicking the **Wireless Link** icon.

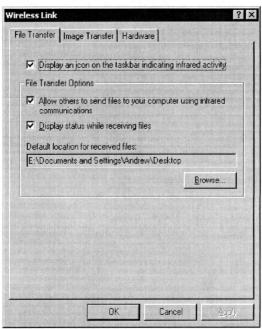

→ Click the **Image Transfer** tab, and press the **Browse** button in order to specify the folder in which you want to store the images that you receive.

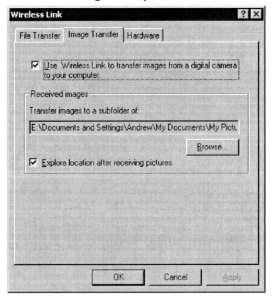

Using the irftp command

The **irftp** command allows you to work, either from a command prompt, or using a graphic interface.

Syntax of the irftp command

Irftp allows you to send files over an infrared link, provided that an infrared device is installed on your computer.

```
irftp[/h][[drive:][path]filename[morefiles]]irftp/s
```

in which:

```
/h
```

specifies hidden mode. This mode allows you to transmit the source files over the infrared link without displaying the **Wireless Link** dialog box.

```
[[drive:][path]filename[morefiles]]
```

specifies the locations and the names of the files that you want to send over your infrared connection. If you do not specify a file, then you will automatically access graphic mode, as the **Wireless Link** dialog box appears and allows you to choose the files that you want to send over your link.

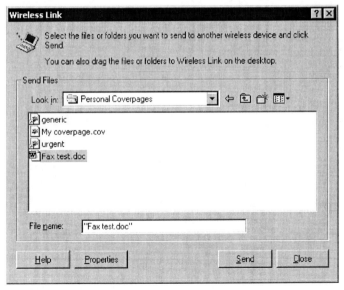

```
/s
```

opens the **File Transfer** page of the **Wireless Link** dialog box. Among other things, this page allows you to specify the **Default location for received files**.

Accessing graphic mode

To access graphic mode, select the **Start - Run** menu option and enter **irftp** in the **Run** dialog box. The **Wireless Link** dialog box then appears, as described above.

15. Universal Serial Bus devices and IEEE 1394 devices

a. Introduction

USB or Universal Serial Bus

A **Universal Serial Bus (USB)** allows you to connect up to 127 devices to your computer.

When you connect a USB device, you do not need to stop and restart your computer as you can make a hot-plug connection. Windows 2000 installs USB devices automatically, and the USB transfer rate is ten times greater than that which you would obtain with traditional serial ports.

IEEE 1394

IEEE 1394 is a high speed serial bus. It offers characteristics similar to those of a USB and in addition, it allows you to interconnect a wide variety of devices such as audio/video components, storage devices and other computers.

Installing a USB or IEEE 1394 printer

If you connect a USB or an IEEE 1394 printer, then Windows 2000 will detect it and then start up the **Add/Remove Hardware Wizard**. You do not need to stop and restart your computer. To complete the installation of your printer you need only follow the instructions that appear on the screen. Windows 2000 automatically adds the icon of your new printer to the **Printers** folder.

b. Troubleshooting USB and IEEE 1394 printers

As USB devices are Plug-and-Play components, they require very little management or configuring.

As a general rule, either they work correctly, or they do not work at all.
Here are some typical problems that you may encounter:

Faulty, or wrong type of hardware

Connecting faulty hardware, or the wrong type of hardware to the serial port will often result in a reset storm on the USB and cause the system to stop responding. Reinitializing the computer will not help in this case. You must switch the computer off so that you can reinitialize the device concerned.

However, it may be very difficult to identify the device that is causing the problem. One approach to solving this problem is to try the different devices one by one on another system in order to see if you can reproduce the problem, and thereby identify the device concerned.

If the device, which you have identified the device that is causing the problem, is connected to a secondary USB hub, then try connecting it to the root USB hub.

With most hardware problems (for example, faulty power supply, overloaded bandwidth or the wrong firmware version) information will be transmitted to the operating system and messages will appear in the **Event Viewer**. To identify any problems, you can consult the Event Viewer log.

→ Use the **Device Manager** to check whether or not the root USB hub is working correctly.

→ Check that the BIOS has assigned an IRQ to the root USB hub.

If none of the devices that are connected to the root hub are working, check that you are respecting the acceptable range of power supplies: USB devices support a maximum supply of 500 mA per connection, and a minimum supply of 50 mA. If the power supply exceeds this range then the port will be suspended, whereas if the power supply falls below this range then the port will be disabled.

Incorrect or missing device driver

Windows 2000 provides classes of device driver for a certain number of USB devices. When you connect a USB device, then Windows 2000 automatically assigns a device driver from one of the driver classes.

If Windows 2000 asks you for a device driver, then consult your vendor to find out whether a suitable driver is available.

If Windows 2000 informs you that a driver has not been signed then you must consider your driver as being suspect. In fact, this means that Microsoft has not tested this driver.

→ Check the **Event Viewer** log to see if there are any errors concerning: Hidclass.sys, Hidusb.sys, Usbhub.sys, Usbd.sys, Uhcd.sys, or Openhci.sys.

The device driver may have been inserted as a replacement in the Windows 2000 device driver stack, which could destablize the whole bus.

Cabling error

There are two types of USB cable: high speed cables and low speed cables.
Low speed cables are not shielded as well as high speed cables are.
Consequently, if you connect a high speed device onto a low speed cable then, over long distances, the signal may be distorted.

→ Check the entire USB chain: some devices must be connected to a powered hub, whilst other devices can be connected to a non-powered hub.

Out-of-date firmware

The firmware contains all the information about the device. All the firmware descriptors must be loaded and checked by the root hub before the port is reset. This is particularly important for printers and modems. You must check then, that you have the right firmware, both for the BIOS of your computer, and for each of the USB devices.

If you have any duplicate devices, take special care to check that your firmware is up-to-date.

Badly configured USB root hub

→) Check that an IRQ has been assigned to the USB controller.

→) More specifically, check that the BIOS system assigns an IRQ to the USB. This will usually be IRQ 9.

16. Tape devices

Windows 2000 does not support QIC (*Quarter Inch Cartridge*) devices, or tape drives that use floppy drive connections.

If you use either of these types of device, contact your vendor to find out whether a driver is available for Windows 2000.

Normally, Windows 2000 should detect and install your device automatically. If this is not the case, then you can install your device manually:

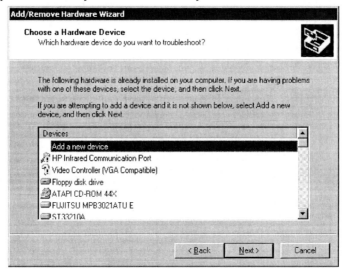

➜) Indicate that you want to choose the driver yourself for a specific device:

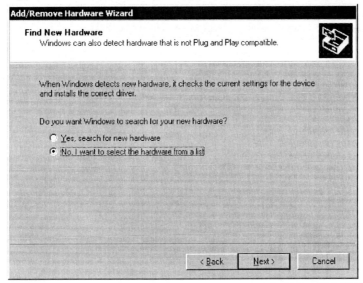

💿 Windows 2000 must be able to detect your device in all cases.

➜) Under **Hardware types**, select **Tape drives**:

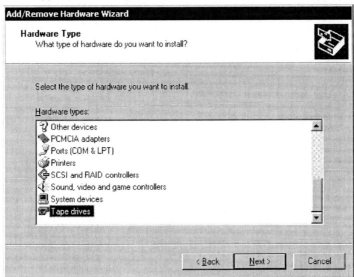

Then, Windows 2000 should detect your device. However, if Windows 2000 is unable to detect your device, then it will display the following message:

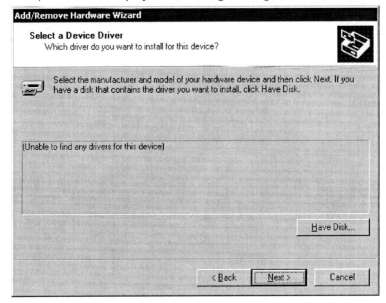

17. Cameras

a. Installing

If you have a USB camera, for example, then you need only plug it into the USB port of your computer. First, Windows 2000 detects the presence of your USB device:

Then, it detects your device in more detail:

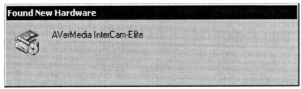

According to the device concerned, Windows will indicate either that it recognizes the driver as having been signed, or that it does not recognize the driver as having been signed:

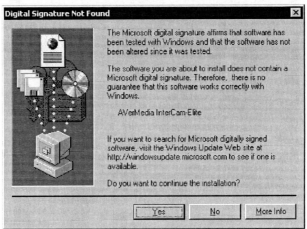

The final step is to install the applications that will use this device.

b. Troubleshooting

If you have any problems, you can update your device driver, with a signed driver for example.

→) Double-click the **Unplug or Eject Hardware** icon on your taskbar. The following dialog box appears:

➜ Click the **Properties** button, then click the **Reinstall Driver** button.

After you have specified appropriate search locations, such as hard disks, floppy disk drives and CD-ROM drives, the **Upgrade Device Driver Wizard** may be able to find a more suitable driver for your device.

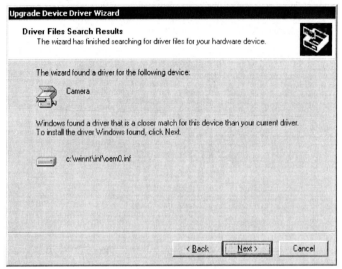

Windows 2000 will then tell you if it recognizes the driver or not.

Otherwise, you can always consult the **Hardware Troubleshooter** to solve any problems that you may have with a device.

18. Multiprocessor platforms

This section discusses how you can upgrade a Windows 2000 monoprocessor computer to a multiprocessor platform.

Upgrading to a multiprocessor platform

To upgrade a workstation to support several processors, you must carry out the following steps.

➜ Open the **Computer Management** console and select **System Tools - Device Manager - Computer - Standard PC**.

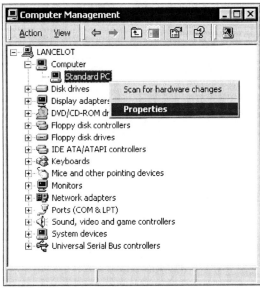

Select the **Properties** of this object.

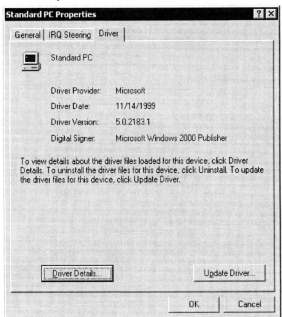

→) Under the **Driver** tab of this dialog box, click the **Update Driver** button. The **Upgrade Device Driver Wizard** starts up.

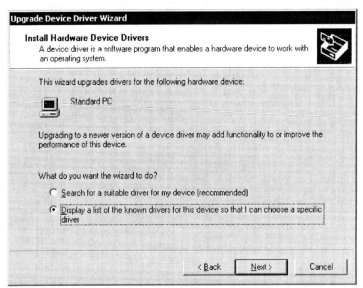

Display the list of drivers and choose the appropriate manufacturer and model.

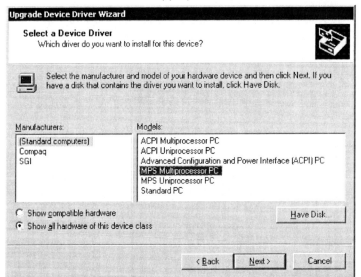

By this means, you can specify the HAL *(Hardware Abstraction Layer)* that Windows 2000 must use.

→ Shut down and switch off your system, physically upgrade your processor and restart your computer

19.Troubleshooting hardware problems

If one of your devices is malfunctioning, you can go into the Control Panel, open the configuration icon of the device that is causing the problem, and then click the **Trouble-shoot** button (for most devices this button is under the **Hardware** tab). The online **Help** will then guide you step by step in an attempt to diagnose the cause of the problem, and thereby to help you to solve it.

In addition, you can use the **Device Manager** program in order to monitor the status of your devices.

An icon with a red cross on it indicates that the corresponding device is disabled.

An icon that is marked with a black exclamation point on a yellow background indicates, either that the device concerned is badly configured, or that a driver has not been installed for this device.

In addition, you can use the **Windows 2000 Hardware Troubleshooter**:

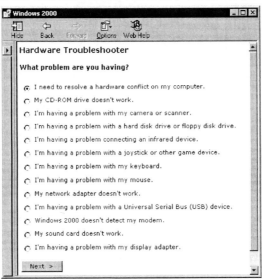

20. Managing device drivers

a. Updating drivers

A device driver is a (binary) software program that allows an operating system to recognize the device. After you have installed these software components, you can update them, either by accessing the **Properties** of the device in the **Device Manager**, or by accessing the **Microsoft Windows Update** Internet site.

b. Device Manager

→) You can start up the **Device Manager** by right-clicking **My Computer**, clicking the **Manage** option, and then selecting the **Device Manager** folder.

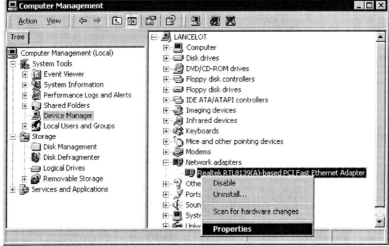

→) You can access the driver of a particular device, by right-clicking the device entry, selecting **Properties** and clicking the **Driver** tab in the dialog box that appears.

→) Click the **Update Driver** button. The **Upgrade Device Driver Wizard** starts up and offers to help:

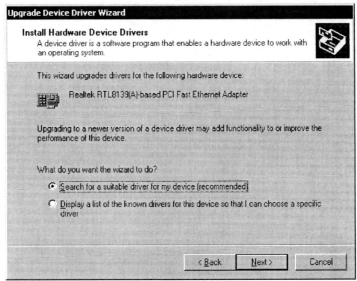

→) This wizard offers, either to search for a driver on a floppy disk, on a CD-ROM or at a specific location, or to display a list of drivers for this type of device in order to help you to find a suitable driver.

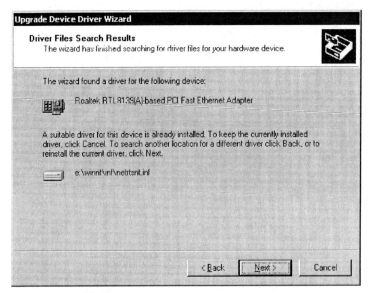

c. Microsoft Windows Update

Alternatively, you can update some of your files and drivers by visiting the Microsoft site on the Internet at the address: http://**windowsupdate.Microsoft.com**/. This site offers drivers, upgrades, help files and Internet products that you can download in order to ensure that you keep your computer up-to-date.

If you have access to the Internet you can visit this site directly from the **Start - Windows Update** menu option.

Then, select the **PRODUCT UPDATES** link.

This link allows you to analyze your workstation in order to find any out-of-date system files and to replace them automatically by the most up-to-date versions.

◐ When you open the **PRODUCT UPDATES** page for the first time, a message appears asking you if you want to install the necessary applications and products: click **Yes** to this question.

d. Overview of signed drivers

Microsoft has digitally signed the drivers and the system files of the WIndows 2000 operating system in order to certify their quality. The Microsoft digital signature is a guarantee that a file has undergone numerous tests and that it has not been modified or replaced during the installation phase of another program.

Depending on the way in which the administrator configured the workstation, when Windows 2000 encounters an unsigned device driver, it will either ignore the lack of signature and install the driver (level 0), or display a warning message (level 1), or prevent the driver from being installed (level 2).

The laboratory that tests and signs drivers is called the **Windows Hardware Quality Lab (WHQL).**

The driver's binary code does not contain the driver signature directly. In fact for each signed driver, Microsoft creates a **catalog** (.cat) file that contains both the binary code and an encoded digital signature that corresponds to this code. Thus, if you modify the binary code then the signature will no longer be valid.

◐ The signature files are contained in the **%SystemRoot%\System32\CatRoot** folder.

◐ The Microsoft Windows Update Web site **http://windowsupdate.Microsoft.com/** offers only signed drivers.

e. Managing signed drivers

→) Go into **Control Panel - System** and select the **Hardware** tab.

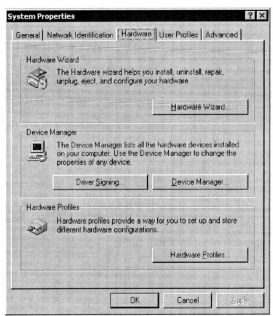

Under **Hardware Wizard**, the **Hardware Wizard** button allows you to start up the **Add/Remove Hardware** module.

Under **Device Manager**, the **Driver Signing** button allows you to specify the security level that the system must respect when it installs new drivers.

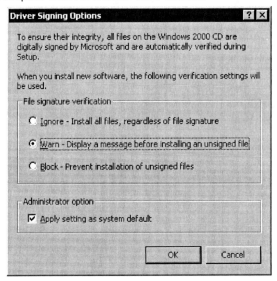

Badly written device drivers are the cause of most system failures. Microsoft guarantees that all drivers that are signed by them are compatible with the Windows 2000 environment. However, some drivers have not received this signature because their manufacturers did not consider it to be necessary. You can enhance the stability of your system by forbidding the installation of unsigned drivers.

Windows 2000 Datacenter version does not allow the installation of drivers that have not been signed.

The **Device Manager** allows you to view the status of your devices. It also allows you to uninstall them, to disable them or to view their properties. An alternative way of accessing **Device Manager** is to right-click **My Computer** and then to select **Manage**.

B. Workstation settings

1. Introduction

Windows 2000 allows you to customize your work environment in many ways. For example, you can choose your own color scheme and screen background, you can specify the use of single clicks, or you can add shortcuts onto your desktop or into your **Start** menu.

Thanks to the automatic management of user profiles, each user can have a custom work environment on the same computer without altering the work environments of the other users. Windows 2000 saves all work environment modifications at the end of the user session.

2. Changing the look of your desktop

The **Control Panel - Display** module offers a number of pages that allow you to customize your desktop.

For a description of this module, see the Display section earlier in this chapter.

In addition, you can customize your **Start** menu and your taskbar as follows:

→) Select **Start - Settings - Taskbar & Start Menu**:

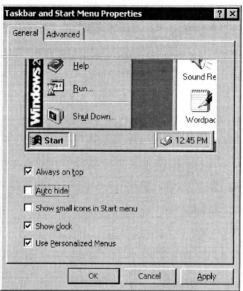

The **Advanced** page of this dialog box allows flexible management of your menus:

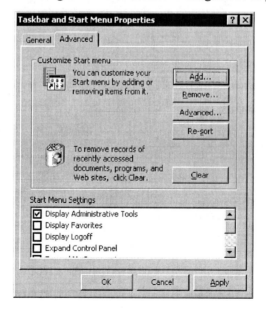

➜) Clicking the **Advanced** button allows you to modify your menu hierarchy manually: either by right-clicking items, or by dragging items to other locations, or by creating new shortcuts.

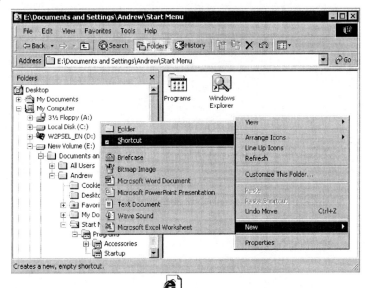

You can create a shortcut, for example  example, so that it will appear automatically in your **Start** menu:

3. Changing the "Send To" destination

When you right-click an item, such as a document for example, you can use the **Send To** option in order to send the document to a specific destination.

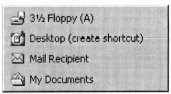

You can change the contents of the **Send To** menu in order to send a document to a printer, for example, or to any other application. In order to do this, go into the folder that contains your profile, and access the **SendTo** subfolder (see important note below):

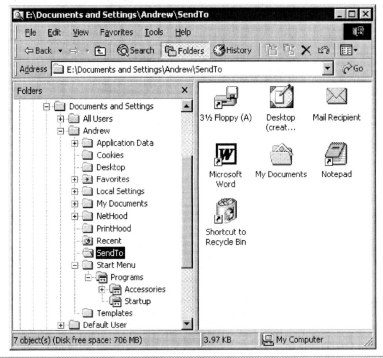

 A simpler way of accessing this folder is to select **Start - Settings - Taskbar & Start Menu** and then click the **Advanced** tab followed by the **Advanced** button. The **SendTo** folder is on the same level as the **Start Menu** folder (see Important note below).

Important note: the **SendTo** folder is hidden by default. If it is not displayed then select **Tools - Folder Options**, click the **View** tab and activate the **Show hidden files and folders** setting.

4. Enabling Active Desktop

Active Desktop allows you to make your desktop display a dynamic page from the Internet, or from your intranet. When you enable this feature, your screen background displays the default page of your Internet browser.

→⟩ Go into **Control Panel - Folder Options**.

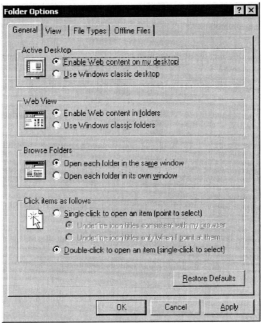

→⟩ On the **General** page, activate the **Enable Web content on my desktop** option. Alternatively, you can right-click your desktop and select **Active Desktop - Show Web Content**.

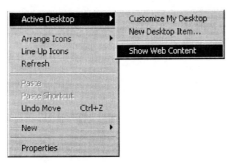

5. Adding a program onto the Quick Launch bar

The simplest way of adding a program onto your **Quick Launch** bar is to select the icon for the program concerned and drag it onto the **Quick Launch** bar. The **Quick Launch** bar appears on the taskbar and contains a number of icons.

Alternatively, you can modify the contents of the **Quick Launch** folder directly in the folder hierarchy:

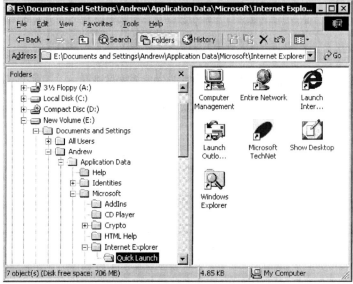

For example, you can specify the following **Quick Launch** bar:

6. Using personalized menus

This feature allows you to display, in the **Programs** menu, only those items that you have used recently and to hide the other items.

Nevertheless, you can still access the hidden programs thanks to the down-arrow that appears at the bottom of the menu. This down-arrow allows you to expand the menu and display these hidden items.

To activate the **Personalized Menus** feature, select **Start - Settings - Taskbar & Start Menu** and then, under the **General** tab, activate the **Use Personalized Menus** option.

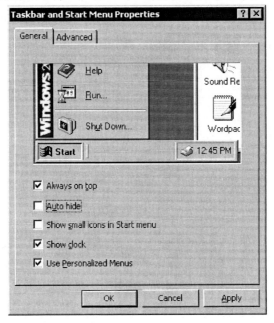

7. Add/remove programs

This module allows you to install, to remove and to modify programs. If you decide to diffuse applications using the publication technique, then users will be able to consult the published applications with a view to installing them using this module.

You can use the **Add/Remove Programs** icon from the **Control Panel**, either to add Windows components, such as, SNMP agent, RIP agent, IIS services and Unix print services:

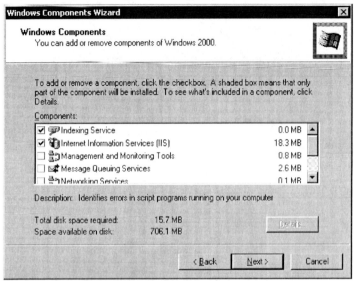

or, you can add programs that are not Windows components:

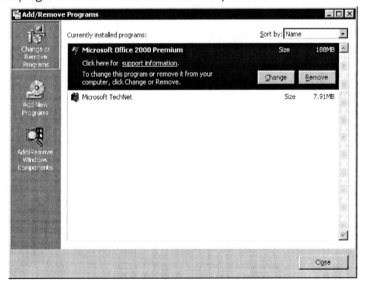

Windows 2000 Professional

In addition, you can install a **Windows Installer** package. For example, you can install the Windows 2000 Administrative Tools on your Windows 2000 Professional workstation (See the **Important note** below):

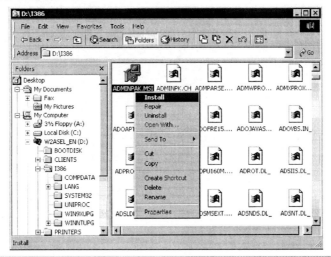

Important note: You can install these administrative tools from the **I386** folder on the Windows 2000 Server CD-ROM.

When you install these tools, Windows 2000 adds a considerable number of extra tools into the **Administrative Tools** folder:

You can access this folder from the **Start - Programs** menu.

8. Date/Time

Date/Time This module allows you to adjust the date, the time and the time zone.

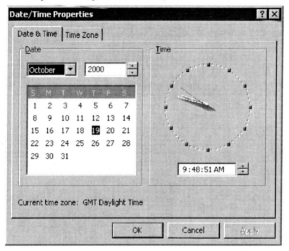

9. Accessibility options

Accessibility
Options This module offers a large number of very useful options that allow you to make Windows 2000 even more accessible.

For example you can specify that the system must make a sound when you press the [Caps Lock] key. In addition, you can use the **StickyKeys** feature. This feature allows you to execute a shortcut key sequence, by pressing one key at a time. For example, with this feature, rather than pressing [Ctrl][Alt][Del] simultaneously, you can execute this shortcut sequence by pressing these three keys, one after the other, in any order. When you enable these features, Windows 2000 automatically displays the corresponding icons.

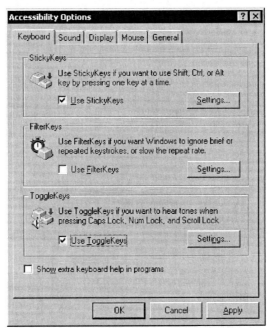

You can use your numeric keypad in order to control your mouse pointer:

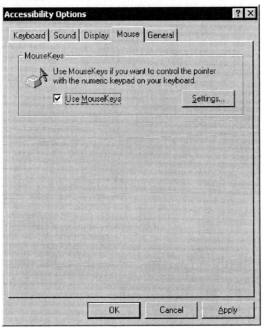

You can specify that Windows 2000 must generate a visual warning when it makes a sound:

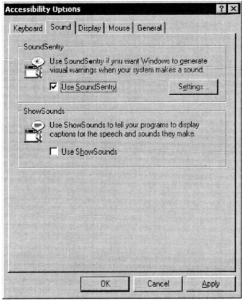

You can use colors and fonts for easy reading:

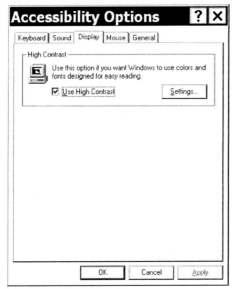

Finally, under the **General** tab of this dialog box, you can specify settings that the system must apply to new user profiles:

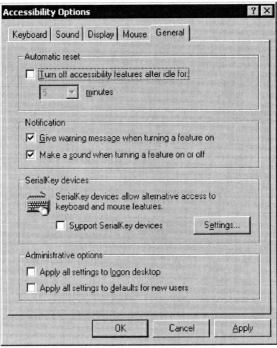

In addition, the **Accessibility** menu provides other features (you can access this menu by selecting **Start - Programs - Accessories - Accessibility**):

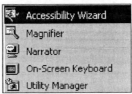

Amongst these features, the **On-Screen Keyboard** allows you to type information by clicking the corresponding on-screen keys using your mouse:

Also, the **Magnifier** allows you to display a magnified image of the screen zone in which your mouse pointer is placed:

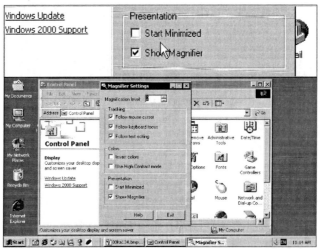

10. Power options

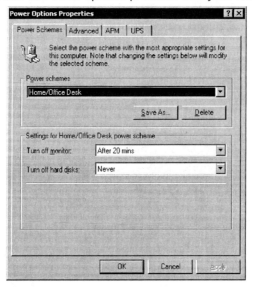

Power Options   This module allows you to reduce the energy consumption of your computer by specifying that the monitor and/or the hard disks must be turned off automatically after a specified idle time. You can use these options provided that your hardware supports them.

11. Folder options

Folder Options This module is covered in Chapter 7: Managing disk resources.

12. Internet options

Internet
Options This module is just a shortcut to the **Internet Properties** dialog box that **Internet Explorer** provides (you can access **Internet Explorer** directly from your desktop).

13. Regional options

a. Configuring local settings

Regional
Options You can configure numerous local and international settings in your work environment. For example, you can specify, the type of keyboard that you are using, the character code page in a given language, how the date and the time must be displayed, and the local currency.

According to the code page that you use, many characters will have a different code, (for example, ANSI, EBCDIC, or ISO). Consequently, in order fully to support international aspects, you must implement character conversion tables that take account of the source language and the destination language. Windows 2000 allows you to do this simply, as it supports Unicode. Unicode is an intenational standard that represents international characters.

You can configure and modify all your local settings in the **Control Panel - Regional Options** module:

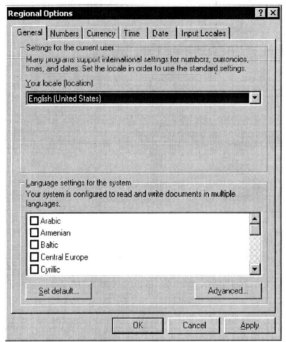

On the **General** page of this dialog box, the upper frame (**Settings for the current user**) concerns the user who is currently logged on.

The lower frame on this page (**Language settings for the system**) concerns the system as a whole.

b. Windows 2000 multiple language support

Introduction

Multiple language support is one of the prime features that Windows 2000 offers. It allows people to work in different languages on the same workstation. This approach allows a multinational company to use a common multilingual interface and to share its workstations amongst several users who work in different languages.

This allows you to simplify the work of the users, and to reduce the Total Cost of Ownership (TCO).

For this purpose, Microsoft offers several versions of Windows 2000 Professional. Each of these versions corresponds to different specific cases. This approach allows you to support a variety of user specific linguistic needs, on a small or large scale. Microsoft offers the following versions of Windows 2000 Professional:

– Windows 2000 English version,

- Windows 2000 Localized version (avalailable in over 20 languages),
- Windows 2000 Multilanguage version.

Windows 2000 Multilanguage version provides extensive support of the specific properties of each language. This version is offered only to clients that have a Microsoft Open, Select or Enterprise license contract.

Options of the different versions

English or localized version

The user interface of this version is fully localized (menus, help files, dialog boxes and file names).
Users can create, display and print documents in over 60 languages.
Advantages: you can work with documents that are written in different languages.

Multilanguage version

Users can switch from one language interface to another (menus, help files, dialog boxes and file names).
Users can create, display and print documents in over 60 languages.
Avantages: This version offers the same features as the English or locatised version, and in addition, it allows you to change the user interface from one language to another.

Activating multiple language support

Go into the **Control Panel** and open the **Regional Options**. Then, in the **Language settings for the system** frame under the **General** tab, enable the check boxes for the languages that you would like Windows 2000 to support.

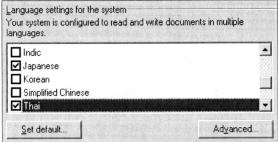

The **Advanced** button provides access to the **Code page conversion tables**.

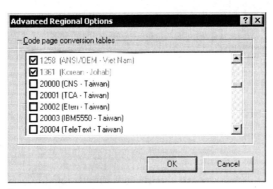

Configuring multiple language support

The **Input Locales** tab of the **Keyboard Properties** dialog box allows you to specify the input language and the type of keyboard that you will be using.

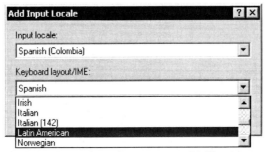

When you have configured the languages that you would like to use, you can switch from one language to another by clicking the language icon on your taskbar (this is the **EN** icon in the example below).

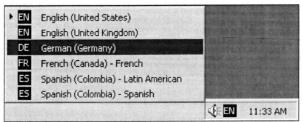

When you have switched languages, the new language icon appears on the taskbar (the German icon, in the example below).

Configuring Windows 2000 Professional for use in multiple environments

According to your geographical location, you can activate Windows 2000 support for the appropriate keyboard. To do this, under the **Input Locales** tab of the **Regional Options** dialog box, configure the appropriate language and keyboard.

When you click the **Add** button on the **Input Locales** page, you must select the **Input locale** along with the **Keyboard layout/IME**.

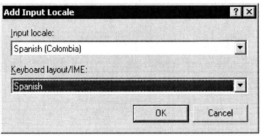

The **Input Locales** page also allows you to define a **Change Key Sequence** in order to switch between input locales. For example:

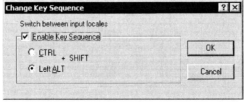

You must configure the general settings in the **Your locale (location)** list in the **Settings for the current user** frame, under the **General** tab. In addition, you must configure the input locale settings in the **Language settings for the system** frame, under the **General** tab and in the **Installed input locales** frame, under the **Input Locales** tab.

Finally, you must restart your computer to apply your settings.

When you have restarted your computer, an icon corresponding to the language that you selected in the **Your locale (location)** list appears in the taskbar. When you click this icon, you can choose from the different input locales that you installed.

Windows 2000 uses these settings to interpret your keyboard and implement its international characteristics. For example, if you select **Spanish** in the **Your locale (location)** list, the **Date/Time Properties** will appear as follows:

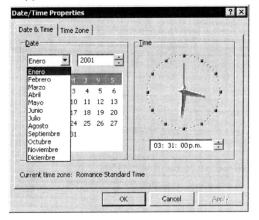

14. Administrative tools

a. Local tools

Windows 2000 groups local administrative tools together. On a Windows 2000 Professional workstation, the **Computer Management** tool groups these tools together. The **Administrative Tools** module contains the **Computer Management** tool.

You can access **Administrative Tools** either from the **Control Panel**, or from the **Start - Programs** menu:

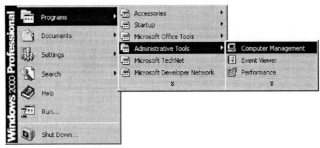

Standard Windows 2000 Professional tools

Component Services

This utility allows administrators to provide access to the objects of an application in a distributed environment.

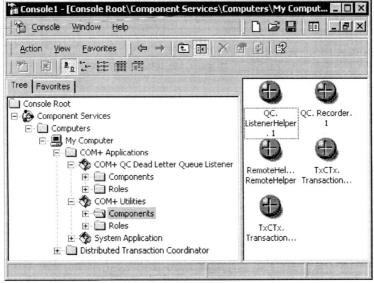

Computer Management

This console groups together the essential tools that you need to administer a Windows 2000 machine that is not a domain controller remotely.

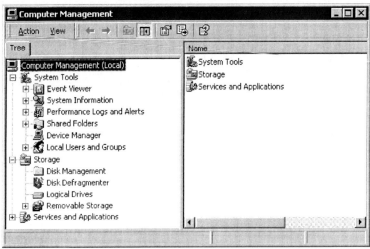

Data Sources (ODBC)

ODBC (*Open DataBase Connectivity*) is a programming interface that allows programs to access data in database management systems that use SQL *(Structured Query Language)* as a data access standard.

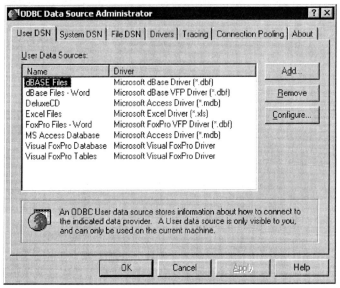

Event Viewer

This tool allows you to view and to manage event logs concerning the system, the programs and the security of your computer. It gathers together information concerning Windows 2000 hardware and software problems.

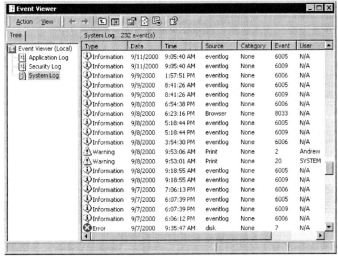

Local Security Policy

This tool allows you to configure security settings for the local computer. These settings include Password Policy, Account Lockout Policy, Audit Policy, IP Security Policy, User Rights Assignment, Recovery Agents for encrypted data, and other security options. You can manage local security only on Windows 2000 machines that are not domain controllers.

If the computer is a domain member then policies that are received from the domain replace these local security policies.

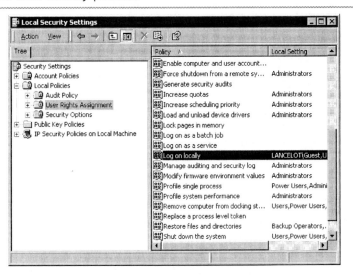

Performance

The **Performance** tool allows you to collect and to view, in real time, data concerning the different resources, such as memory, disk, processor, and network interface. You can view this data, either in graphic form in the **System Monitor**, or in a log in **Performance Logs and Alerts**.

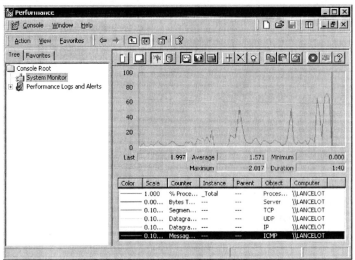

Services

The **Services** tool allows you to manage the services on your computer. In particular, it allows you to define recovery actions in the case of a service failing, and customize names and descriptions so that you can identify them more easily.

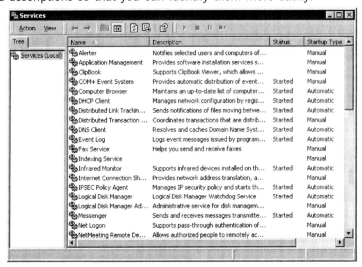

Windows 2000 Professional

b. Administrating a domain

You can add additional domain administration tools by installing the **Adminpack.msi** Windows Installer Package from the **i386** folder of the Windows 2000 Server CD-ROM.

You can install this package using the **Add New Programs** button in the **Add/Remove Programs** module of the **Control Panel**.

Customizing your administrative tools

A customized console is a file that has an .MSC extension. You can add snap-in components to this file. A snap-in is an application management component.

To create a customized MMC, run the **mmc.exe** program.

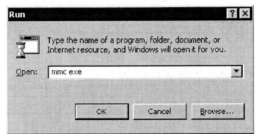

A blank console appears, into which you can add snap-in components.

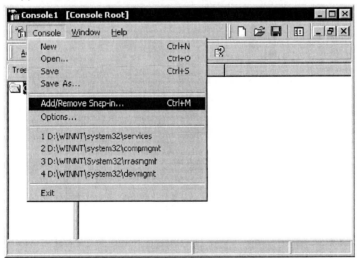

➜ For this purpose, open the **Console** menu and select the **Add/Remove Snap-in** option.

➜ Click the **Add** button and select the snap-ins you want to add to your console.

When you have created your console, you must save it so that you will be able to re-use it. You can create as many MMCs as you like. In addition, you can add as many snap-ins as you like into each console.

⊙ If user profiles have been implemented, you must place this MMC in your own profile to be able to use it from any machine in the network.

⊙ In this way, you can create customized consoles so that you can delegate certain administrative tasks to other users. These customized consoles can be sent by e-mail for example.

Terminology

As an example, take the following MMC:

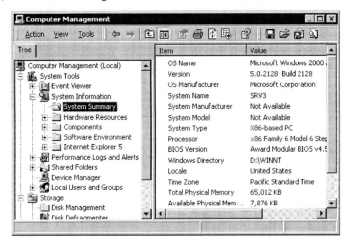

- This section deals with the Snap-ins for **Computer Management**
- A snap-in can have one or more **extensions**. In the example above, the snap-in **Computer Management** has extensions that include **Event Viewer** and **Device Manager**. An extension is a snap-in attached to a parent snap-in. Some snap-ins can be both snap-ins and extensions. This is the case for **Event Viewer**.

When you create your own MMC, you can use an extension as a snap-in for the console that you are designing. To do this, run an MMC, and then add a snap-in.

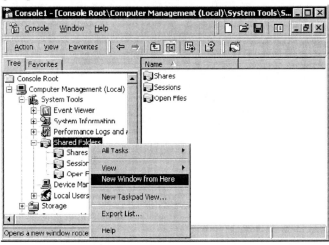

Right-click the extension that you want to use as a snap-in for your console and select **New Window from Here**. Then, all you have to do is to save your console.

You may wish to add a snap-in and then remove a few of its extensions. You can do this when you add the snap-in, by clicking the **Extensions** tab.

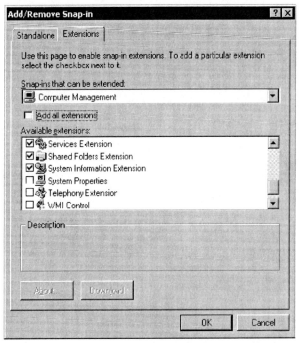

Deactivate the check boxes for the extensions that you do not want to display.

If you create customized consoles for users whose administrative roles are limited, you can design your consoles so that the users will be able to modify them, or so that they will not be able to modify them.

By default, a console is created in **Author mode**. This means that you allow full access to all the features of the MMC. Consequently, the users will be able to add or to remove snap-ins, to create windows, to display all parts of the console tree and to save all their modifications.

To change the mode, open the **Console** menu and select **Options**.

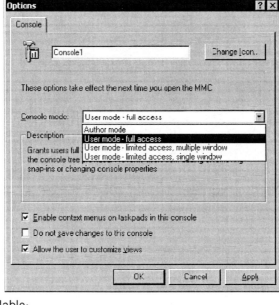

Four modes are available:

- **Author mode**: allows users to modify the console (for example to add/remove snap-ins, modify extensions and create new windows).

- User mode - **full access**: allows users to explore the console, create new windows and open new windows. However, it does not allow users to add or remove snap-ins, nor does it allow them to save the console.

- **User mode - limited access, multiple window**: allows users to display several windows in the console, but it does not allow them to create other windows. In this mode, users can neither add snap-ins nor remove them.

- **User mode - limited access, single window**: this mode is similar to the previous one, except that users are not allowed to open several windows.

There is a difference between displaying a new window and creating a window:

- To display a new window, right-click the snap-in that you want to display and select **New Window from Here**.

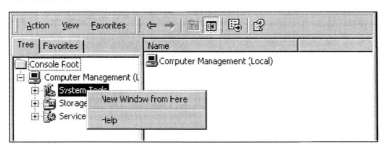

- To create a new window, right-click **Console Root** and select **New Window from Here**.

15. Fonts

Fonts   This **Control Panel** icon allows you to view and print specific character fonts.

→) Double-click this icon to view the list of fonts that are installed on your system.

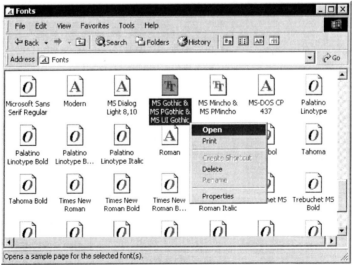

→) To view a specific font, right-click its icon and choose **Open**.

16. Find Fast

This tool creates indexes to help you find Office documents, either from **Microsoft Outlook**, or from the **Open** dialog box of other Microsoft Office applications.

You install **Find Fast** when you install Microsoft Office. This tool allows you to create indexes on all the local disks of your computer for all your office documents.

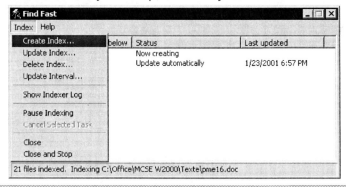

Important note: **Find Fast** does not create indexes for read-only documents or for documents that reside on removable disks. Once **Find Fast** has created an index, it updates it as a background task, every two hours by default.

You can create indexes for other folders, such as network folders, for example.

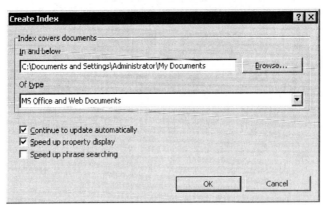

To view information on a specific index, select the drive or the folder in the **Find Fast** window, open the **Index** menu, choose the **Update Index** option and click the **Information** button.

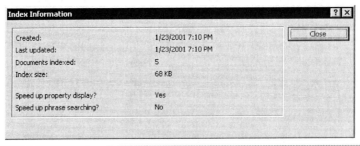

⊙ To manage its indexes, **Find Fast** automatically creates hidden files in the root folder concerned.

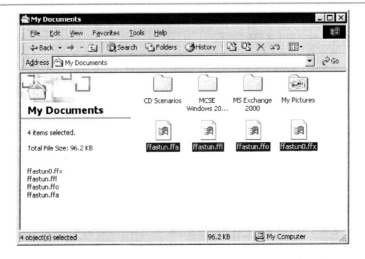

Windows 2000 Professional

Find Fast logs all the events that occur when it is working on indexes in the **%System-Root%\System32\ffastlog.txt** file.

You can view this log by selecting the **Index - Show Indexer Log** menu option. This command automatically opens the log in **Notepad**.

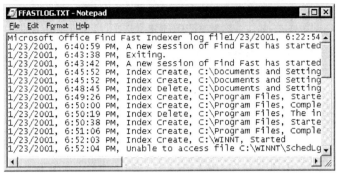

⓪ **Find Fast** automatically deletes the oldest records when the size of this log exceeds 24 MB.

17. System

System   This module allows you to access a certain number of tabs that concern system properties.

General tab

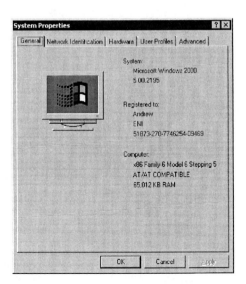

This page displays general information, including the registered user, the type processor and the amount of RAM.

Network Identification tab

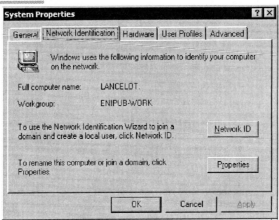

This page allows you to join a domain or a workgroup. You can even change the name of your computer provided that your computer is not a domain controller.

Advanced tab - Performance Options

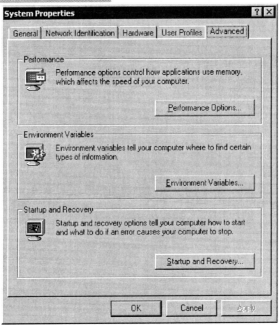

Performance Options allow you to optimize execution priority for applications and services that run in the background.

The application that is running in the foreground is the one whoose title bar appears in dark blue (provided that you are using standard colors). This is the application with which the user is currently working. Select **Applications** in order to define a priority level that is higher than that of the background application. If you select **Background services**, then all the applications will have the same priority.

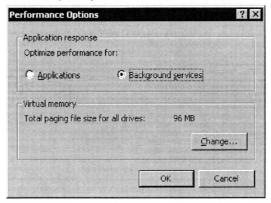

⟳ By default, Windows 2000 Server privileges the applications that run in the background (this improves the performance of network services). On the other hand, Windows 2000 Professional privileges the applications that run in the foreground.

Configuring the paging file

In order to modify the size or the location of the paging (swap) file, click the **Change** button in the **Performance Options** dialog box.

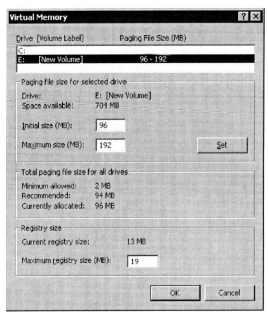

By default, the paging file is located in the root of the partition that contains system files. Its name is **pagefile.sys**. You can resize this file in order to optimize the functioning of the system. In addition, you can move the file so as to optimize read/write access to the disk. In order to do this, select the drive on which you wish to place your paging file, and define the **Initial size (MB)** and the **Maximum size (MB)** in the corresponding text boxes. Then click **Set** in order to fix these values.

Sizing the paging file

For both Windows 2000 Server and Windows 2000 Professional, by default, the initial size of the paging file is based on the following relationship:
Pagefile.sys = size of the computer's RAM + 50%

If there is not enough free disk space on the system partition, then Windows 2000 will use the partition that contains the most free disk space.

The size of the paging file will never fall below its initial size, and although it will increase according to its needs, it will never exceed its maximum size. The performance of your system will deteriorate if certain applications need to swap to disk.

The minimum size of a paging file is 2 MB.

When you restart your computer, Windows 2000 resizes your paging file to its initial size.

In order to view information concerning the paging file, select **Folder Options** in the **Tools** menu of **Windows Explorer**. Then click the **View** tab and deactivate the **Hide protected operating system file** option.

Optimizing the paging file

If your system has several hard disks, it might be a good idea to place a paging file on each of them. This can be particularly useful if your disk controller handles simultaneous read/writes. When there are several paging files, the virtual memory manager balances the load between these different files.

As part of the optimization process, it is helpful to separate the hard disks according to types of activity. For example, it is useful to create a paging file on a different partition from the one which contains the system files. However, if the size of your paging file on the system partition is less than that of the RAM on your system, Windows 2000 will not be able to create a debugging information file in the event of an error.

In any case, to avoid slowing down the system, you must ensure that the minimum size of the paging file is always adequate. If this is not the case, the paging file will grow up to the maximum size that was specified, to the detriment of the overall performance of the machine.

 You can also define a maximum size for the registry. As soon as the size of the registry comes close to the maximum size, you must increase this maximum size. Otherwise, you might lose configuration information.

Advanced tab - Environment Variables

Environment variables contain information that is used by the system. For example, the **TEMP** variable specifies where temporary files must be stored.

There are two types of environment variable:
- user variables,
- system variables.

The user variables vary according to the user concerned. Users can add, modify and delete user environment variables.

System variables do not apply to an individual user, they apply to the whole system. Consequently, they apply irrespective of the user who is logged on. Only administrators can modify system variables.

Advanced tab - Startup and Recovery

This dialog box allows you to specify the default options that must be configured upon startup. It also allows you to specify what the system must do in the event of a fatal error.

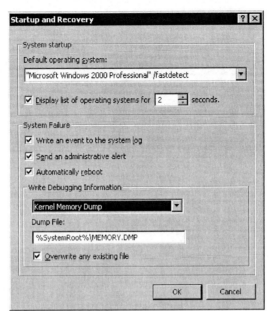

Under **System startup** you can specify the system that must be booted by default (this is the option that is highlighted in the startup menu). In addition, you can indicate for how long the startup menu must be displayed.

In reality, this graphic tool modifies the **boot.ini** file, which contains startup options.

The following options are used in order to define the actions of the system in the event of a fatal error:

– Write an event to the system log.

– Send an administrative alert so that a recipient will receive a message concerning the problem.

– Reboot, copying the contents of volatile memory to a file (which is called **memory.dmp** by default). This file will help the Microsoft technical support to diagnose the causes of this error. In fact, when a failure occurs, the contents of volatile memory are written to the paging file, which is then copied to the **memory.dmp** file upon the next startup. A new paging file is then created.

The default option is Small **Memory Dump (64 KB)**. If you specify this option then the system will store a minimum amount of diagnostics information. This option requires that the boot volume must contain the paging file, which must have a size of at least 2 MB. It will create a file on your computer in the **%SystemRoot%\MiniDump** folder.

➔ The other options are **Kernel Memory Dump**, which saves information concerning system processes, and **Complete Memory Dump**, which saves the entire contents of the RAM.

19. Scheduled Tasks

This module allows you flexibly to manage the execution of single run and periodical tasks.

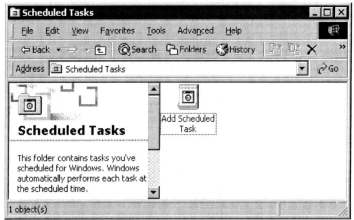

→) You can launch the **Scheduled Task Wizard** by double-clicking the **Add Scheduled Task** icon.

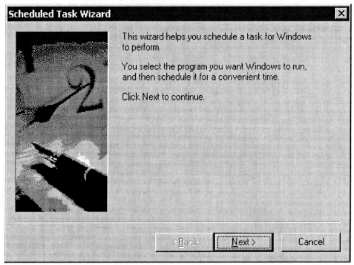

The wizard then displays the list of installed applications.

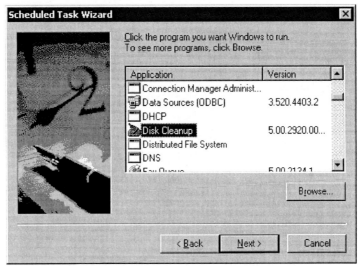

→) Choose the application that you require.

→) Specify how often the system must run this task.

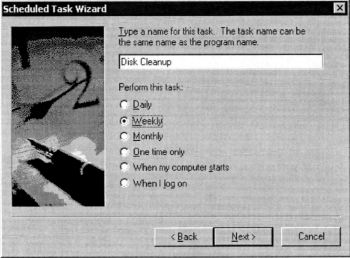

→) Then, specify the dates and the time when the system must run this task.

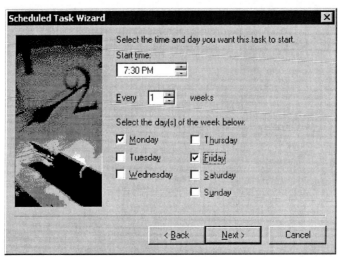

→) Enter the name and password of a user. This user must have enough rights to be able to carry out this task.

→) On the final screen, click **Finish** to confirm your instructions.

⊙ By double clicking your task icon, you can access the **Properties** of your task, and you can view and modify the settings for this task.

You can select other useful options in the **Advanced** menu:

20. Hardware profiles

The **Device Manager** allows you to define several hardware profiles. For example, you could define one hardware profile for your portable computer when you use it in your company's network, and another hardware profile for when you use your portable computer as a stand-alone machine.

→) For this purpose, access **Control Panel - System** and select the **Hardware** tab.

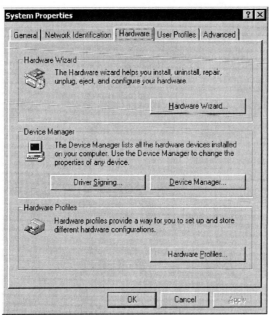

The **Hardware Profiles** button allows you to create different startup configurations. For example, if you use a portable computer, you could create two hardware profiles: one in which the network adapter is disabled, and the other in which the network adapter is enabled.

By default, only one hardware profile is created. This hardware profile is called **Profile 1**, and it contains the current hardware configuration. In order to create a second hardware profile, click **Copy**.

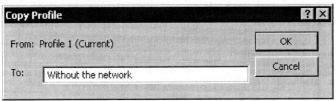

⊚ A configuration name cannot contain extended characters.

When you have created your alternative hardware profile, all you need to do is to start up your machine on the profile that you wish to configure and then start up the **Device Manager**.

Select the device that you want to deactivate for the current hardware profile. Then, in the drop-down list that appears under **Device usage,** select **Do not use this device in the current hardware profile (disable).**

Using this technique, you can also specify your profiles so that you will be able to activate or deactivate the services of your computer according to the profile that you select:

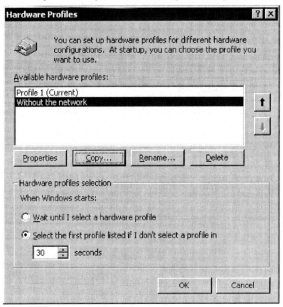

Chapter 5: Configuring the network

A. Configuring the network

1. Overview of networking components

In order to communicate on a network, you need a number of components:

Network interface card driver

This driver is the interface of the network adapter. It allows Windows 2000 to work with this device.

Communication protocol

This protocol allows computers to communicate with each other.
It can be TCP/IP, NetBEUI, DLC, AppleTalk or Transport Compatible Nwlink IPX/SPX.
The communication protocol comprises a set of rules that allows network interface cards to exchange information.

Network client

The **Network client** is a software component that is able access the **Network Server**, with which it is associated.
For example, the **Client for Microsoft Networks** accesses the **File and Printer Sharing for Microsoft Networks**. This client component is able to communicate with a server that uses the same protocol in order to access specific resources: in this case shared queues and folders.

2. Choosing a protocol

Windows 2000 manages several protocols. Each of them has its peculiarities and its fields of application.

This section will describe the cases in which you must use one protocol rather than another.

TCP/IP (Transmission Control Protocol/Internet Protocol)

The Internet is based on this protocol. It is a routable protocol that handles extended networks. It requires an explicit addressing scheme.

Transport compatible Nwlink IPX/SPX/NetBIOS

This is an NDIS (Network Device Interface Specification) 5.0 version of the Novell IPX/SPX *(Internetwork Packet eXchange/Sequenced Packet eXchange)* protocol.
NWLink allows communication between MS-DOS, OS/2, Windows and Windows 2000 computers, by means of RPCs *(Remote Procedure Calls)*, or Windows sockets or by Novell NetBIOS IPX/SPX. IPX is a routable protocol. IPX addressing is implemented dynamically on the clients.

NetBEUI (NetBIOS Extended User Interface)

This protocol is used on Lan Manager, Lan Server, Windows 95 and Windows for Workgroups systems. This is a fast and efficient protocol that is usable only on small LANs. It is not a routable protocol and is based on broadcasting.

▶ The computers identify themselves on the network by broadcasting packets to all the other machines each time they need to communicate.

However, it has the advantage that it does not need configuring.

DLC (Data Link Control)

This protocol provides access to SNA systems and to certain network print devices.

AppleTalk

This protocol allows a Windows 2000 server that runs services for Macintosh, to communicate with Macintosh clients. This is also a routable protocol.

3. Overview of TCP/IP

a. Internet services

TCP/IP offers services:
- at application level,
- at network level.

Interconnection services at application level

The user perceives TCP/IP as a set of programs that offer services that use the network for different purposes. Here are the main application services:
- electronic mail,
- file transfer,
- remote connections.

Interconnection services at network level

Programmers who develop applications using TCP/IP have a different perspective from that of the users. Programmers use various interconnection services:

Packet delivery service in connectionless mode

This service underlies all the other services. The data packets are transmitted from one machine to another, and each machine is identified by an address.

At this level, the packets are routed independently from each other. Also, there is no guarantee of a reliable delivery, and neither is there any guarantee that the packets will arrive in the correct order.

Reliable transport service

Network applications require error-free communications. This is achieved principally thanks to techniques of automatic recovery in the event of errors.

The reliable transport service manages these sorts of problems. It allows an application to set up a connection with another application that runs on another machine, just as if there was a direct and permanent connection.

b. The advantages of TCP/IP

Even though many other protocols offer identical services to those that TCP/IP provides, the set of TCP/IP standards offer a number of advantages:

Independence from the network technology

TCP/IP is independent of any hardware or manufacturer. It can run with a wide range of technologies. It uses a transmission unit, called a DATAGRAM, which specifies how the information must be transmitted on a given type of network.

Universal connectivity

Each machine that is connected via TCP/IP is assigned a unique address, and each pair of machines can communicate with each other. The intermediate nodes use addresses that are contained in the DATAGRAMS in order to decide how the packets must be routed.

End to end acknowledgement

TCP/IP ensures direct acknowledgement between the source machine and the destination machine, even if the machines are not connected on the same physical network.

Standardized application protocols

Apart from transport protocols, TCP/IP includes various application protocols. In particular, these application protocols concern the mail service, file transfer (FTP, TFTP) and remote login (rlogin).

Programmers who develop applications are often able to use existing programs, which provide the services that they need.

c. Internet addressing

An Internet address is called an *IP address*. It uniquely identifies the machine, and also the network in which the machine is situated. This feature allows efficient routing of information. This address is encoded on 32 bits, and is used for all communications with the machine.

Each address is made up of a network identifier and a machine identifier. A first set of bits corresponds to the network, and a second set of bits corresponds to the machine. Under no circumstances must the bits in either the machine part or network part, be all set to one or all set to zero.

IP address classes

The IP address class can be determined from the address' heavy weight bits. Only the first three address classes can be used for machine addresses.

Class A

Class A addresses correspond to networks that contain more than 2^{24}-2 machines. 7 bits are used for the address of the network, and 24 bits are used for the address of the machine.

0	8	16	24	31
0	Network ID		Machine ID	

- The first byte is between 1 and 126 (inclusive).

Class B

This class corresponds to networks in which the number of machines varies from 2 to 2^{16}-2. 16 bits are available for the number of the machine, and 14 bits are available for the number of the network.

0	8	16	24	31
1 0	Network ID		Machine ID	

- The first byte is between 128 and 191 inclusive.

Class C

21 bits are used for the number of the network, and 8 bits are used for the number of the machine. Consequently, you can use this class for small networks that contain from 2 to 2^8-2 (254) machines.

0	8	16	24	31
1 1 0	Network ID		Machine ID	

- The first byte is between 192 and 223 (inclusive).
  For example, a router is a machine that has several addresses. It cannot have a unique address, as it must have as many addresses as it has accesses to different networks. One IP address identifies one access to the network, and not one machine on the network.

Class D

0	8	16	24	31
1 1 1 0	Broadcast address			

A multicast address can be attributed to a host, in addition to its unique address. This technique allows several peripherals to be identified simultaneously (so that they can receive a multimedia emission, for example).

◐ The first byte is between 224 and 239 (inclusive).

Network address and broadcast address

An address in which the machine number is equal to zero is used to refer to the network itself. Consequently, a machine cannot have an address in which all the bits of the machine number are reset to zero.

If all the bits of an address that correspond to the machine number are set to one, then it is a broadcast address. A broadcast address references all the machines in the network.

◐ On some UNIX systems, an address with all its bits set to zero is used in order to signify a broadcast from the host.

Local broadcast address

An address in which all the bits are set to one, corresponds to a local broadcast address that is intended for all the machines in the network of the machine that is emitting the address. In this case, the emitting machine does not need to know its own network address.

Network address that is completely reset to zero

If a machine does not yet know its network number, it can send a message in which the network number is zero. In this case the destination of the message will be interpreted as being the current network. The workstations that respond to the request will return a network address that is completely formed. This will allow the emitter to know the address of its network.

Drawbacks of Internet addressing

One drawback of Internet addressing is that if a machine is moved from one network to another then its address must be modified accordingly.

Another difficulty of Internet addressing is that, if a class C addressing scheme is used, and the number of machines subsequently exceeds 254, then a class B scheme must be used and the network address must be modified accordingly. Typically, this can be a problem for a portable computer.

The most important drawback of IP addressing is that the path that is followed depends on the network number, which is contained in the address.

In the event of failure of one of the networks, a machine that has several addresses (a multi-homed machine) might be accessible through one address, and not through another.

Dotted decimal notation

IP addresses are composed of four decimal integers that are separated by dots when they are intended for users, or for programmers. For example: 128.10.2.30.

Local loopback address

The local loopback address is equal to 127.0.0.1. This address is used for inter-process communications on the local machine. An address in which the network number is equal to 127 is never emitted on the network.

NIC (Network Information Center)

All the IP addresses are allocated by a central organization that is called the NIC. This is done in order to guarantee the uniqueness of the network part. However, an organization that is assigned a network number can choose its own machine numbers.

A network number is assigned only when an organization wishes to connect to the Internet. On the other hand, if an organization decides to operate autonomously, it is free to choose whatever network number it considers to be appropriate.

d. IP configuration

IP Address

It is essential that you do not choose the IP address of a LAN arbitrarily. Such an approach could have undesirable effects for you, and for others, and in any case would not allow you to work on the network.

Subnet mask

In order to understand the role of the subnet mask, you must write it in binary (for this purpose you can use the Windows 2000 Calculator in scientific view!). The purpose is to identify precisely the bits that encode the IP network number, from amongst the bits that are used to encode the host number. A bit that is set to '1' in the subnet mask signifies that the corresponding bit in the IP address is part of the network number. On the other hand, a '0' in the subnet mask designates a bit that is used in the IP address so as to encode part of a host number.

For example, suppose you have an IP address of 192.142.1.15 that is associated with a subnet mask of 255.255.255.0. In binary, this IP address is 11000000.10001110.00000001.00001111 whilst the subnet mask in binary is 11111111.11111111.11111111. 00000000. By carrying out a LOGICAL AND between the address and the subnet mask you determine the IP address of the network.
With a LOGICAL AND, the association of two 1s produces 1, and the association of two 0s, or of one **1** and one **0**, produces **0**. The result in binary is 11000000.10001110.00000001.00000000, which equals 192.142.1.0 in decimal.

Default gateway

The default gateway is the IP address of the router interface that allows you to leave the LAN. Without this indication, a network peripheral cannot communicate beyond a router, and the information could not leave the LAN.

> A Windows 2000 computer that has two network interface cards can act as a router for a given protocol (IP, IPX or AppleTalk). Windows 3.11 can also act as an IP router.

4. Network settings

a. Configuring network interface cards

If your network interface card is not automatically detected and installed by Windows 2000, then you must use the **Add/Remove Hardware** program from the **Control Panel** in order to install it.

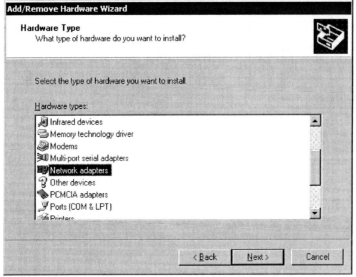

Windows 2000 will then automatically configure your network card.

There are two ways of viewing the properties of your card:

– Right-click **My Network Places** and select **Properties**. Then, right-click **Local Area Connection** and again select **Properties**.

– Alternatively, go into **Control Panel** and double-click the **Network and Dial-up Connections** icon. Then, right-click **Local Area Connection** and select **Properties**.

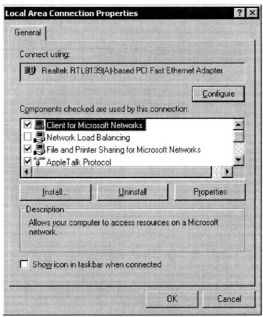

If you activate the **Show icon in taskbar when connected** check box, then you will be able to double-click the 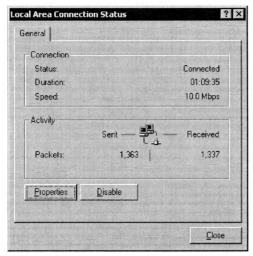 icon in order to display the connection status of your local area network.

If you click the **Disable** button, then you will disable your network interface card. In order to re-activate the network connection, select the properties of **My Network Places** and double-click the graycd-out **Local Area Connection** icon. Alternatively, you can right-click this grayed-out icon and then select **Enable**.

Coming back to the **Local Area Connection Properties** dialog box, the **General** tab shows the card by which the network connection has been made, along with all the items that this connection uses. These items must include a communications protocol. By clicking the **Configure** button, you can view the properties of your network interface card.

- The **General** tab allows you to enable or to disable this device with respect to the different hardware profiles. It also allows you to run the **Troubleshooter** program, which is useful if you have a problem with your network interface card.
- The **Advanced** tab provides access to settings that you can configure for the card. The settings that are proposed will depend on the card concerned.

- The **Driver** tab provides information on the driver that the card uses (concerning the files that correspond to the driver). This tab also allows you to uninstall or to update this driver.
- The **Resources** tab allows you to view the resource settings that your card uses (such as the IRQ and input/output address).

b. Configuring TCP/IP

Automatic configuration

For the automatic configuration of TCP/IP protocol, the network must contain a server that will distribute IP configurations to clients that request them. This type of server is called a DHCP (*Dynamic Hosts Configuration Protocol*) server. A DHCP server must have a static IP configuration. Windows 2000 Server can perform this function.

In order to transform your computers into DHCP clients you must:

- Right-click **My Network Places** and then select **Properties**.
- Right-click **Local Area Connection** and then select **Properties**.
- Under the **General** tab, select **Internet Protocol (TCP/IP)** and then click the **Properties** button.

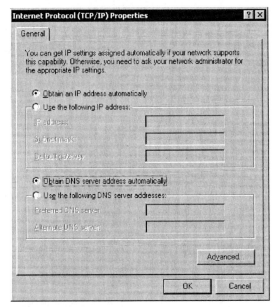

- Select **Obtain an IP address automatically**.
- Then, you can choose automatically to obtain the address of the DNS server for which your machine is a client via the DHCP server. Alternatively, you can choose to enter this address manually.

The DHCP server can supply many items of information, including the following:
- IP address (compulsory).
- Subnet mask (compulsory).
- Default gateway(s).
- The IP address of one or more DNS servers.
- The IP address of one or more WINS servers.
- Node type (the resolution mode of NetBIOS names).
- Domain name.

Manual configuration

For the client computers in your network, it is convenient to use the DHCP protocol in order to distribute IP configurations. This technique avoids any duplication of addresses. In addition, this approach simplifies and speeds up the administration.

However, your servers require a fixed addressing scheme. This is particularly important if services such as DNS, DHCP and WINS run on these servers.

In order to configure the IP addresses of your servers manually, check to ensure that the addresses that are used by your servers do not correspond to addresses that could be allocated by a DHCP server.

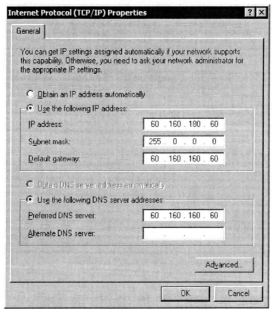

The **Advanced** button allows you to apply advanced IP settings.

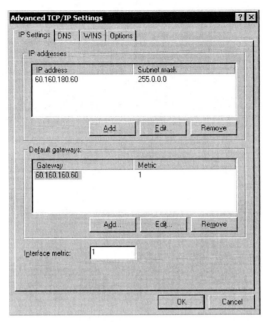

- The **IP Settings** tab allows you to add one or more IP addresses for the same interface, along with several gateway addresses.

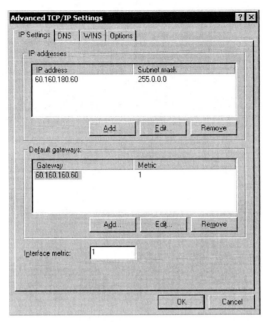
Important note: if you specify several gateway addresses for an interface, the first will always be used if it is accessible. For example, if you attempt to contact a host that is not on your sub-network, then the query will be directed to the first default gateway. If this gateway knows the destination host (from its routing table), then it will forward the packet. Otherwise, it will return a message stating that the host is inaccessible, even though it might be accessible via another gateway. These other gateways will be used only if the first gateway is physically inaccessible.

A **metric** is associated with each network interface. This value is integrated into the routing table of the computer. It indicates the cost of reaching a given network. If, in a routing table, a network is accessible via two separate interfaces, then the interface that has the smaller metric will be used.

- The **DNS** tab allows you to specify the IP addresses for supplementary DNS servers, with a view to providing fault tolerance. A DNS server allows you to resolve host names into IP addresses (for example: **ping merlin**, or **ping merlin.enipub.com**).
- The **WINS** tab allows you to specify a list of the WINS servers that will be used for resolving NetBIOS names (for example: **net view \\merlin**). This tab also allows you to disable NetBIOS. By default, NetBIOS is enabled on TCP/IP. If you disable NetBIOS, you will no longer be able to use **My Network Places** in order to display the list of servers that are available on your network.

Example:

With:

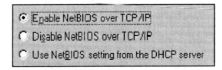

the result is as follows:

With:

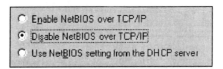

the result is as follows:

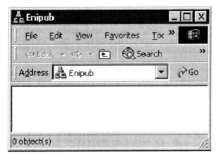

– The **Options** tab allows you to filter IP packets.

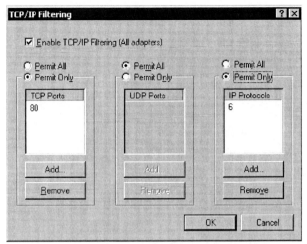

In this example, the filtering is enabled. Only Web queries (TCP port number 80) will be accepted. In addition, only TCP protocol will be authorized (port number 6 in an IP packet is used for TCP transport protocol; port number 17 is used for UDP).

To test the filtering, you can run an ftp command to a server (SRV3 in the example below) on which the filtering is enabled:

```
D:\>ftp srv3
> ftp: connect :Connection refused
ftp> dir
Not connected.
ftp>
```

The ftp application runs on ports TCP 20 and 21, whereas the filter specifies that packets will be allowed through only if the TCP port number is 80.

If you disable this filter:

```
E:\>ftp galahad
Connected to galahad.enipub.com.
220 GALAHAD Microsoft FTP Service (Version 5.0).
User (galahad.enipub.com:(none)): administrator
331 Password required for administrator.
Password:
230-Welcome to the Galahad FTP server
230 User administrator logged in.
ftp> dir
200 PORT command successful.
150 Opening ASCII mode data connection for /bin/ls.
03-31-00  03:17PM       <DIR>          RFC
03-31-00  03:17PM       <DIR>          Utilities
03-31-00  03:12PM       <DIR>          White papers
226 Transfer complete.
ftp: 147 bytes received in 0.01Seconds 14.70Kbytes/sec.
ftp> quit
221 See you later

E:\>
F:\>
E:\>
```

Again in the **Options** tab, you can disable IP security.

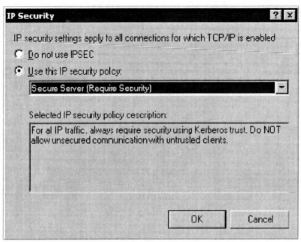

To make IP traffic secure, Microsoft has included the IPSec (*IP Security*) standard in the Windows 2000 products. IPSec is an industry standard that was produced by the IETF (*Internet Engineering Task Force*) to ensure the security of IP traffic. By default, it is disabled.

B. Security of IP network traffic

With Windows 2000, Microsoft allows you to encrypt the IP traffic that circulates on your LAN, or even across extended networks. The main objective of this feature is to provide security for data that circulates on a network that is not itself secure, like Internet for example.

Windows 2000 uses **IPSec** (*IP Security*) for this purpose. This is an open standard and not a proprietary invention. Because of this, a Windows 2000 machine is able to communicate securely with any type of computer (client, server or router) that runs IPSec.

 IPSec is described in RFC 1825.

Implementing IPSec

It is very simple to implement IPSec. You can implement IPSec either machine by machine or using group policies.

➜) Right-click **My Network Places** then select **Properties**.

➜) Right-click the **Local Area Connection** for the network interface card on which you want to enable IP security.

➜) Select **Properties**, then select **Internet Protocol (TCP/IP)** and click the **Properties** button.

→) Click the **Advanced** button.

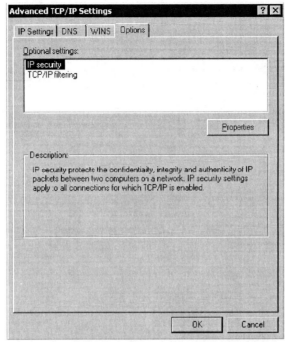

→) Click the **Options** tab, then select **IP security** and click **Properties**.

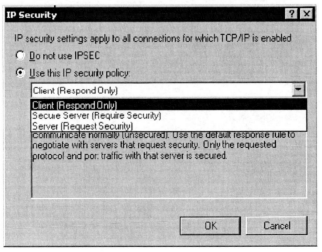

By default, IP security is not enabled. You can choose from three security levels:

Client (Respond Only)

> This option allows IP traffic to circulate normally. Encrypted response is provided to clients that request it.

Secure Server (Require Security)

> This option does not allow unsecured communication.

Server (Request Security)

> This option implements encrypted messages, but accepts unencrypted client requests.

C. Remote access

Windows 2000 allows users to access a company's network remotely (from a hotel, or from home, for example). You can configure a Windows 2000 server so that it will act as a remote access server and a VPN server. On the client side, the user will connect to the server using the remote access client. The two sides must be linked using a communications medium that is suitable for remote communication. Therefore, a WAN link must be used. This can be a Switched Telephone Network (STN), an Integrated Services Digital Network (ISDN), an X25 medium (packet switching), a frame relay (frame switching) or an Asynchronous Transfer Mode (ATM) connection. You can even use a serial cable in order to link together the two computers. A WAN link communication protocol must be used on this physical medium. With Windows 2000, you can use PPP, Microsoft RAS, ARAP and SLIP protocols.

1. Transport methods

In order to send data between the remote client and the server, you must encapsulate it in a suitable protocol.

a. WAN link protocol

You need a specific protocol in order to transmit information across remote links. Microsoft allows you to use several protocols:

- **SLIP** *(Serial Line Internet Protocol)*: You must use this protocol in order to connect to a SLIP server via a modem. This is an old communication standard that is used in UNIX environments. It was originally written in order to support low throughput networks. It does not support automatic negotiation of the network configuration and can encapsulate only the IP. It does not support encrypted authentication either.

> ◐ Windows 2000 includes a SLIP client but it does not support the role of SLIP server as this lacks the security and the efficiency of PPP.

- **PPP** *(Point to Point Protocol)*: This is an improvement on SLIP. Unlike SLIP, which supports only IP, PPP allows you to encapsulate other protocols such as IPX/SPX, and NetBEUI, in addition to TCP/IP. The great advantage of PPP is that it is not a proprietary protocol. Because of this, any client that supports PPP can connect to a Windows 2000 remote access server.
- **Microsoft RAS**: This proprietary protocol allows Windows for Workgroups clients, Windows NT 3.1 clients, MS-DOS clients and Lan Manager clients that use NetBEUI protocol to access a Windows 2000 remote access server. The Windows 2000 remote access server acts as a gateway for these clients in order to allow them to access the server, even if the server uses another protocol.
- **ARAP** (AppleTalk Remote Access Protocol): Windows 2000 can act as a remote access server for Macintosh clients. Macintosh clients use the ARAP protocol to connect to Windows 2000 servers.

Windows 2000 clients cannot connect to an ARAP remote access server.

b. LAN protocol

The section above describes the different protocols that allow you to set up a connection with the remote access server. Once the connection has been set up, the client uses resources as if they were located on the local network. In order to allow this, the data is encapsulated in a local network protocol. Windows 2000 allows you to use TCP/IP, Nwlink IPX/SPX, NetBEUI and AppleTalk protocols. In turn, these LAN protocols are encapsulated into a WAN link protocol such as PPP so that they can be transmitted on the remote links.

This means that you can use Windows 2000 remote network access services to allow a client that runs the NetBEUI protocol, for example, to communicate with a UNIX server located on the company's local network. In this way, the remote access server acts as a NetBEUI / TCP-IP gateway. However, both of these protocols must be installed on the remote access server.

c. Virtual Private Networks (VPN)

The main advantage of virtual private networks is that you can use them in order to connect together two computers irrespective of the physical level (LAN or WAN connection). This allows you to create a VPN between two machines using either the Internet, or simply the local network as the communication medium. VPNs use tunneling protocols. Windows 2000 allows you to use VPNs with PPTP or with L2TP. The purpose of these two protocols is to provide encrypted tunnels in an insecure network (such as the Internet).

- **PPTP** *(Point to Point Tunneling Protocol)*: This protocol allows you to interconnect networks using an IP network.
- **L2TP** *(Layer Two Tunneling Protocol)*: Unlike PPTP, this protocol allows you to interconnect networks when the tunnel offers only a packet oriented point-to-point connection. They allow you to operate on an IP network using Frame Relay, X25, ATM, and IP Permanent Virtual Circuits (PVC).

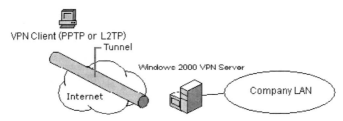

Both PPTP and L2TP use PPP protocol in order to transfer data (IP, IPX/SPX...). They provide an extra envelope for data transport via VPNs. This envelope adds headings that allow you to transport the information.

L2TP offers the following advantages:
- It allows you to compress headers (4 bytes, instead of 6 bytes with PPTP)
- It allows authentication to take place in the tunnel.

These two protocols offer different levels of security. PPTP uses the encryption that is offered by PPP. L2TP uses IPSec in order to encrypt data. However, IPSec and L2TP are totally independent from each other. You can use L2TP without IPSec.

If you use IPSec in a PPTP tunnel then the PPTP will provide authentication in the tunnel, in the same way as L2TP does.

2. Configuring a remote access server

Windows 2000 provides two utilities that allow you to configure remote network access:
- **Network and Dial-up Connections**

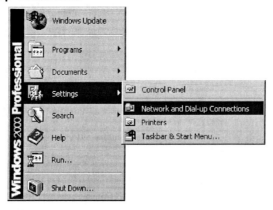

– and the **Routing and Remote Access** console.

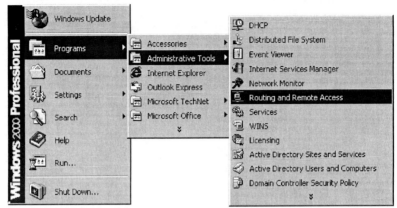

You can use this console in order to configure incoming connections when your server is either a domain controller or a domain member.

If this is not the case, then you can configure both incoming and outgoing connections using the **Network Connection Wizard**. You can access the **Network Connection Wizard** by opening the **Start - Settings** menu and then selecting **Network and Dial-up Connections**.

a. Incoming connections

Network and dial-up connections

When you authorize incoming calls, you configure your server as a remote access server:

→) Open the **Start - Settings** menu and then select **Network and Dial-up Connections**.

→) Double-click the **Make New Connection** icon.

→) The welcome screen of the **Network Connection Wizard** appears. Click the **Next** button.

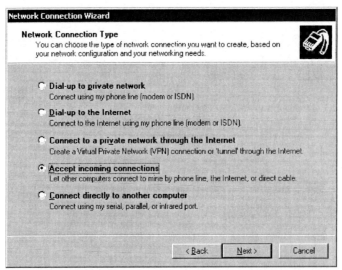

→) Select **Accept incoming connections,** and then click the **Next** button.

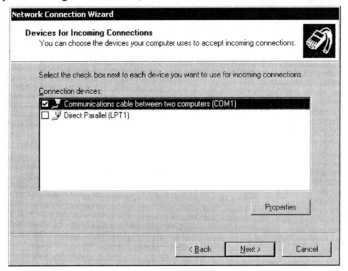

➔) Select from the list, the devices that you want to use for your incoming connections. If your modem does not appear in the list, then you can install it using the **Phone and Modem Options** program that is located in the **Control Panel**. Click **Next**.

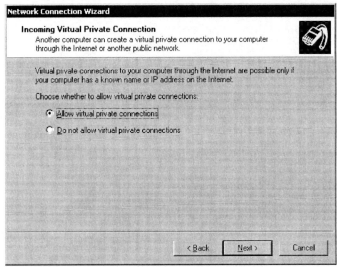

➔) Indicate whether or not you want to allow VPN connections, and then click the **Next** button.

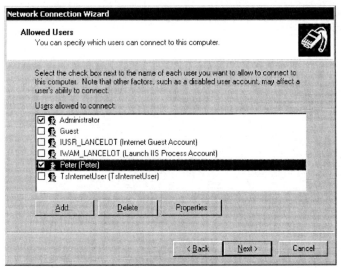

➔) Select the users that will be allowed to use the remote access. You can grant permission to other users at any time by displaying the properties of the accounts concerned, and selecting the **Dial-in** tab.

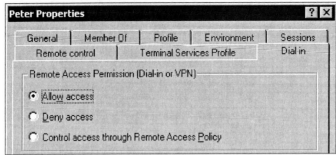

Users who dial in to a server that is not a domain controller must have an account in the SAM database of this server.

→) The next step allows you to modify the dial-in properties, such as the LAN protocol that must be used.

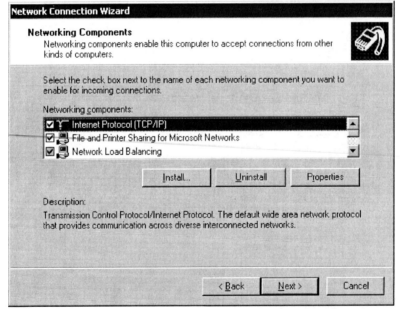

This screen allows you to add a new protocol, or to set up the addresses that must be used by remote access clients. In order to do this, select the **TCP/IP** protocol and then click the **Properties** button.

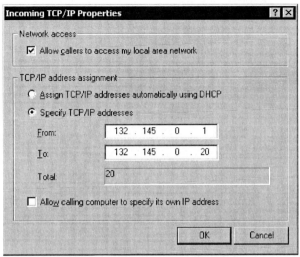

You can use DHCP to attribute IP addresses to remote clients automatically, or to specify a range of addresses for these clients. In this case, the first address in the range will be assigned to the remote access server. This technique allows you to use a different network address in order to communicate with remote clients.

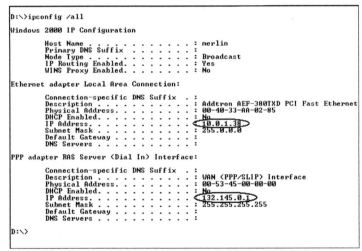

→) Click the **Next** button, and then click the **Finish** button to complete the operation.

Routing and Remote Access (Windows 2000 server)

To accept incoming connections on a domain controller or on a member server, you must use the **Routing and Remote Access** console.

When you use this console for the first time, you must enable the Routing and Remote Access service.

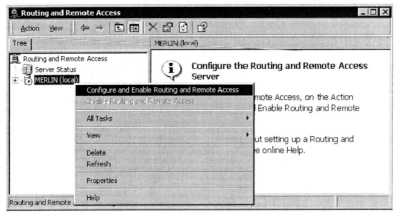

→) Right-click the name of your server and select **Configure and Enable Routing and Remote Access**.

→) Click the **Next** button in the welcome window that appears.

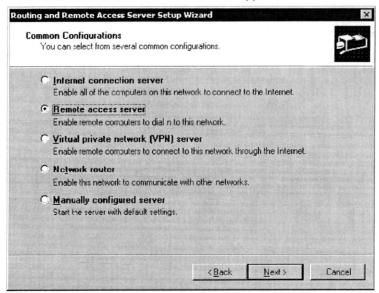

→) Select **Remote access server** and click the **Next** button.

→) Check the list that appears to make sure that it contains all the protocols that you require and click the **Next** button.

→) Indicate whether you use a DHCP server to assign IP addresses to your remote clients, or whether you prefer to specify a range of addresses. If you prefer the latter option, enable **From a specified range of addresses** and click the **Next** button.

→⟩ Click the **New** button, then enter a start address and end address for your address range.

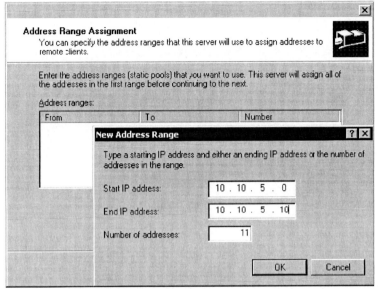

→⟩ Click the **OK** button, followed by the **Next** button.

→⟩ For the last step, you are asked if you want to install the RADIUS server. Select **No, I don't want to set up this server to use RADIUS now** and click the **Next** button followed by the **Finish** button.

If you have used this console already for a reason other than for the remote access service (for example to configure a DHCP relay agent or to configure a router), then you can configure your remote access server by right-clicking its icon in this console and selecting **Properties**.

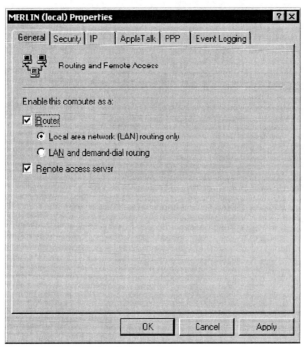

Activate the **Remote access server** check box.

⊙ When the remote access service is started for the first time, it automatically creates 5 PPTP ports and 5 L2TP ports. The number of these ports is not limited and you can configure them using the **Ports** icon in the **Routing and Remote Access** console.

b. Outgoing connections

In order to access a remote access server, you must configure an outgoing connection. You must use the **Network Connection Wizard** for this purpose. In order to access this wizard, you must open the **Start - Settings** menu, select **Network and Dial-up Connections** and double-click the **Make New Connection** icon.

You can configure three types of outgoing connections:

- Remote access connection (which covers the options, **Dial-up to private network** and **Dial-up to the Internet**).
- Connection to a virtual private network.
- Direct connection using a cable.

Remote access connections

The Dial-up to private network option allows remote clients to connect directly to the remote access server using a modem.

In this case you must know the telephone number of the server to which you want to connect.

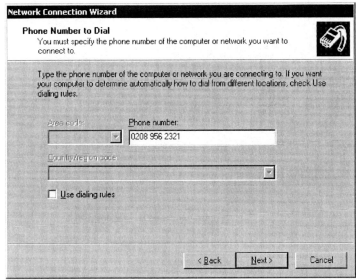

The **Dial-up to the Internet** option allows you to connect to an Internet Service Provider (ISP). The **Internet Connection Wizard** will help you to set up this connection. You can connect via your LAN, in which case you must indicate the address of your proxy server. Alternatively, you can use your modem in order to connect to your ISP.

Connecting to a Virtual Private Network (VPN)

In order to create a virtual private network you need to know only the IP address of the destination machine. Select the **Connect to a private network through the Internet** option, and then click **Next**.

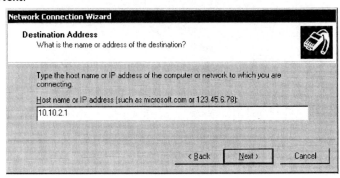

➝) Indicate the host name or the host IP address, and click the **Next** button. Then, indicate whether you will be the only user with access to the connection that you are creating, or whether you want to share it with other users, who will then be able to log on to your machine.

➝) The next step allows you to share this connection with other users of your LAN. Click **Next**, enter a name for this connection, and then click the **Finish** button.

The wizard creates a new icon in the **Start** menu:

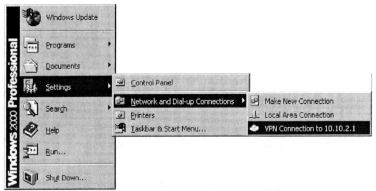

In order to connect, click the icon that represents the connection.

Enter a user name and a password for an account that has dial-in permission, and then click the **Connect** button.

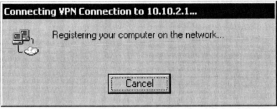

When the connection has been set up you will receive the following message:

Connecting directly using a cable

You can link two computers together by connecting a cable between the serial ports, the parallel ports or the infrared ports. In this case, select **Connect directly to another computer**, and then click the **Next** button.

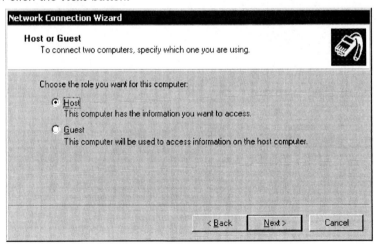

For this type of connection to work, one of the computers must be configured as a **Host**, and the other computer must be configured as a **Guest**. The host computer will act as a sort of access server, and the guest computer will act as the client. With both of these configurations, you must specify the device that will be used for the connection (and also the port that will be used for the connection). In addition, for the host you must indicate the users who will be allowed to connect.

Connecting to the Internet

Connecting to the Internet by remote access

As with any TCP/IP network, you need a correct IP configuration before you can connect to the Internet. This configuration must include the following items: an IP address, a subnet mask, the IP address of a default gateway, and the IP address of a DNS *(Domain Name System)* server. The DNS server must be able to resolve host names (such as **www.eni-publishing.com**, for example) into IP addresses (such as 212.155.178.51, for example).

 Once you have set up your connections, you can display this information by opening a command prompt and entering the command **ipconfig /all**.

Go into the **Control Panel**, start up the **Network and Dial-up Connections** module, and activate the **Make New Connection** icon. This starts the **Internet Connection Wizard**. Click **Next** and select the **Dial-up to the Internet** option.

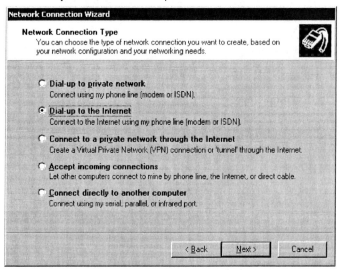

The Internet Connection Wizard will then allow you to choose to access the Internet, either using an ISDN card (or modem) and a telephone line or through a Local Area Network (LAN). The LAN itself must be a remote access client that shares its connection:

If you intend to share an Internet connection, you will probably need an additional username and password for this connection.

The Internet Connection Wizard provides a short **Tutorial** that provides essential information on setting up an Internet connection:

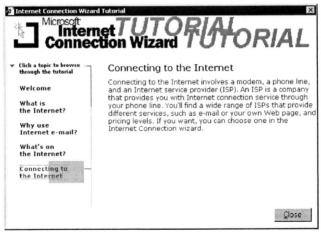

The next screen of the Internet Connection Wizard allows you to choose either a unique local access connection or a shared access connection:

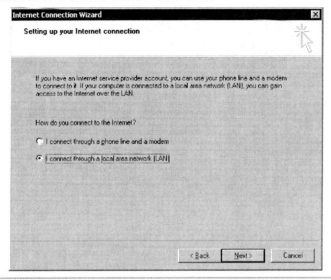

⊙ A home user who wants to connect to the Internet will generally need to set up a connection that uses PPP *(Point-to-Point Protocol)* across the Switched Telephone Network, and an external modem (**I connect through a phone line and a modem**).

If you choose the shared access option
(I connect through a local area network (LAN)):
then you can ask the wizard to detect your configuration automatically:

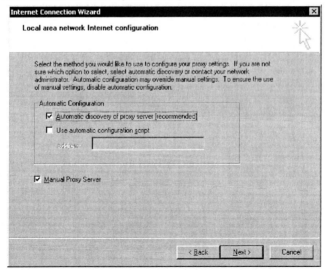

Windows 2000 Professional

Alternatively, you can opt to configure your access manually:

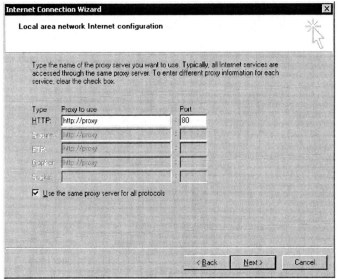

In this case, Windows 2000 will ask you for a username and a password that will allow you to *go out* onto the Internet from your company's network:

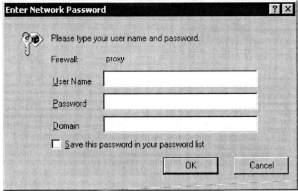

If you choose the local internal access option (I connect through a phone line and a modem):
then you must specify the settings concerning your Internet Service Provider (ISP). These settings include: a **telephone number** corresponding to your ISP, and a **username** and **password** that will allow you to use the remote access.
The wizard helps you to set up this connection in three steps.

In the first step, you must specify the telephone number of your ISP:

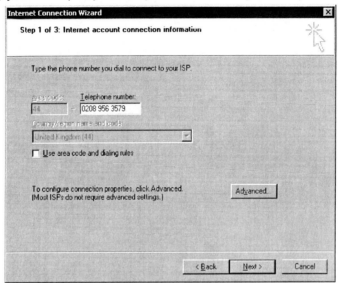

Notice the **Advanced** button on this screen. It allows you to specify advanced settings for your Internet access. In particular, you can choose your WAN protocol: either PPP or SLIP or CSLIP:

→⟩ The **Addresses** page of the **Advanced Connection Properties** dialog box allows you either to indicate that the wizard must use the IP address that your ISP provides or to specify the IP address yourself:

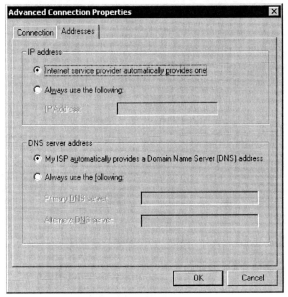

⟩ If you are in any doubt, then choose the default options.

In the second step of setting-up your connection, you must indicate the username and password that you use to log on to your ISP.
The third step concerns the name of the dial-up connection. The wizard allows you to customize this name.

You can then set up your Internet mail account:

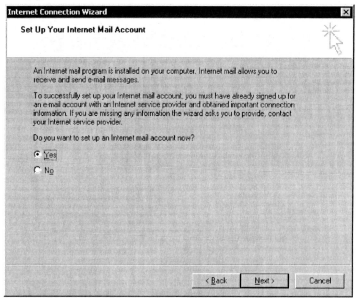

→) First you must enter your name as you would like it to appear in the **From** field of your outgoing mail messages:

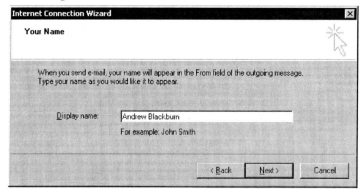

→) Then, you must specify your e-mail address:

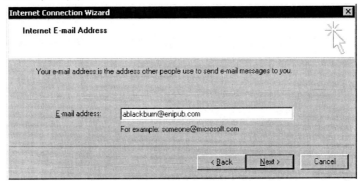

The next step is to specify the names of your incoming mail server and your outgoing mail server:

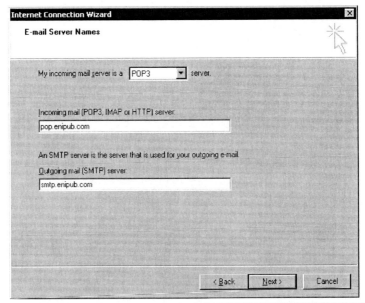

In general, you will specify server names here and not IP addresses. These names must be resolved into their corresponding IP addresses in order to allow data exchange to take place. Consequently, you must also set up the means of resolving names into IP addresses. In particular, this operation involves indicating the IP address of a DNS server.

Finally, you must specify an **Account name** and a **Password**. If your ISP also manages your mail account, then these details can be the same as those that you specified for your Internet connection:

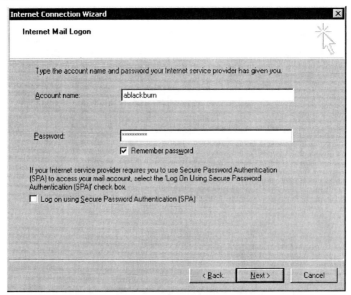

Finally, in order to communicate via the Internet you will need certain client software components, such as an Internet browser, a mail client, and possibly a newsgroup client.

3. Authentication

When you allow remote network access connections, you must implement an authentication mechanism that will run during the logon process, to prevent any unauthorized people from getting into your company's network.

Logging on via a WAN takes place in three phases:

- Setting up a physical link. This first phase allows the two parties to negotiate the connection by sending LCP (*Link Control Protocol*) packets. These packets contain the connection's negotiation settings on the physical level, such as the compression, the type of authentication that is used and whether links are shared or not.
- The second phase covers the authentication. It runs after the line has been set up and before the network level is set up.
- When the authentication has been completed, then the network level-3 protocol that must be used (IP for example) is negotiated. NCP (*Network Control Protocol*) packets are sent for this purpose.

Here are the layers of the PPP architecture:

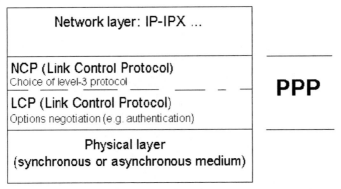

Windows 2000 supports several authentication methods that offer differing security levels. You can configure these authentication methods using the **Routing and Remote Access** console.

➜) Right-click the name of your remote access server then select **Properties**.

➜) Select the **Security** button then click the **Authentication Methods** button.

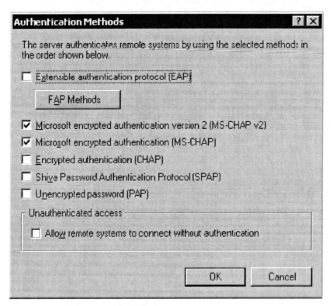

Several authentication protocols are provided:

- **PAP (*Password Authentication Protocol*)**: this method is relatively simple and not very secure. The remote client sends the password as clear text. The client sends the user name and password to the remote access server. The remote access server then checks this information against its own information.

- **SPAP** (Shiva Password Authentication Protocol): this is a proprietary protocol supplied by the vendor Shiva. It allows a Shiva client to connect to a Windows 2000 remote access server, or a Windows 2000 client to connect to a Shiva server. The passwords are encrypted.

- **CHAP** (*Challenge Handshake Authentication Protocol*): this is a sophisticated authentication protocol. The remote access server sends a "challenge" to the client after the first phase of the logon has completed. This is an identifier that is sent to the client after being randomly generated by the server. Only the remote access server knows this identifier. The client sends its password in a hashed format, together with the "challenge" that was sent by the server. This method is called hashing. (it is used by MD5: *Message Digest*). The server restores the message and checks that the password corresponds to the user name.

- **MS-CHAP (*Microsoft Challenge Handshake Authentication Protocol*)**: this protocol uses the same principle as CHAP. In addition, MS-CHAP allows you to use MPPE (*Microsoft Point-to-point Protocol*) encrypting in order to secure data on PPP or PPTP links.

- **MS-CHAP version 2**: this is a development of MS-CHAP. It is more secure than MS-CHAP v1. It is the most secure authentication protocol that Windows 2000 offers. You can use this protocol only if you have Windows 2000, Windows NT 4.0 or Windows 95/98 clients.

- **EAP** *(Extensible Authentication Protocol)*: this is not a single protocol. It is a set of protocols that provide other methods of authenticating PPP protocol. EAP is used for smart-card authentication by TLS (*Transport Layer Security*) protocol, by MD5-CHAP protocol and by other authentication methods that have not yet been developed such as biometric recognition.

▶ As with the MS-CHAP protocol, you can use MPPE encryption with the TLS protocol.

4. Internet connection sharing

a. Overview

Windows 2000 allows you to share a dial-up Internet connection that you have configured.

▶ The **Microsoft Proxy Server for Windows 2000 Server** product offers enhanced share and control features for Internet access.

To use a shared Internet connection, other computers in your local area network must be able to access the computer on which you have configured the Internet connection.

Before you can share an Internet connection, you need to understand a certain number of concepts. These concepts include private addresses, network address translation, automatic dialing, remote access and filtering.

Private Internet Addresses

The following IP address ranges are private and are never used on the Internet:

10.0.0.0 10.255.255.255

172.16.0.0 172.31.255.255

192.168.0.0 192.168.255.255

▶ RFC 1918 defines these private address ranges. The following Web page provides a complete list of RFCs: *www.cis.ohio-state.edu/hypertext/information /rfc.html*.

Companies can use these private address ranges to connect to the Internet via a computer that has a private IP address (network interface card) and a public IP address (WAN connection). The public IP address is associated with a connection as a remote access client.

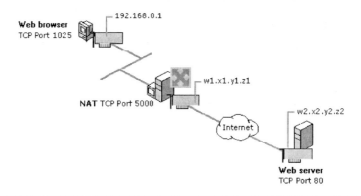

⏩ On the LAN side, Windows 2000 assigns the IP address 192.168.0.1 automatically to the computer that is sharing its Internet connection.

Network Address Translation (NAT)

In addition to sharing its Internet access, the sharing computer must send queries to the Internet via a Proxy server and translate the IP addresses that it uses. This technique is known as **Network Address Translation**, or **NAT**.

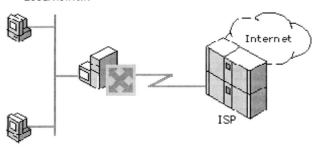

Autodial

Furthermore, if the sharing computer uses a switched link as a remote access client, the line must be available on demand.

The Autodial service manages this on-demand dialing.

Remote access filtering

In addition, to secure this access you can apply restrictions according to the services that you need (known TCP or UDP ports).

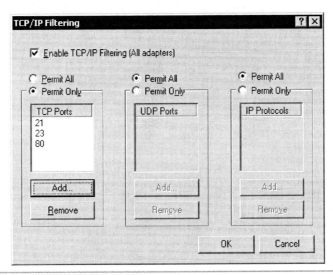

▶ If you decide to use a Windows 2000 Proxy Server in an Active Directory domain environment, you can also filter additional information, such as incoming and outgoing IP addresses, computer name, username, password and connection schedules.

You can enable IPSec for your Internet connection. To do this, open the **Network and Dial-up Connections** tool and right-click your Internet connection to access its **Properties**. Under the **Networking** tab, select **Internet Protocol (TCP/IP)** and click the **Properties** button. Click the **Advanced** button, activate the **Options** tab, select **IP security** and click the **Properties** button. Then, select the **Use this IP security policy** option.

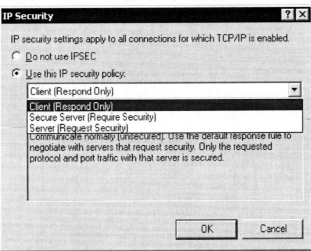

b. Implementing Internet connection sharing

Once you have configured the remote access for outgoing calls (remote access client) you can open the **Properties** for this access.

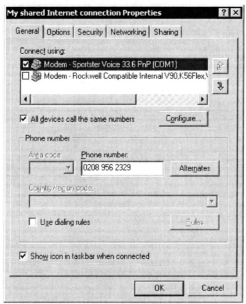

You can share this connection by activating the **Sharing** tab.

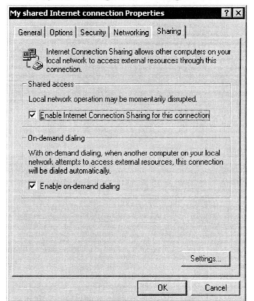

> If you are working with a WAN dial-up connection (for example ISDN or PSTN), then make sure that you Enable on-demand dialing.

When you apply this sharing, the **Network and Dial-up Connections** tool reminds you that it will modify your LAN configuration by implementing a specific address setting.

c. Configuration changes that apply when you enable Internet connection sharing

When you enable Internet connection sharing for an outgoing connection on a Windows 2000 Professional machine, the system automatically changes a certain number of settings. This section describes these changes to illustrate how a shared Internet connection works.

IP address of the Internet Proxy server network adapter

On the machine with a direct Internet connection, the system changes the IP address of the network adapter connected to the company's LAN to **192.168.0.1**, with a class C mask (**/24**).

> Microsoft refers to this working environment as **SOHO (Small Office or Home Office).**

Automatic dialing

As an Internet access can use a switched link, you need an automatic dialing mechanism in order to ensure that the line will be used on demand. The system automatically enables the **Autodial** feature on a machine that shares an Internet connection.

Internet connection sharing service

The system starts up the Internet connection sharing service to manage the shared connection.

Default IP route

When you set up the direct dial-up connection from the machine that shares the Internet connection, the system automatically modifies the static default IP route so that it will transmit all the data packets to the remote access server at the other end of the extended connection.

Forwarding DNS requests

In addition, the machine that shares the Internet connection will forward all name resolution requests from the clients in its LAN to the DNS server that the remote access server offers.

For this purpose the system enables the **DNS proxy**.

D. Troubleshooting

1. Shared Internet connection

Failure of shared Internet connections

– Check that you have shared the Internet connection and not the LAN network adapter.
– Check that the TCP/IP protocol is installed on the LAN from which you are trying to access the Internet via the shared connection.
– Check the following TCP/IP settings on the LAN machines: IP address and subnet mask (use the DHCP for this purpose to avoid any configuration conflicts) and the IP addresses of DNS servers (that are obtained automatically). Check that the machines have direct access to the Proxy server (the machine that shares the Internet connection). In addition, you must define the IP address of a default gateway.
– Check the Internet options of the LAN machines: you must specify the name or the IP address of the proxy server.
– Check that the Internet connection sharing service is started (using the **Event Viewer**).
– Check that the proxy machine is correctly configured to use DNS (and possibly WINS).
– Check to see if you can access the Internet by specifying an IP address. If you can do this, then your problem probably concerns name resolution.

2. IP configuration errors

Even the slightest error in your TCP/IP configuration can prevent your network from working correctly.

For example, an IP network number must be unique on the same section of a network between two routers. You must also be careful to enter the subnet mask correctly, as this information will be used in order to determine the IP network on which a destination machine is located.

Finally, before two hosts that are situated on separate IP networks can exchange information, both of them must have the IP address of a default gateway.

Troubleshooting IP configuration errors

First, you must examine the network topology, in order to identify the different logical networks.

Then, check the IP configuration on your workstation, in order to ensure that it is compatible with your local area network.

Determine whether or not you need the IP address of a default gateway; in other words, decide whether or not your workstation needs to communicate with other IP networks. If your workstation does need to communicate with other IP networks, then you must configure the IP address of a default gateway.

Carry out a local test on your network interface card, followed by a connectivity test with another machine on the same local area network. Finally, if these first two tests are successful, carry out a further connectivity test with a host that is situated on a remote network.

IP connectivity tests

When you have ensured that your IP configuration is correct, then you can check that another host is present by sending it an echo packet.

You can display your IP configuration by opening a **Command Prompt** and then entering the command: **ipconfig /all**.

You can carry out three types of test:

- a local loopback test,
- a test with a local host (with a host that is on the same local area network, or on the same IP network)
- a test with a remote host (with a host that is located on the other side of a router)

You do not need the IP address of a default gateway in order to carry out the first two types of test. On the other hand, you must have the IP address of a default gateway in order to carry out the third type of test.

You can exchange packets with either local or remote TCP/IP machines using the **ping** command.

First, you can carry out a local loopback test via the address 127.0.0.1, or using the name **localhost**. This name is defined in the file: **%Systemroot%\system32\drivers\etc\hosts**.

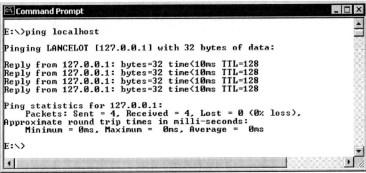

If this command is successful then you can try another **ping** command, this time with a remote machine.

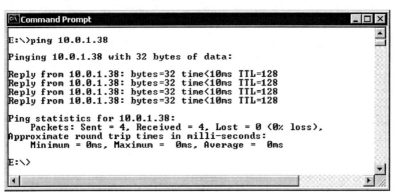

```
Command Prompt                                              _ □ X

E:\>ping 10.0.1.38

Pinging 10.0.1.38 with 32 bytes of data:

Reply from 10.0.1.38: bytes=32 time<10ms TTL=128
Reply from 10.0.1.38: bytes=32 time<10ms TTL=128
Reply from 10.0.1.38: bytes=32 time<10ms TTL=128
Reply from 10.0.1.38: bytes=32 time<10ms TTL=128

Ping statistics for 10.0.1.38:
    Packets: Sent = 4, Received = 4, Lost = 0 (0% loss),
Approximate round trip times in milli-seconds:
    Minimum = 0ms, Maximum =  0ms, Average =  0ms

E:\>
```

If this command runs successfully, then your TCP/IP configuration is correct, and you can now use tools such as **FTP** or **TELNET**.

Chapter 6: Managing users and groups

A. Authentication and logon methods

1. Introduction

For authentication purposes, Windows 2000 uses Kerberos version 5. This system supports authentication by public key. Windows 2000 implements the Kerberos client as security provider and the **winlogon** logon process integrates the initial authentication.

The **Key Distribution Center** security service runs on domain controllers. This service uses the Active Directory as a security accounts database.

Windows 2000 identifies users with a number of protocols. These protocols authenticate remote access sessions and users who access the network via the Internet. However, in a Windows 2000 domain environment you can choose from only two authentication systems:

Windows NT LAN Manager (NTLM)

The Windows NT 4 operating system uses this authentication system by default.

Windows 2000 implements this authentication system for backwards compatibility reasons, to support users of previous versions of the Windows operating system. Windows 2000 also uses NTLM to authenticate sessions from Windows 2000 stand-alone computers.

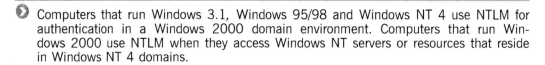

Computers that run Windows 3.1, Windows 95/98 and Windows NT 4 use NTLM for authentication in a Windows 2000 domain environment. Computers that run Windows 2000 use NTLM when they access Windows NT servers or resources that reside in Windows NT 4 domains.

Kerberos version 5

Windows 2000 uses this protocol by default to authenticate computers in a Windows 2000 domain environment.

2. Advantages of Kerberos authentication

Windows 2000 aims to allow network administrators to stop using NTLM authentication, once all the network clients are able to support Kerberos authentication. Kerberos has a number of advantages with respect to NTLM: it is more flexible, it is more efficient and it provides enhanced security.

Quicker logon

With NTLM authentication, a server must contact a domain controller in order to authenticate each of its clients. With Kerberos authentication, a server does not need to contact a domain controller. The server can authenticate the client simply using the characteristics that the client transmits. A client need access a server only once and the system can then reuse these logon characteristics throughout the duration of the network connection.

Mutual authentication

NTLM allows servers to check the identity of each client. It does not allow clients to check the identity of the server, nor does it allow a server to check the identity of another server. With Kerberos, each participant in a network connection is sure that it is dealing with the right correspondents. This is not the case with NTLM, which allows only the server to identify the client.

Delegating authentication

Kerberos offers a delegation feature called proxy Kerberos. This mechanism allows a service to provide access to its clients needing to connect with other services. NTLM does not offer a similar feature.

Simplified management of trust relationships

Thanks to the Kerberos mutual authentication feature, the trust relationships between Windows 2000 domains are two-way and transitive. This means that you no longer need to set up complex infrastructures of one-way trust relationships in order to manage a complex network that contains many domains.

Instead, you can organize the numerous domains of a large network into a hierarchy of two-way transitive trust relationships. Consequently, the security authority of any domain can authenticate an access to the entire Active Directory tree. In addition, if the network contains more than one tree, then the security authority can operate in any tree in the forest.

Compatibility

Microsoft has implemented the Kerberos system according to an international standard (that was published by the Internet Engineering Task Force). This approach allows Windows 2000 to offer an authentication method common to all networks supporting Kerberos version 5.

3. How Kerberos authentication works

Kerberos allows mutual authentication between a client and a server, or between two servers, before they set up a connection. Kerberos considers that clients and servers exchange data in an environment in which no computer is physically secure and that you can capture and modify the data packets that computers send via the cable. These assumptions are fully justified on today's Internet.

The Kerberos v5 authentication mechanism assigns access **tickets** to network services. These tickets contain encrypted data, such as an encrypted password, which confirms the identity of the user to the requested service. The authentication process is invisible to the user, apart from the password or the smart card identification that the user must provide.

Here are the different steps of the Kerberos authentication process:

1 - By supplying a password or using a smart card, the user requests authentication from a **Key Distribution Center** on one of the domain controllers.

2 - The Key Distribution Center returns a special ticket to the client that is called the **Ticket Granting Ticket**, or **TGT**. This ticket allows the client to access the **Ticket Granting Service**, or **TGS.** The TGS is part of the Kerberos v5 authentication system on the domain controller.

3 - The Ticket Granting Service issues a **service ticket** to the client.

4 - The client then presents this service ticket to the network service that the client requests. Not only does this service ticket prove the identity of the user to the service, but it also proves the identity of the service to the user.

4. Local authentication

When you log on to a Windows 2000 machine that is not a domain controller using a user account that Active Directory does not support, you obtain only local authentication.

With a local user account, you log on to a local computer using the information that the computer stores in its local accounts database (handled by the Security Account Manager).

Each Windows 2000 Professional workstation, or Windows 2000 server, that is not a domain controller uses a local database to authenticate users when they log on.

5. Authentication in a Windows 2000 domain

The use of a centralized database allows Windows 2000 to offer the **single sign-on** feature. With single sign-on, the user need log on to the domain only once to access resources that are distributed throughout the network.

When a user logs on to a Windows 2000 computer with a domain account, the logon process is different from the logon process that takes place when a user logs on with a local account.

First the user enters a password, or uses a smart card. The system then consults the Active Directory in order to authenticate the user. If the logon is successful, then the user will be able to access not only resources that reside in his/her domain, but also resources in any trusting domain for which he/she has the required permissions.

🔾 If you log on with a password, Windows 2000 uses the normal Kerberos mechanism to authenticate your logon. On the other hand, if you log on with a smart card, Kerberos will use certificates.

6. Network Authentication

Network authentication allows a user to access a remote network service. Windows 2000 uses various authentication methods for this purpose. These methods include Kerberos v5, SSL/TSL (*Secure Socket Layer/Transport Layer Security*) and NTLM for backwards compatibility reasons.

Thanks to the single sign-on feature, network authentication is invisible to the user. On the other hand, a user with a local account must supply a valid username and password to the remote server each time that the remote server requires them.

To administer user and group accounts, you can use two different consoles:

- The **Active Directory Users and Computers** console allows you to manage the domain.
- The **Computer Management** console allows you to manage local users and groups on a Windows 2000 member server, Windows 2000 stand-alone server or Windows 2000 Professional workstation.

B. Managing a local computer

1. Users

A local user account is an account that can be used to log on locally to a computer. With this type of account, you can access only the local resources of a machine.

These accounts are stored in the accounts database of the local computer. This is the SAM database, which is stored under the folder **%systemroot%\system32\config**. These account data-bases are present only on workstations and on member and stand-alone servers. On a domain controller, accounts and groups are stored in Active Directory.

If a user who is logged on locally wishes to access resources that are situated on another computer, then the user must have an account on the other machine.

a. Predefined accounts

When you install Windows 2000, two user accounts are created:
- the Administrator account,
- the Guest account.

Administrator

The administrator has maximum power on a machine. The administrator manages the system configuration. This includes the following tasks:
- managing security policy,
- managing user accounts and group accounts,
- managing the software configuration of the operating system,
- creating folders and installing files on the hard disks,
- installing and configuring printers,
- administrating the sharing of file and printer ressources,
- logical and physical organisation of data on the disks (including formatting, and partitioning),
- backing up and restoring data.

You cannot delete the Administrator account, but you can rename it.

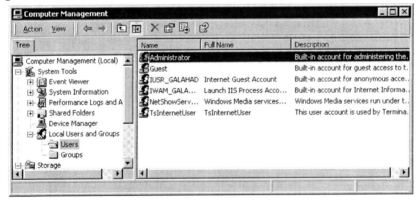

You are recommended to rename the Administrator account because it is more difficult to find the password of an account when you do not know its name.

From a security viewpoint, you may find it useful not to display the name of the last user who logged on. You can specify this in your local security policy as follows:
Open a console using the MMC tool and add the **Group Policy** snap-in. Under **Console Root**, expand **Local Computer Policy - Computer Configuration - Windows Settings - Security Settings - Local Policies - Security Options**. Then, enable the **Do not display last user name in logon screen** policy.

Guest

As the name indicates, this account is intended for occasional users, or for inexperienced users. For security reasons, the *Guest* user has a minimum amount of rights on the system.

b. Creating a user account

You can create a local user account using the **Local Users and Groups** folder of the **Computer Management** console.

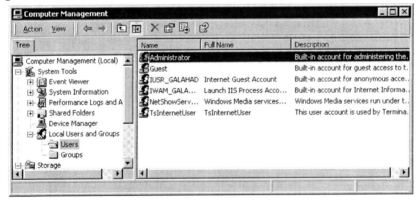

To create a new user account, right-click **Users** and select **New User**. Then fill in the following fields:

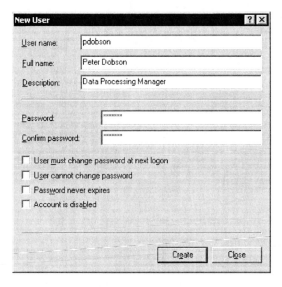

User name

This is the name that the user must enter in order to log on to the machine. This field is obligatory and must not exceed 20 characters.

Full name

This is the user's full name. It is used for administrative purposes.

Description

This field allows you to specify such details as the user's position in the company, and the user's geographical location.

Password and Confirm password

The administrator can assign a password to the user.

User must change password at next logon

If you enable this option, then the user must choose a password when he/she logs on for the first time. Then, the user will no longer have to choose a password on subsequent logons, and will be able to use the password that he/she entered upon the first logon. This option allows the administrator to let the user choose his/her own password. However, in this case the administrator will have no means of finding out a user's password.

User cannot change password

This option is useful so as to fix certain passwords, such as that of the guest user and those of accounts that are used by several people. This option helps the administrator to manage user passwords.

Password never expires

You must use this option if you do not want the password to expire. This option can be useful with an account that is used by an application or by a service.

Account is disabled

You must enable this option if you do not want anyone to use an account (for example, when a user goes on holiday). When you disable an account a cross appears on the icon: 🖼.

➲ If you select the **User must change password at next logon** option, then the **User cannot change password** option, and the **Password never expires** option, are grayed out.

---

c. Modifying a user account

Once you have created a local account, then it appears in the **Computer Management** console, in the user list under the **users** folder.

You can modify the characteristics, which you have defined for a user, later. In order to do this, select the user concerned and then press the `Enter` key. Alternatively, you can open the **Action** menu and select **Properties**.

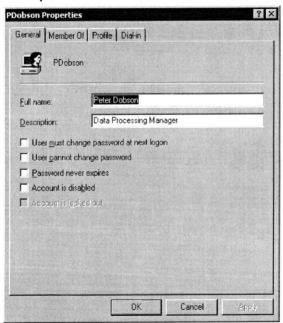

It must be noted that this dialog box contains a new option that is grayed out: **account is locked out**. This option will become available if you define an account policy that indicates that the account must be locked out after a specified number of failed logon attempts.

The user **Properties** dialog box offers a number of additional tabs:

- The **Member Of** tab indicates the groups to which the user belongs. If you wish to include the user in a new group, then click the **Add** button and select the desired group.
- The **Profile** tab allows you to specify the path of the user's profile. This topic will be covered in greater detail later on in this chapter.
- The **Dial-in** tab allows you to specify how this account must be used via remote network access or via VPN *(Virtual Private Networking)*.

When you rename a user account you do not lose all the information that is associated with the account (such as group memberships and permissions). In fact, although you use the login name of the user, when you handle a user account, Windows 2000 associates this name with a security identification number (SID). This number is unique, and has the following format:

$$\text{5-1-5-21-527237240-2111687655-1957994488-500}$$

When you rename an account you will modify the login name on the other hand the SID never changes. When you grant permissions to a user account, then these permissions are attributed to the SID that is associated with the account.

If you delete an account, and then recreate the account with the same name, then you will have created a new account that is associated with a new SID. Because of this, you will not recover the permissions that had been granted to the previous account.

If you wish to rename, or to delete an account, then you can either right-click the account concerned, or you can use the **Action** menu.

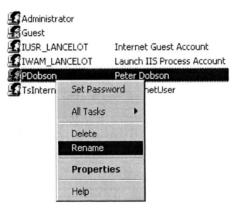

d. Modifying a password

With Windows NT 4.0, you could change the password that is associated with a user account by modifying the properties of the account. With Windows 2000 however, you must right-click the account concerned and then select the **Set Password** option (alternatively, you can use the **Action** menu).

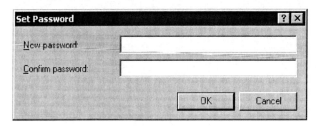

You cannot modify a password via the properties of the account so that the administration of this item can be delegated. With the Windows 2000 approach, you can grant to users, or to groups of users, the sole power of changing their passwords, without allowing them to change any other characteristics of their accounts.

⊚ An administrator cannot find out a user's password.

2. Groups

a. Introduction

Groups allow you to simplify user administration. A group contains a set of user accounts that have the same administrative needs. Thus, rather than granting permissions to each user individually, an administrator can simply grant the permissions to a group.

The permissions and rights that are assigned to a group apply to all the users who are members of the group.

⊚ A user can be a member of several groups.

In the local accounts database of a member/stand-alone server, or of a workstation, only one type of group can be created: a local group. Local groups are represented by the 🖥 icon.

b. Creating a group

You can create a group by expanding **Local Users and Groups** and right-clicking the **Groups** folder in the **Computer Management** console, and then selecting **New Group** (alternatively you can select the **Groups** folder and then use the **Action** menu).

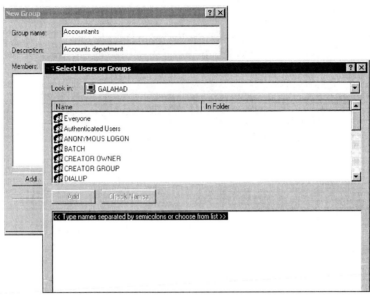

Give the group a meaningful name, and possibly a description, and then click the **Add** button. You can choose to include users either from the local accounts database or from a domain.

c. Predefined groups

On member/stand-alone servers, and on Windows 2000 Professional workstations, a number of groups are predefined during the installation of Windows 2000.

These groups have rights that allow them to carry out a certain number of tasks on the local machine, such as making backups, and administering resources.

These predefined groups are as follows:

- **Administrators**: the members of this group can carry out all the computer's administrative tasks. By default, the only member of this group is the administrator account. When you include a workstation, or a stand-alone server, in a domain, then the global administrators group of the domain is included automatically in the local administrators group of your computer. This is done so that the domain administrators can manage all the machines that are in their domain.

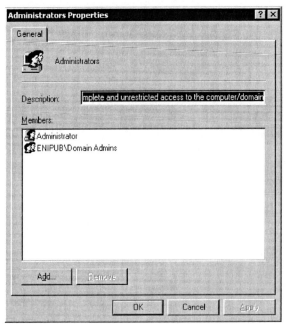

In the example above, the Administrators group of the ENIPUB domain have been included in the local Administrators group of the member server. Thanks to this approach, the domain administrator can administer this computer in the same way as the local machine administrator.

- **Guests**: as the name indicates, this group is used for occasional access. For security reasons, the users of this group are granted only a minimum number of system rights. By default, the **Guest** account is automatically included in this group.

- **Backup Operators**: the members of this group can use the Windows 2000 Backup utility in order to back up and to restore data.

- **Users**: all the user accounts that you create are included in this group. They can carry out only the tasks that you specify and have access only to those resources for which you have granted permissions. When your workstation, or your server joins a domain, the users group of the domain is automatically included in the users group of your machine.

- **Power Users**: the members of this group can share resources, and they can create and modify user accounts from the computer's local accounts database. They can carry out certain administrative tasks without being in total control of the machine.

In addition to these groups, every computer that runs Windows 2000 has system groups. You cannot modify the membership of these groups, which reflect the status of your system at a given time.

- **Everyone** group: this group includes all users: those you have created, the guest account, and all the users of the other domains. It must be noted that, when you share a resource, this group has **Full Control** permission.

- **Authenticated Users** group: this group includes all users that have a user account and a password for the local machine, or for Active Directory. It is preferable to grant permissions to this group, rather than granting them to the **Everyone** group.
- **Creator Owner** group: every user that has taken possession of a resource is a member of this group, for the resource concerned. The owner of a resource has full powers on this resource.
- **Network** group: this group includes all users that access a resource via the network.
- **Interactive** group: this group contains all the users who are logged on locally (in the case where you use Terminal Services, this group contains all the users who are logged on to the Terminal Server).

C. Managing in a domain

Every person who uses the network must have a user account in order to log on to the domain and have access to the network resources. These user accounts are created in the Windows 2000 directory database.

When a user logs on to the domain, the logon information is sent to the domain controller, which compares it with the information contained in the Active Directory database. When the logon has been validated, the user can access all the network resources which he/she has the permissions to access.

When you promote a Windows 2000 server to domain controller (by installing active directory), the group and user information contained in the SAM database is migrated to the Active Directory database.

1. Managing domain users

a. Predefined accounts

When you install Windows 2000, two user accounts are created:
- the Administrator account,
- the guest account.

Administrator

The administrator has the maximum power on a machine. The administrator manages the system configuration, which includes the following tasks:
- managing security policies,
- managing user accounts and group accounts,
- managing the software configuration of the operating system,
- creating folders and installing files on the hard disks,
- installing and configuring printers,
- administrating the sharing of file and printer ressources,

- logical and physical organisation of data on the disks (including formatting and partitioning),
- backing up and restoring data.

You cannot delete the Administrator account, but you can rename it.

❿ You are recommended to rename the Administrator account because it is more difficult to find the password of an account when you do not know its name.

❿ In addition, it is useful not to display the name of the last user who logged on to a machine. You can use group policies for this purpose.

Guest

As the name indicates, this account is intended for occasional users, or for inexperienced users. For security reasons, the Guest user has a minimum amount of rights on the system.

By default, this account is disabled and does not have a password. You can rename this account. When you enable this account, you introduce a major weak-point into the security system.

b. Creating a user account

Before you start creating users, you might find it useful to define a naming convention that will allow you to identify each user and, above all, that will allow you to ensure that each logon name is unique in the domain. For example, one possible naming convention could be to use the first letter of the user's first name, followed by the users surname. If this rule leads to a duplication of logon names, one way of solving the problem could be to add the second letter of the first name. For example, suppose you have one user who is called Peter Jenkins and another user who is called Paul Jenkins. Then, you could define their login names as **pejenkins** and **pajenkins**, respectively.

To create domain user accounts, you must use the **Active Directory Users and Computers** console.

You must create this user object in a container. To do this, right-click the organizational unit in which you want to create the account, then select **New** followed by **User** (alternatively, you can use the **Action** menu).

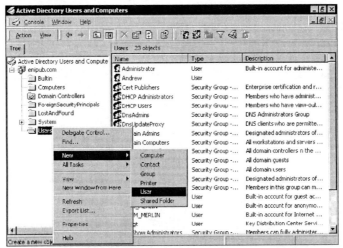

The **New Object - User** dialog box appears:

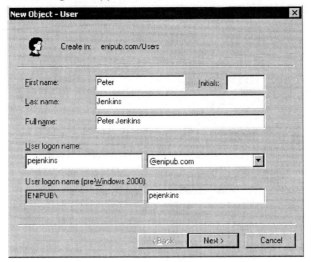

First name
This field is obligatory. It allows you to enter the user's first name.

Last name
The user's surname is also obligatory.

Full name
This name must be unique on the organizational unit in which you are creating the user account.

User logon name

The user will enter this name so that it can be authenticated by the domain controller. This name must be unique in the domain and must be in conformity with your naming convention. This logon name is followed by the name of the domain in which you are creating the user. In the example above, the user will be able to log on as **pejenkins@enipub.com**.

User logon name (pre-Windows 2000)

Users who work with a pre-Windows 2000 version must log on with this name. This name must not exceed 20 characters.

When you have completed these fields, click **Next**.

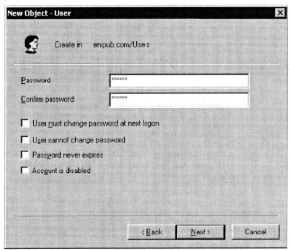

Password and Confirm password

The administrator can provide a password for the user.

User must change password at next logon

If you enable this option, the user must choose a password when he/she logs on for the first time. The user will no longer have to choose a password on subsequent logons and will be able to use the password that he/she entered upon the first logon. This option allows the administrator to let the user choose his/her own password. However, in this case the administrator will have no means of finding out a user's password.

User cannot change password

This option is useful for setting certain passwords, such as guest user's and those of accounts that are user by several people. This option helps the administrator to manage user passwords.

Password never expires

You must use this option if you do not want the password to expire. This option can be useful with an account that is used by an application or by a service.

Account is disabled

You must enable this option if you do not want anyone to use an account (for example, when a user goes on holiday). When you disable an account a cross appears on its icon.

If the predefined OUs do not suit your needs, then select the name of your domain in the **Active Directory Users and Computers** console and open the **Action** menu and select **New** followed by **Organizational Unit**.

When you create an object it is replicated automatically on all the other domain controllers.

c. User account properties

Personal properties

Personal properties are the attributes of the user. This information includes such items as the user's geographical address, telephone numbers. This information is stored in the Windows 2000 directory database so that users will be able to find it.

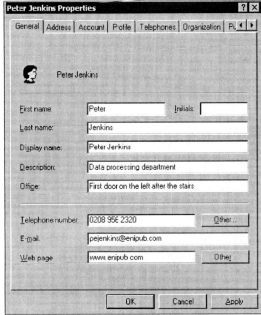

This information allows you to find a user very easily.

You can look for a user in two ways:

- Open the **Start - Search - For People** menu and select **Active Directory** in the **Look in** drop-down list.

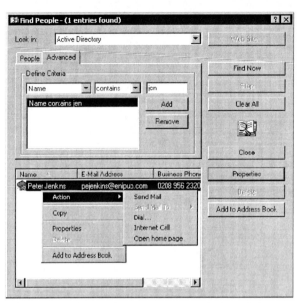

When you have found your contact, you can carry out a certain number of actions. For example, you can send the user an electronic mail message, you can open the user's Web page, or you can view the user's properties to find out his/her geographical address.

- Alternatively, using the **Active Directory Users and Computers** console you can open the **Action** menu then select **All Tasks** followed by **Find**. This method allows you to carry out searches according to more advanced criteria.

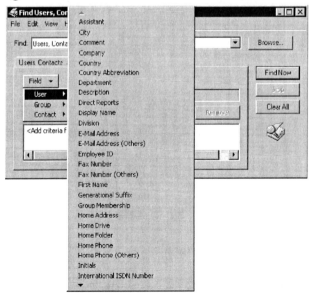

Account properties

Unlike personal properties, account properties do not supply information about the user. They supply information concerning the running of the account (including items such as time period restrictions and account expiry).

To view or to enter account properties, double-click the user concerned and select the **Account** tab.

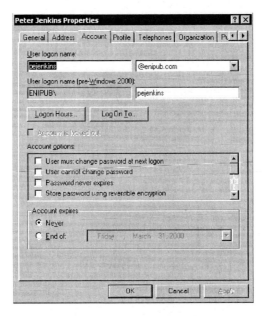

Under **Account options** you can modify the settings that were specified when the account was created. These settings include the following:

- Password never expires,
- User must change password at next logon,
- User cannot change password,
- Account is disabled.

In addition, the following options are also available:

Smart card is required for interactive logon

Windows 2000 allows you to request authentication using a smartcard, provided that your system is equipped with a card reader.

Account is sensitive and cannot be delegated

This option ensures that control of this account will not be delegated.

Account is trusted for delegation

This option allows the user to delegate administrative tasks to other users.

Store password using reversible encryption

You must use this option if there are any users in the Windows 2000 network who work with Apple computers.

Do not require Kerberos preauthentification

You must use this option if the user account uses another version of the Kerberos protocol.

Use DES encryption types for this account

You must enable this check box if you use DES (*Data Encryption Standard*) encryption. DES supports encryption methods such as IPSec and MPPE.

Account expiry

You can set an account expiry date (this may be useful in the case where you know that a user will leave the company on a fixed date, for example on May 12th, 2001). You can set an expiry date as follows:

Under **Account expires** select the **End of** option and open the list box to display the calendar. Select the date on which you want the account to expire.

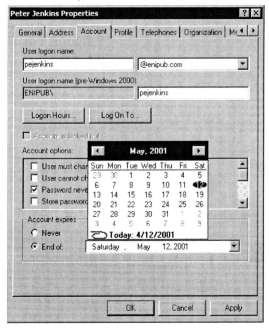

Time period restrictions

For security reasons, you may want to define the time periods during which a user will be allowed to log on. In order to do this, select the **Logon Hours** button.

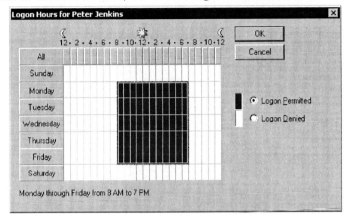

Select the desired logon hours then enable either the **Logon Permitted** or the **Logon Denied** option button according to your requirements.

Access restrictions

You can restrict the access of the user to certain, specified machines. In order to do this, click the **Log On To** button, then add the names of the computers onto which the user must be allowed to log.

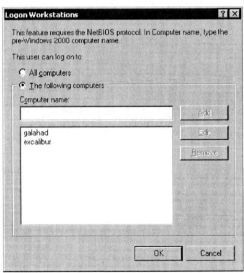

d. Copying user accounts

If you must create a large number of user accounts with the same characteristics, you may find it quicker to create a template account that includes all the common characteristics, then to copy it.

When you copy an account, certain settings are maintained:
- logon hours.
- the following account options:
- User must change password at next logon,
- User cannot change password,
- Password never expires,
- Account is disabled.
- access restrictions (Log On To).
- account expiry date.
- profile options and the home directory (for these settings you must use the **%username%** variable).
- group membership.

To copy an account, right-click the account concerned, then select **Copy**.

e. Modifying an account

Resetting a password

If a user forgets his/her password, then you must reset it (after verifying the user's identity). You can reset a password by right-clicking the user's account and selecting **Reset Password**.

Moving a user object

As the organizational unit tree structure is not fixed, you can move a user account (or any other object) from one OU to another OU. To do this, right-click the account that you want to move, then select **Move**.

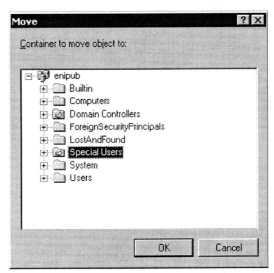

Select the OU to which you want to move the user object, then click **OK**.

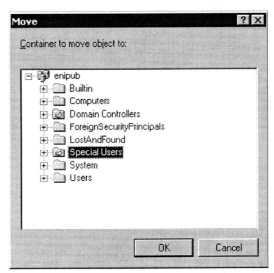 You can move objects from an OU in a domain to another OU in another domain by using the **MOVETREE** command from the Windows 2000 resource kit.

2. Managing groups

a. Group Types

As has been discussed earlier on in this chapter, groups help you to manage user accounts so that you can allow them to access resources. They allow you to simplify administrative tasks.

Active Directory has introduced a number of group features that were not avaiable with Windows NT 4.0.

There are two types of group:

- **Security groups** which are used to manage the resources of one or more domains.
- **Distribution groups** which can be used, for example, to send electronic mail messages to all the users in such groups. These groups cannot be used for security purposes. Applications such as Exchange 2000 work with the Windows 2000 directory database and can use distribution groups.

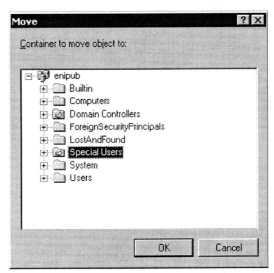 Although you can use security groups as you would use distribution groups, you are strongly recommended not to do so, as some applications are able to read distribution groups only. In addition, when a user logs on, Windows 2000 creates an **access token** that contains the list of all the security groups to which the user belongs. If you use security groups for distribution purposes, you may slow down the logon process.

Each of these group types has a scope that specifies the people who can belong to them (user accounts, group accounts or computer accounts) along with the extent to which they can be applied.

There are three types of group scope:

- **Domain local**: allows you to apply permissions.
- **Global**: allows you to organize user accounts.
- **Universal**: allows you to group together users that come from any domain and to grant them permissions in any domain.

The contents of these groups will differ according to whether the domain configuration is in native mode, or in mixed mode.

A mixed mode domain allows Windows NT 4.0 domain controllers to operate in a Windows 2000 domain.

When you have upgraded all pre-Windows 2000 domain controllers, you can switch to native mode. When you have switched to native mode, you will be able to use universal groups and you will be able to nest groups inside other groups (for example, a global group can be a member of another global group in native mode).

 After you have installed your Windows 2000 domain controllers, your domain will be in mixed mode. Switching to native mode is irreversible. To switch to native mode, go into your domain properties in the **Active Directory Users and Computers** console.

In mixed mode:
- A **domain local** group can contain users and global groups that come from any domain.
- A **global** group contains users that come from the same domain as that of the global group.
- **Universal** groups do not exist in mixed mode.

In native mode:
- A **domain local** group can contain user accounts, global groups and universal groups that come from any domain in the forest. It can also contain domain local accounts that come from its own domain.
- A **global** group can contain user accounts and global groups from the same domain.
- A **universal** group can contain user accounts, global groups and universal groups from any domain in the forest.

A domain local group can obtain permissions on the domain in which it is located. Global groups and universal groups can obtain permissions on all the domains in the forest.

b. Creating groups

To create these groups, go into the **Active Directory Users and Computers** console.

→) Select the OU in which you want to create your group.

→) Open the **Action** menu, and select **New** followed by **Group**.

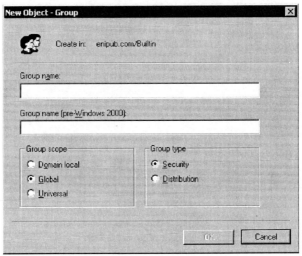

→) Select the **Group type** (**Security** or **Distribution**) along with the **Group scope** (**Domain local**, **Global** or **Universal**).

→) Give a meaningful name to the group.

It must be noted that you can specify a different name for use with a pre-Windows 2000 machine.

When you have created your group, you can double-click it to edit its properties:

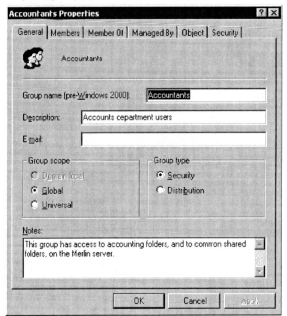

If the domain is in native mode, you will be able to modify the **Group type** at any time. You can also modify the **Group scope**:

- You can change from a global group to a universal group provided that your global group is not a member of another group. This is because a global group cannot contain a universal group.
- You can change from a domain local group to a universal group provided that your domain local group does not contain any other domain local groups. This is because a universal group cannot contain a domain local group.

The **Members** tab allows you to view, add or remove user accounts or computer accounts in this group. An alternative way of adding a user to a group is to display the properties of the user concerned then to use the **Member Of** tab in this dialog box.

The **Member Of** tab allows you to display the list of the groups to which your group belongs. This tab also allows you to insert your group into another group.

The **Managed By** tab allows you to specify the person or the group that must manage your group. For example, a user can look on this tab for the telephone number of the person who is responsible for the group, so that he/she can contact this person if any problem occurs.

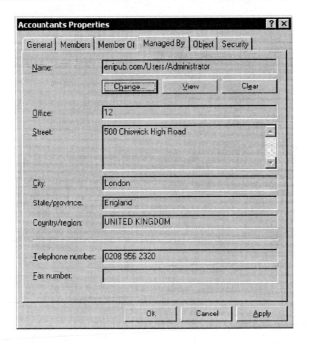

c. Carrying out actions on a group

Finding a group using Active Directory

If you have many different groups that are in different OUs, you might find it useful to search for a group using Active Directory so that you can administer the group.

→) Open the **Active Directory Users and Computers** console, open the **Action** menu and select **Find**.

→) Enter the name of the group that you are looking for then click **Find Now**.

→) When your group has been found, you can double-click it, or right-click it, in order to administer it.

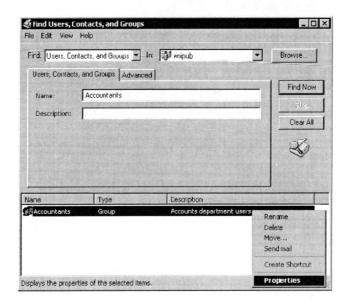

Deleting a group

When you delete a group, you do not delete the accounts that are members of the group.

The rights and the permissions that are associated with this group are deleted. When you create a group, a security identifier (SID) is associated with it. This SID is unique and cannot be re-used. Consequently, if you delete a group and then create a group with the same name, then a new SID will be associated with this group. The permissions of the former group will not be applied to the new group.

To delete a group, right-click it and then select **Delete**. Alternatively, you can use the **Action** menu.

Renaming a group

When you rename a group, you will change the name of the group, but the SID that is associated with the group will stay the same. The members of this group are retained, and they can carry on using the resources for which the group has permissions.

d. Strategies for using groups

A domain local group can have permissions only on the domain in which it is located. Consequently, whenever possible you must try to organize users into global groups, then include these global groups (which can come from any domain in the forest) in domain local groups.

You can then assign permissions for resources to the domain local groups and these permissions will automatically apply to the members of the global groups.

e. Predefined groups

Remember that all the computers that run Windows 2000 have a certain number of predefined groups, which are created when Windows 2000 is installed.

Predefined global groups

Domain Guests

The **Guest** user account is automatically included in this group. In addition, this global group is itself automatically included in the **Guests** domain local group.

Domain Users

All the user accounts that you create are included in this group. These accounts can carry out only those tasks that you specify and have access only to those resources for which you grant permissions. These accounts are automatically included in the **Users** domain local group.

Domain Admins

The Administrator account belongs to this group, which itself is included in the **Administrators** domain local group. In fact, the Administrator user account has no particular rights as a user account. The Administrator obtains its rights by being a member of this global group, which itself belongs to the **Administrators** domain local group.

Enterprise Admins

The members of this group have administrator rights on the whole network (they are not limited to the domain).

Predefined domain local groups

Account Operators

The members of this group can administer user accounts and groups (they can add, remove and modify these items). However, they cannot touch the Administrator account, nor can they touch the accounts of the other members of the **Account Operators** group.

Server Operators

The members of this group can share resources, and they can back up and restore data on the domain controllers.

Print Operators

The members of this group can manage the network printers of the domain controllers.

Administrators

The members of this group can administer the domain controllers, along with any machine that is included in the domain. By default, the **Domain Admins** global group and the Administrator account belong to the **Administrators** domain local group.

Guests

This group includes the **Domain Guests** global group and the **Guest** user account. Members of the **Guests** domain local group have few rights.

Backup Operators

The members of this group can backup and restore on all of the domain controllers.

Users

This group includes the **Domain Users** global group. You can use this group to apply rights and permissions to everybody that has an account in the domain.

By default, the different operator groups do not have members. You can include user accounts in these groups in order to assign specific rights to your users.

If a user must carry out backup operations, it is better to include this user in the Backup Operators group, rather than in the Administrators group. To control security, it is preferable to limit a user's rights to those functions that the user must carry out.

It must be remembered that, in addition to these groups, every computer that runs Windows 2000 has system groups. You cannot modify the membership of these groups, which reflect the status of your system at a given time.

- **Everyone** group: this group includes all users: those you have created, the guest account and all the users of the other domains. When you share a resource, this group has **Full Control** permission.
- **Authenticated Users** group: this group includes all users with a user account and a password for the local machine, or for Active Directory. It is preferable to grant permissions to this group, rather than granting them to the **Everyone** group.
- **Creator Owner** group: every user that has taken possession of a resource is a member of this group, for the resource concerned. The owner of a resource has full powers on this resource.
- **Network** group: this group includes all users that access a resource via the network.
- **Interactive** group: this group contains all the users who are logged on locally (in the case where you use Terminal Services, this group contains all the users who are logged on to the Terminal Server).

3. User profiles and home directories

a. User profiles

A local user profile is a file that is stored locally in a folder with the user's logon name. This folder is stored in the **Documents and Settings** directory. When no roaming profile exists for a user on a server, a new folder is created locally with the name of the user and the contents of the **Default user** profile. The user environment is then built up by adding the information that is contained in the **All Users** folder. All modifications made by the user are saved in the new user profile. The initial **Default user** profile is unchanged. If the user has the same account name to log on locally and to log on to the domain, then two separate folders are created. In particular, this is the case for the administrator:

Windows 2000 Professional

The user's environment is contained in each of these folders. The profile file is called **ntuser.dat**.

The profile provides the user's environment (including such items as screen background colours and customized **Start** menu) each time that the user logs on.

b. Roaming user profiles

With local profiles, the user will go into his/her environment only if the user logs on to the machine on which his/her environment has been configured.

In many networks, users move from machine to machine. It is useful then, for the user to be able to go into his/her environment whatever the machine where he/she logs on. This can be achieved by configuring roaming profiles.

When a user logs on, Windows 2000 automatically downloads the user's profile. However, before it does this, Windows 2000 compares the user's profile with the one on the machine where he/she is logging on. This approach allows Windows 2000 to download only the differences between the two profiles, speeding up the logon process.

D. User rights policies

You can use group policies, in order to modify certain rights on the operating system. These user rights include the rights to log on locally, to change the system time, to shut down the system, to add workstations to domain and to manage the auditing and security log.

To modify these rights, select the container concerned, and then select **Properties - Group Policy - Edit**.

In a Workgroup, you can apply group policies only to your local computer, using the Group Policy snap-in on your local computer.

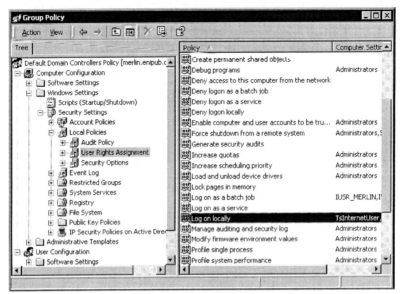

For example, suppose you want to grant to a specific user, the right to log on locally onto a domain controller (by default, only the administrators and the operators have this right on domain controllers). In order to do this, select the organizational unit that represents the domain controllers. Then edit this group policy in order to add the user concerned for the **Log on locally** right, in the **User Rights Assignment** that is situated under **Local Policies.**

E. Account policies

1. Introduction

You can define accounts and password security using group policies. Several templates are provided that offer different levels of security. You can modify existing templates, or you can create new ones, in order to meet your own specific security needs.

Once you have configured a template it is imported into the group policy so that it can be applied to users or to computers.

You can store Group Policy objects in an Active Directory database. Alternatively, you can store these objects in the local database, either of a Windows 2000 Professional workstation, or of a Windows 2000 Server that is not acting as domain controller.

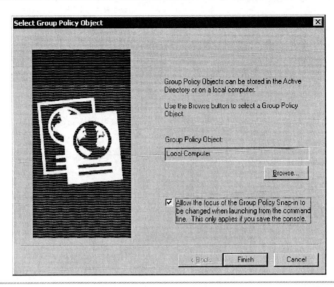

With Active Directory, group policies are associated directly with the container to which they apply. On the other hand, with a local database, group policies will be local to the computer and to the users who will log on locally.

In addition, policy settings that are defined at domain level override those that are defined locally.

You can access security templates by creating an MMC and adding into it, the **Security Templates** snap-in.

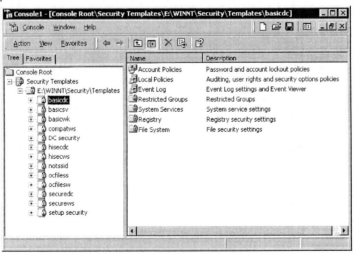

The security templates are text files that have **.inf** name extensions. They are located in the directory **%systemroot%\security\templates**.

❂ You can display a description of the contents of a template by right-clicking the template concerned and selecting the **Set Description** option.

To create a new template, right-click **%systemroot%/security/template**, and then select **New Template**.

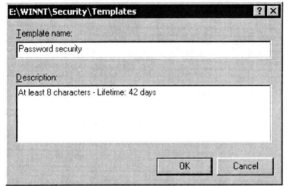

Give a significant name to your new template, along with a description that will help you quickly to remember its purpose.

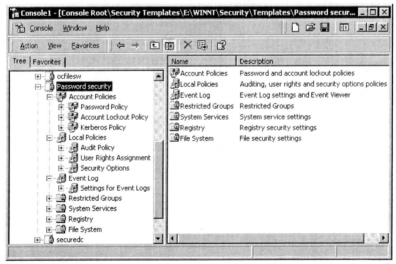

Finally, you must set up the security actions that your template must implement.

2. Implementing a group policy in a domain environment

To apply a security model to a group policy, you must use either the **Active Directory Sites and Services** console or the **Active Directory Users and Computers** console.

➔) Right-click the container for which you want to apply the policy.

➔) Select **Properties** then select the **Group Policy** tab.

➔) Select, or create a policy, then click the **Edit** button.

➔) Right-click **Security Settings** (under **Computer Configuration - Windows Settings**), then select **Import Policy**.

➔) Select the security template that you wish to import then click the **Open** button.

3. Security options

In addition to account, password and auditing options, group policies allow you to add an extra security level using the **Security Options**, which are situated under the **Local Policies**.

These security options allow you:

- not to display the logon name of the user who last logged on (this policy allows you to prevent users from guessing the name of the administrator, in the case where you renamed this account),
- to display a logon message title,
- not to allow unsigned drivers to be installed,
- to log off users automatically when their logon time expires,
- to prevent users from installing printer drivers,
- to warn users that they must change their passwords, before their passwords expire,
- to rename the administrator account and the guest account,

And they also allow you to carry out many other actions.

4. Analyzing the security

When you have set up and applied your security templates, you cannot be completely sure that the actions that will be applied are really the ones that you wanted.

In order to check the security that is applied against the security that you planned, a snap-in is provided that allows you to carry out this diagnosis.

→) Open an MMC. Then, add the **Security Configuration and analysis** snap-in.

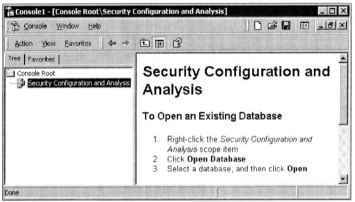

→) Right-click **Security Configuration and Analysis** and select **Open Database**.

→) Enter a name for your database. Then click **Open** and select the template that you want to analyze.

→) Click the **Open** button.

→) Right-click **Security Configuration and Analysis** and select **Analyze Computer Now**.

→) Enter a name for your log file, in which the analysis results will be stored, and then click **OK**. The security analysis can then begin:

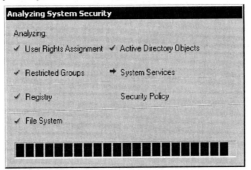

→) The result appears in your console:

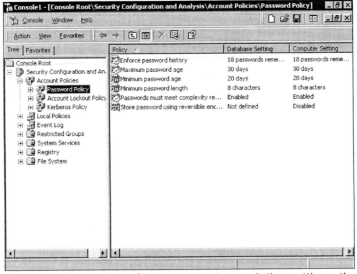

The difference between the status of your computer and the settings that are required by your template, is shown for each of the elementary policies. A ![symbol] symbol indicates that your computer setting is different from that of the template, and a ![symbol] symbol indicates that your computer setting is the same as that of the template.

If the security that is applied to your computer is not the one that you wanted, then right-click **Security Configuration and Analysis** and select **Configure Computer Now**. The system will then apply your security template as you intended.

F. Audit

The audit is a system tool that allows you to log the events and the activities that are carried out, either by the system or by the users that you want to monitor. Events can be audited when they are successful, and/or when they are unsuccessful.

The results of these audits are stored in the **Security** log of the Event Viewer. They provide information on the action that was carried out, they tell you by whom it was carried out, and they tell you whether the action was successful, or whether it was unsuccessful.

If you are working in a Windows 2000 Server environment that is based on an Active Directory domain, then you are advised to define your audit policies at the level of the organizational units that contain the computers that you want to audit.

In this case, you should use the **Active Directory Users and Computers** snap-in, and access the **Properties** of the container to which you want to apply your audit policy.

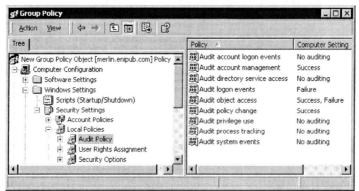

In addition, you can use a security template, after you have imported it into a group policy.

➜ Double-click the event that you want to audit.

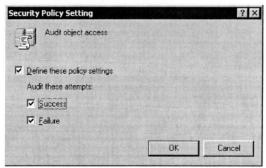

➜ Activate the **Success** check box, and/or the **Failure** check box.

⊕ Do not choose to audit all the types of event on success and on failure, as this will make it more difficult to extract relevant information from the **Event Viewer**.

If you want to audit the actions that are carried out on your resources (such as files, folders, printers and drives), then you must activate the **Audit object access** policy, and set up the audit on the resource concerned. You can do this as follows:

→) Edit the properties of the resource.

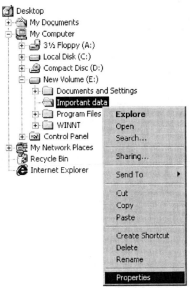

⊕ You can audit only files and folders that are located on NTFS partitions or volumes.

→) Select the **Security** tab, and click the **Advanced** button.

→) Select the **Auditing** tab, and click the **Add** button.

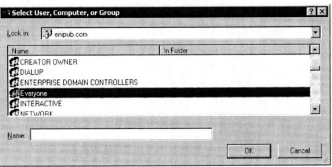

→) Add the users that you want to audit and then click the **OK** button.

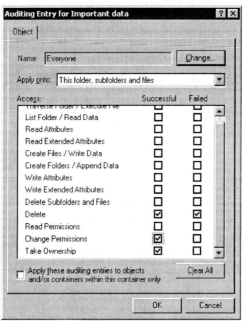

→) Enable the actions that must be audited when they have been **successful**, and/or when they have **failed**, and then click **OK**.

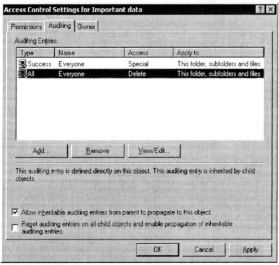

→) Click **OK** to finish the operation.

⚬) Important note: If you select only **Failure** for the **Audit object access** policy, then you will not be able to audit the events that are successful, even if you define them as such at resource level.

⚬) You can audit a printer for invoicing purposes, for example. You can audit the following actions for a printer: Print, Manage Printers, Manage Documents, Read Permissions, Change Permissions and Take Ownership.

Viewing the audited events

You can consult the audited events using the **Security** log of the **Event Viewer**.

The 🔒 icon represents failure, and the 🔑 icon represents success.

→) Open the **Event Viewer** console that is situated in the **Administrative Tools** menu.

→) Click the **Security Log**. The list appears of all the actions that have been audited.

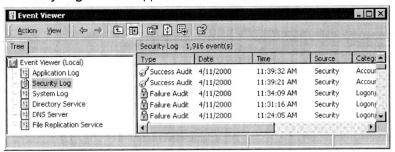

→) Double-click the event for which you want to view the details.

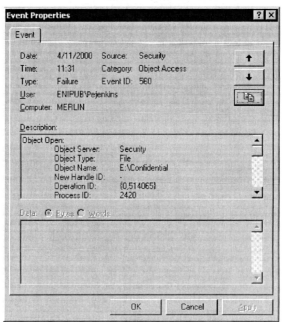

This dialog box shows information on the action concerned, and provides the name of the user who carried it out. If you click the button, then you will take a copy of the description, which you can then insert into a text file.

```
Event Type:      Failure Audit
Event Source:    Security
Event Category:  Object Access
Event ID:        560
Date:            4/11/2000
Time:            11:31:16 AM
User:            ENIPUB\Pejenkins
Computer:        MERLIN
Description:
Object Open:
        Object Server:   Security
        Object Type:     File
        Object Name:     E:\Confidential
        New Handle ID:   -
        Operation ID:    (0,641816)
        Process ID:      1124
        Primary User Name:     Pejenkins
        Primary Domain: ENIPUB
        Primary Logon ID:      (0x0,0x108BF)
        Client User Name:      -
        Client Domain:   -
        Client Logon ID:       -
        Accesses         DELETE
                         READ_CONTROL
                         SYNCHRONIZE
                         ReadAttributes
```

In this description, note that the user Pejenkins of the ENIPUB domain, tried unsuccessfully to delete the folder **e:\Confidential** on 04/11/2000 at 11:31 on the computer that is called Merlin.

You define audit policies in order to monitor your network so as to counter any intrusions or incorrect usage. Consequently, it is important that you cover all the relevant events. Group policies allow you to set up the **Event Viewer** in order to:

- Stop the computer when the security log is full. This technique allows you to ensure that you will not miss any event audit.
- Set a maximum size for the security log, the system log and the application log.
- Set a time period, during which data will be stored in the different logs.
- Define how you want to store the different logs (by overwriting events that are older than a certain number of days, by overwriting events when necessary, or by not overwriting events at all).

You can define these settings in the **Event Log**, of the group policies, under **Security Settings**.

G. Troubleshooting accounts and policies

1. Troubleshooting audits

If you have problems setting up your audits, then the following points may be of assistance:

- To ensure that Windows 2000 will apply to the auditing of file and folder access, you must enable the **Audit object access** option in the audit policy, using the **Group Policy** snap-in. If you do not enable this policy, then Window 2000 will display an error message when you define the file and folder audit, to notify you that no files or folders will be audited.
- In order to audit files and folders, either you must log on as a member of the **Administrators** group, or you must have been granted the **Manage auditing and security log** users right, in the **Group Policy**.
- By default, Windows 2000 does not enable any event category. You can enable the categories that you require using the **Local Computer Policy**. To do this, go into the **MMC** and add the **Group Policy** snap-in. The console then displays the **Local Computer Policy** folder under the **Console Root**. Expand this folder as follows: **Computer Configuration - Windows Settings - Security Settings - Local Policies**. Then, select **Audit Policy** and enable the required policies.
- You can define file and folder audits only on NTFS partitions.
- When you set up the audit, if the check boxes in the **Access** frame of the **Auditing Entry** dialog box are grayed out, or if the **Remove** button is unavailable on the **Auditing** page of the **Access Control Settings** dialog box, then the audit settings will be inherited from the parent folder.
- The audit log has a limited size (this is the **Security** log of the **Event Viewer**). Consequently, you must ensure that you audit only those files and folders that you really need to audit.
- Check that you have enough disk space for the audit log.

2. Troubleshooting user rights

User rights problems often concern the specific user rights policies that are listed below. If you have access problems then you should check that the corresponding user right has been assigned.

User rights policies

The predefined user rights allow users to carry out actions such as, accessing a computer via the network, opening an interactive session, or running a script as a batch job.

Access this computer from the network

This right allows users to access a computer via the network. By default, Windows 2000 assigns this right to the following groups of users: Administrators, **Everyone**, and **Power Users**.

Log on as a batch job

This right allows users to open a session using a batch-queue. By default, Windows 2000 assigns this right to the **Administrators** users group.

Log on as a service

This right allows security principals (users or computers) to open a session as a means of setting up a security context. The **LocalSystem** account always has the right to log on as a service. This right must be assigned to any service that runs under a separate account. By default, Windows 2000 assigns this right to the **Administrators** users group.

Log on locally

This right allows users to open an interactive session on a computer. By default, Windows 2000 assigns this right to all users of a Windows 2000 Professional workstation, and to the following user groups on a Windows 2000 Server domain controller: Administrators, Account Operators, Backup, Operators, Print Operators, and Server Operators.

If you do not have this right then Windows 2000 will display the following message: **The local policy of this system does not permit you to logon interactively**.

3. Troubleshooting account configurations

When you log on, check that the required servers are available, especially if you meet any of the following problems:
- Roaming profile is not available.
- Remote server is not available to connect you to your home directory.
- No domain controller was found.
- The DNS service has not started.
- The machine onto which the user attempts to log is not a DNS client (or is no longer a DNS client).

In addition, check that you entered your username and password correctly:
- Check your username.
- Check that the ⌨️Caps Lock key was not activated (as passwords are case sensitive).
- Check that the system recognizes your keyboard correctly when you enter your password (for example, you could try entering a letter sequence, such as "QWERTY" in the **User Name** field, and check that your entry is correctly displayed).
- Check that you entered the correct computer name, or the correct domain name.

4. Troubleshooting account policies

Certain account restrictions can prevent you from logging on. In particular, you should check the following settings:
- Any specific logon hours.
- Any specific logon machines.
- Account lockout.

5. Troubleshooting a security configuration

If you are unable to log on, or to change your password, then you should check the following points:
- Any account expiry date (if this feature is selected, then your account will expire after 42 days, by default).
- Minimum password length.
- Minimum and maximum password age.
- Password history.
- Password complexity requirements.

Chapter 7: Managing disk resources

A. Managing disks, volumes and partitions

1. File systems

a. FAT16

This file system is present on a large number of operating systems, including the following:
- OSA/2
- MS-DOS
- Windows 3.x
- Windows 95/98
- Windows NT
- Windows 2000

The FAT system was designed for low-volume partitions (for partitions of up to 500 MB). For partitions of this size, FAT uses only a very small amount of disk space for its internal management.

The FAT structure is very simple. One reason for this simplicity is that the FAT does not manage an Access Control List (ACL) for each file and folder. FAT addressing is coded on 16 bits. This means that a FAT partition can be divided into 216 clusters.

b. FAT32

FAT32 is a development of FAT16 file systems. Whereas FAT16 does not support partitions of over 2 GB, FAT32 allows you to go beyond this limit. This file system is used with OSR2 versions of Windows 95, and also with the Windows 98 operating system. Windows NT 4.0 does not recognize FAT32. However, Windows 2000 does support this file system.

c. NTFS 5.0

NTFS *(NT File System)* allows you to manage security locally using ACLs. NTFS also supports individual compression, disk quota management, and file encryption by public key/private key.

NTFS offers a transactional mode at file system level. This mode allows NTFS to ensure that the internal structures will be coherent, in most cases. This is possible because all actions that are carried out on the file system are logged. In addition, NTFS supports 64-bit addressing. This feature allows NTFS to divide its partitions into elementary allocation units, which are known as clusters. Not only does this technique allow NTFS to manage larger partitions, but it also allows this file system to waste less disk space when it manages small files.

With NTFS, search operations are much quicker thanks to the use of a B-tree structure. This structure, which is complicated to set up, allows you to write algorithms that have Log N complexity, whereas classical algorithms offer a complexity that is a function of N/2.

In other words, if you want to look for an item amongst N items (for example, N=100), then with classical algorithms you will need to search for a length of time that is proportional to N/2 (for example 100/2 = 50). On the other hand, with B-tree structures you will need to search for a length of time that is proportional to Log N (for example Log 100, which equals 2). Suppose that your reference time is one second. Then, with classical N/2 algorithms your search will take 50 seconds, whereas with B-trees your search will take only 2 seconds.

The higher the value of N, the greater this difference will be.

When a file is fragmented, then fewer disk accesses will be necessary in order to re-assemble it with NTFS than would be necessary with FAT.

NTFS uses a particular table called the *Master File Table*. This table allows you to accommodate small files, and to access them very quickly.

You can extend an NTFS volume, or an NTFS disk stripe. This technique allows you to increase the size of a data volume, without losing information.

Finally, with NTFS, there is no specific limitation on the number of directories that you can create.

d. Choosing the most suitable file system (FAT or NTFS)

For partitions that are smaller than 500 MB, the FAT file system is the most suitable.

NTFS is particularly suitable for high-volume disks. You must use NTFS when you want to:
- implement data security (for files or for folders),
- compress individual items,
- have a stable file system,
- manage data encryption,
- apply disk quotas,
- make your server a domain controller (in order to store Active Directory).

e. Converting a partition to NTFS

You can convert a partition from FAT16 or FAT32 format to NTFS format without losing data.

To do this you can use the **convert** command from a command prompt.

On the other hand, if you wish to convert from NTFS to a FAT format, then you must back up your data and format the partition for the desired file system. You can then restore your data.

Enter **convert /?** to obtain online help for this command.

Here is the syntax of the **convert** command:

```
Convert volume /FS:NTFS [/V]
```

in which:

volume   specifies the drive letter (a colon must follow the drive letter), or the mount point, or the volume name.

/FS:NTFS   specifies that the system must convert the volume to NTFS.

/V   specifies that convert must run in verbose mode.

2. Configuring disks

The disk management of Windows 2000 has evolved with respect to earlier Windows versions. Although there is nothing new about the contents of primary partitions, extended partitions and other logical drives, you can now optimize your disks by creating volumes.

a. Basic disks

With Windows 2000, a basic disk is a disk structure on which you can create primary partitions and extended partitions.

There is a limit to the number of partitions that a basic disk can support. On a basic disk, you cannot have more than:

– 4 primary partitions,
– or, 3 primary partitions and 1 extended partition. In this extended partition you can create one or more logical drives.

On Windows 2000, you can manage your disks using the **Disk Management** snap-in that is situated under the **Storage** node of the **Computer Management** console tree.

Alternatively, you can create your own console and add the **Disk Management** snap-in into it.

You can manage the disks of any computer by selecting the **Connect to another computer** option, or by creating a console that points to the computers that you want to manage, provided that you are a member of the **administrators** group, or of the **server operators** group.

In order to do this, open an MMC and add the **Disk Management** snap-in.

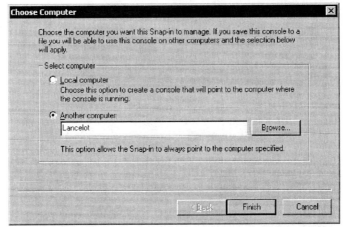

Enter the name of the computer for which you want to manage the disks, and then repeat the operation for any other machines for which you want to manage the disks.

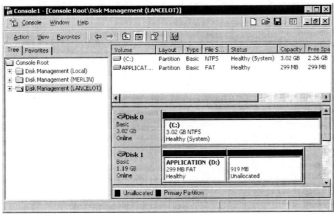

You can now use this console in order to carry out operations on your physical disks such as creating and deleting partitions.

Creating a primary partition

In order to create a primary partition, right-click an unallocated disk space:

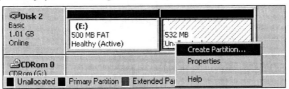

Then, select **Create Partition** so as to start up the **Create Partition Wizard**.

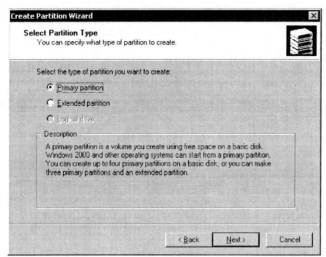

Select **Primary partition**. Note that the **Logical drive** option is grayed out. This is because you can create a logical drive only within an extended partition.

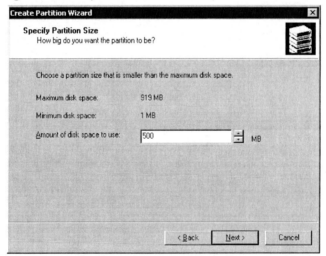

Enter the size that you want for the primary partition. If you decide to create a partition that will occupy all the available disk space, then you should leave at least 1 MB of free space, as you will need this should you want to convert your basic disk into a dynamic disk. This is because the conversion processes will need this space in order to store their working information.

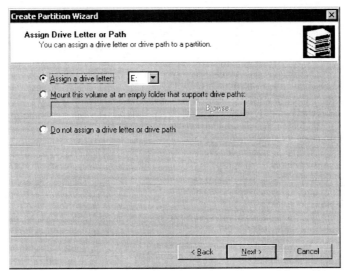

Windows 2000 suggests a drive letter by default for this partition. If you wish, you can choose another letter that is not being used by the other drives. You can change this drive letter after the partition has been created.

You can choose to mount your partition in an empty folder in an NTFS partition. Alternatively, you can choose not to assign either a drive letter or a drive path. In this case Windows Explorer will not be able to access this partition (you can always assign a drive letter later).

The next step consists of formatting the partition.

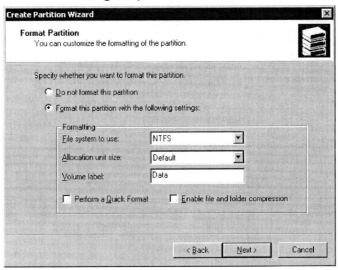

You can choose to use either the FAT, FAT32 or NTFS file systems. In addition, you can customize the size of the allocation unit (cluster). If you choose to format your partition in FAT with a cluster size of over 32 KB, then your partition will not be compatible with previous operating system versions. Be careful of this point then, if you have a multiple boot facility. However, pre-Windows 2000 operating systems would still be able to access the resources that are located on this partition via a network share.

Note that you can choose to enable file and folder compression if you format your partition in NTFS.

When you have finished indicating your settings, the system will format your partition. When your partition is ready to be used it will be marked as being **Healthy**.

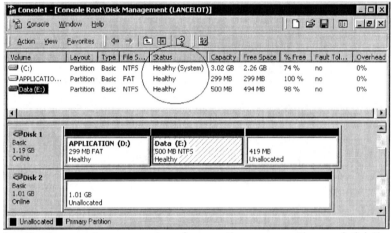

In addition to allowing you to carry out such operations as creating and deleting partitions, this **Disk Management** program provides information concerning disk type (basic or dynamic), file systems, capacities, free space, percentage of free space, and whether or not your partitions belong to a fault-tolerant set.

Creating an extended partition

If you have already three primary partitions on your disk, then your extended partition must occupy the rest of the available space (leaving 1 or 2 MB in order to allow for possible conversion to a dynamic disk). Otherwise, you will lose any remaining space because you cannot create more than four partitions on your disk.

In order to create an extended partition you must carry out the following steps:

→) Right-click an unallocated space and then select **Create Partition**.

→) Select **Extended partition** and then click **Next**.

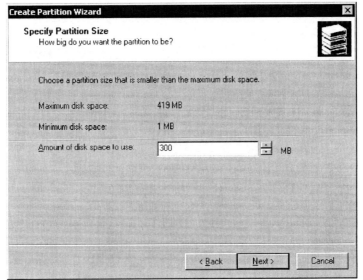

→) Enter the size that you require for your extended partition and click **Next**.

The extended partition is then created and appears in the Disk Management console in green (when standard colors are used).

This extended partition is no longer considered as being **Unallocated**, but it is considered as **Free Space** (free for the creation of a logical drive).

Creating logical drives

After you have created an extended partition, you must create one or more logical drives. You can create as many logical drives as you have drive letters available.

In order to create a logical drive, right-click the extended partition and then select **Create Logical Drive** so as to start the **Create Partition Wizard**.

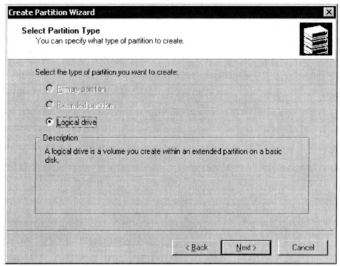

The **Logical drive** option is then selected automatically.

→ Choose the size that must be allocated to this logical drive. If you wish to create several logical drives within this extended partition, then do not take up all the available space in order to create the first one!

→ The following step involves, either choosing the letter that you want to assign to this drive, or deciding not to assign a letter, or mounting the drive at an empty folder in an NTFS partition.

→ Then, define the type of formatting (FAT, FAT32 or NTFS, and the cluster size) and click **Finish**.

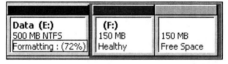

The system then formats the logical drive. If you have not used all the free space for the creation of this logical drive, then you can use the rest of the free space in order to create other logical drives. Once the drive has been formatted it is marked as **Healthy**.

You can change the letters that are attributed to your partitions or to your logical drives at any time. In order to do this, right-click the partition or the drive for which you want to change the drive letter and select **Change Drive Letter and Path**.

Removable storage devices contain only primary partitions. You can create neither extended partitions nor volumes on this type of storage device. In addition, you cannot mark a partition that is on a removable storage device as active.

You can alter the colors and the schemes that are used to represent the different partitions using the **View - Settings** menu option.

b. Dynamic disks

A dynamic disk does not have partitions. It has volumes. A volume is a part of a disk that runs like a separate physical disk. The information concerning the disk is not written in the registry, but on the disk itself.

Here are the advantages of dynamic disks:
- You can use fault tolerance (without having to restart the computer),
- You can create as many volumes as you like,
- You can extend NTFS volumes.

You can still use the partitions on basic disks, which ensures compatibility with existing configurations. However, volumes cannot be read by pre-Windows 2000 systems.

Upgrading to a dynamic disk

You can upgrade from a basic disk to a dynamic disk without losing data. However, once you have upgraded to dynamic disks, if you wish to return to basic disks, then you will have to delete all the disk volumes (therefore, you must remember to back up your data first).

On a dynamic disk, you can have the following volume types:
- Simple volumes
- Striped volumes
- Spanned volumes
- Mirrored volumes (Windows 2000 Server only)
- RAID 5 volumes (Windows 2000 Server only)

If there are partitions on your basic disks when you upgrade them to dynamic disks, then they will become volumes as follows:
- A primary partition will become a simple volume.
- Each logical drive of an extended partition will become a simple volume.
- The free space of an extended partition will become unallocated space (you can then create volumes using this space).
- A partition mirror will become a mirrored volume.
- Stripe sets with parity will become RAID 5 volumes.
- Stripe sets will become striped volumes.
- Partition stripes will become spanned volumes.

In order to upgrade from a basic disk to a dynamic disk, go into the **Disk Management** program and right-click the disk that you want to upgrade:

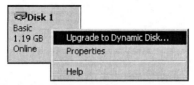

→) Then, select **Upgrade to Dynamic Disk**.

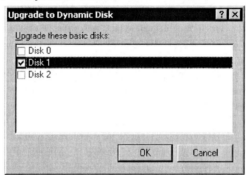

→) Select the disk(s) that you wish to upgrade, and then click **OK**.

→) If you click the **Details** button in the dialog box that appears, a further dialog box appears indicating all the partitions of the disk that must be upgraded.

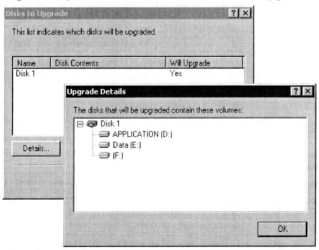

→) Click **OK** so as to return to the previous dialog box, and then click the **Upgrade** button in order to start the upgrade process.

When the upgrade operation has finished, the modifications are updated in the **Disk Mana-gement** console.

Simple volumes

A simple volume corresponds to the space of a single disk. Unlike partitions, volumes are limited neither to a maximum size nor to a maximum number.

On a dynamic disk, simple volumes can be formatted in NTFS, FAT 16 or FAT 32.

A simple volume that is formatted in NTFS can be extended in order to create a volume that will cover the initial space of the volume, plus one or more unallocated disk spaces that can either be contiguous or not.

To create a simple volume, right-click a part of a dynamic disk that is not allocated.

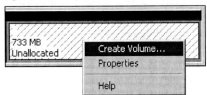

→) Select **Create Volume** to start up the **Create Volume Wizard**.

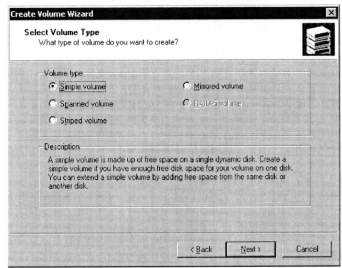

→) Select **Simple volume** then click **Next**.

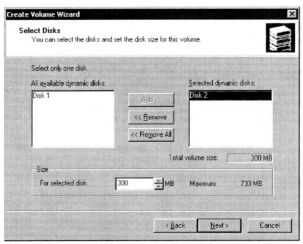

To create a simple volume, you must select only one disk and set the size for this volume.

→) The next step consists of assigning a drive letter (or not assigning a drive letter), or mounting the volume at a folder.

→) Then, select the file system that must be used for this volume.

Extending a simple volume

If your volume is formatted in NTFS, then you can extend it by combining the disk space that is occupied by the volume with one or more unallocated spaces.
The new size of the volume will then be the initial size of the volume, plus the sum of all the spaces that have been added.

To extend your volume, right-click it and then select **Extend Volume**.

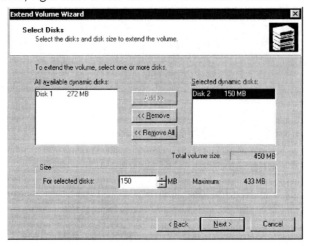

As you can extend your volume over unallocated portions of dynamic disks, you must select the disk(s) on which you want to extend your volume. When you have selected a disk, click the **Add** button to add the disk concerned under **Selected dynamic disks**. Then, set the extra size that you want to add to your initial volume. If you are extending your volume using unallocated spaces from several disks, then you can define a different size that must be added from each space.

If you extend your volume over unallocated spaces on another disk, then your volume will become a spanned volume.

You cannot extend a volume that is the result of an upgrade from a partition. The volume must have been created on a dynamic disk. This means that you cannot extend system volumes or boot volumes.

Spanned volumes

A spanned volume is composed of unallocated spaces that have been grouped together from a minimum of 2 disks, and a maximum of 32 disks. Data is written first to free space on one disk and, when this disk is full, data is written to free space on the next disk.

In order to create a spanned volume, right-click an unallocated space and then select **Create Volume**.

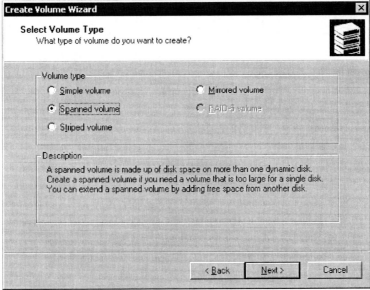

→ Select **Spanned volume** and then click **Next**.

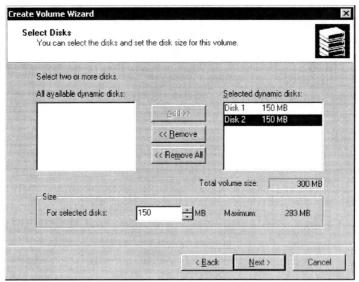

You must select at least two dynamic disks to create a spanned volume. Indicate the size that you want to use for each disk, and then click **Next**.

Assign a drive letter or a mount point. Finally, you must specify the file system that must be used for this spanned volume to finish the operation.

As with simple volumes, you can extend a spanned volume.

You cannot re-use a space that is situated on a disk that is included in a spanned volume, without deleting all the volume. Before you carry out this operation then, you must back up the volume, as all the data will be lost.

Striped volumes

A striped volume groups together, into one logical volume, unallocated space from at least 2 disks and at most 32 disks. The data is written to stripes of 64 KB. This means that 64 KB will be written to the first disk, the next 64 KB will be written to the second disk, and so forth. This type of volume optimizes read and write access.

However, it must be noted that this type of volume does not provide fault tolerance. If a disk fails, then all the data that is written to all the member disks of the striped volume will be lost.

As all the data is written in stripe sets, each of the stripe members must have the same amount of disk space. For example, if you want to create a striped volume on three disks, for which the first disk has 300 MB of free space, the second disk has 350 MB of free space, and the third disk has 280 MB of free space, then your striped volume will be created according to the smallest amount of disk space. In this example, the size of the striped volume will be 840 MB (3 x 280 MB).

In order to create a striped volume, right-click an unallocated space and then select **Create Volume**:

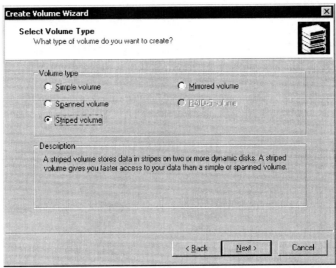

→) Select **Striped volume**, and then click **Next**. If this option is grayed out, then you do not have unallocated spaces on at least two different dynamic disks.

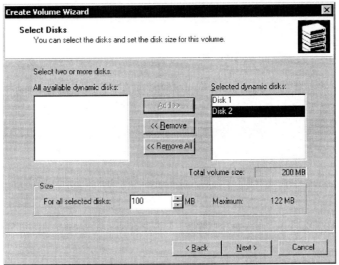

Add the disks on which you want to create the striped volume.
Then select either a drive letter for your striped volume, or a mount point.
Finally, choose the format for your volume (FAT16, FAT32 or NTFS).

You can neither extend nor mirror a striped volume.

c. Mounting volumes

In order to go beyond the limit that is imposed by drive letters (due to there being only 26 alphabetical letters), you can mount volumes in empty directories that are in local NTFS partitions or volumes. Although these volumes are mounted in NTFS partitions or volumes, they can themselves be formatted in NTFS, in FAT or in FAT32.

You can mount your partitions or your volumes when you create them. Alternatively, you can mount them at any time after you have created them.

→) Right-click the volume or the partition that you want to mount.

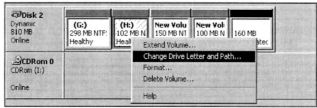

→) Click **Change Drive Letter and Path**.

→) Click the **Add** button to display the dialog box that will allow you to select the directory in which you want to mount this volume.

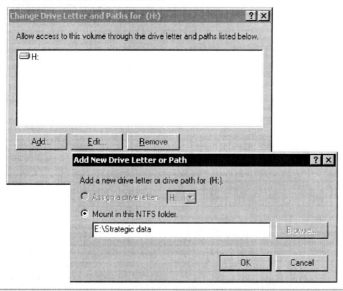

🜚 Remember to delete the drive letter that you associated with the volume or the partition when you created it.

Windows 2000 Professional

d. Adding disks

If the computer on which you want to add a disk does not support hot plugging (the feature that allows you to add and remove disks without stopping the machine), then you must stop your computer, add your disk(s), and then restart your computer. Windows 2000 then recognizes the new disk(s) and adds them to the **Disk Management** console.

On the other hand, if your hardware supports hot plugging, just add or remove your disk(s), then select **Action - Rescan Disks**:

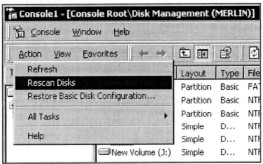

The new disk(s) then appear in the console without you having to restart your computer.

> ➲ If however, your disks do not appear, then restart your computer!

If you add a disk that comes from another computer, it should be recognized automatically. If it is not recognized for any reason, then it will be marked as **Foreign**. In this case, you must right-click this disk and then select **Import Foreign Disks**.

If you import a disk from another computer and the Disk Management displays a **Failed: incomplete volume** message, then the disk was taken from a spanned volume, or from a stripe set.

e. Monitoring and optimizing disks

Disk Defragmenter

When you use a disk heavily, it can become fragmented (this occur when files and folders are saved on non-contiguous disk spaces). This does not prevent you from accessing these files and folders, but your computer will perform better if your files and folders are stored in contiguous disk spaces.

Windows 2000 provides a utility that allows you to defragment volumes, whether they are formatted in FAT, FAT32 or NTFS.

To start up this utility, go into **Windows Explorer**, activate the properties of the volume that you want to defragment, and select the **Tools** tab.

Then click the **Defragment Now** button.

Alternatively, you can use the **Computer Management** console:

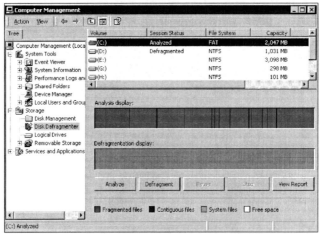

→) Click the **Analyze** button to find out whether or not you need to defragment your disk. In addition, this option tells you which of your files are fragmented.

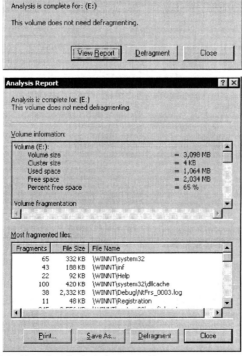

→) Click the **Defragment** button to start defragmenting.

Checking a disk

Under the **Tools** tab of the volume properties dialog box, you can error-check your volume by clicking the **Check Now** button.

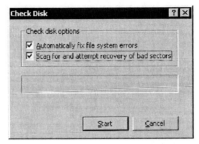

Cleaning up a disk

The volume properties dialog box also allows you to clean up your volume, by clicking the **Disk Cleanup** tab.

The **Disk Cleanup** program examines the volume in order to determine how much space it will be able to free up:

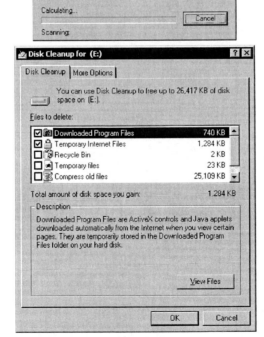

Select the actions that you want to carry out, and then click **OK**.

B. Managing disk resources

1. Sharing folders

a. Overview

The main purpose of a network is to allow you to access files that are situated on another workstation or server. By default, operating systems such as Windows for Workgroups, and the different versions of Windows 95, do not share directories (folders) or files that are on the hard disk, for security reasons. The administrator must set up the sharing of the resource in order to allow users to access it via the network. According to the users who must access it, this resource is shared with different rights (for example, write, read, or delete).

Resource level security

On Windows for Workgroups operating systems, access security is ensured by passwords. A password is allocated per resource and per type of access, independently of the users. For example, no password is necessary for read-only access, where as a password is necessary in order to allow full access (read and write).

User level security

With Windows 98, you can operate with user level security, or with resource level security.

With Windows NT and Windows 2000, only user level security can be used. In this mode, initial authentication is compulsory. Each user is designated as being authorized a particular type of access to a resource. For any given resource, you can designate several users, and/or groups of users, and you can define a specific type of access for each of them.

It must be noted that, with Windows for Workgroups and Windows 98, you can share resources only if you have explicitly enabled this feature by activating the options **I want to be able to give others access to my files** and **I want to be able to allow others to print to my printers**.

When you have activated these options, and after you have restarted your machine, the server service that allows you to share these resources is loaded into memory.

❂ With FAT, sharing folders is the only means of ensuring the security of network access to resources.

b. Predefined administrative shares

On Windows 2000, the files are not shared. Only the folder that contains the files can be shared.

By default, certain resources are shared on Windows 2000. These are administrative shares that are reserved for the configuration management of remote workstations. These files are hidden, and only the administrator can access them.

Shared Folder	Shared Path	Type
ADMIN$	E:\WINNT	Windows
C$	C:\	Windows
D$	D:\	Windows
E$	E:\	Windows
IPC$		Windows
print$	E:\WINNT\System32\spool\drivers	Windows

C$, D$, E$, device_letter$ This share provides the administrator with full access to drives. The administrator can connect to a remote machine by entering **computer_name\c$**.

Admin$ This share is used in order to manage a workstation via the network. This refers to the **%systemroot%** directory.

IPC$ This share allows processes to communicate with each other. It is used to administer a workstation remotely or to consult a shared directory.

Print$ This share is used in order to administer printers remotely.

Notice that the names of administrative shares finish with a **$** sign, which causes them to be hidden. You can add this symbol at the end of a share name so as to hide the share concerned.

c. Sharing a folder

To share a folder, right-click the folder that you want to share, and then select the **Sharing** option.

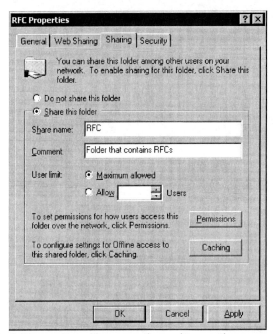

Enable the **Share this folder** option. You can then change the name of your share, if you wish. This is the name that will be seen via the network. By default, the share name is the same as that of the folder, but this is not obligatory. You can also add a comment that describes the folder's contents.

On Windows 2000, a shared folder is reserved for certain users. In order to access a shared folder on a domain controller, you must be either a member of the administrators group, or a member of the server operators group. On a Windows 2000 member server, or a Windows 2000 Professional workstation, you must be a member, either of the administrators group, or of the power users group.

You can choose to restrict the number of simultaneous connections on this share.

If you have MS-DOS or Windows for Workgroups clients, then you must use short names (in the 8.3 character format).

In order to modify network access permissions, click the **Permissions** button.

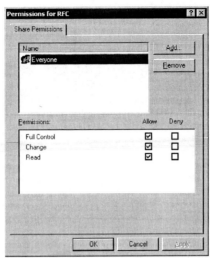

This dialog box displays the share permissions that are currently applied to the folder. Note that the system grants **Full Control** permission to the **Everyone** group, by default.

Under **Permissions**, the list of permissions that apply to the shared folder is displayed. These permissions are as follows:

- **Read**: The user who has this permission is allowed to read the files, to run the programs, and to browse the subfolders.
- **Change**: The user who has this permission has the **Read** permission, plus the right to modify and to delete folders and files.
- **Full Control**: The user who has this permission has the **Change** permission plus the right to change share permissions.

In order to apply these permissions to the users, you can use two columns of check boxes:

To grant a permission, click the corresponding check box in the **Allow** column. To deny a permission, click the corresponding check box in the **Deny** column.

If a user is a member of several groups to which different permissions have been granted, then the users permissions will be the combination of the permissions that have been granted to the different groups. However, this rule does not apply in the case of a permission for which the **Deny** check box has been enabled. The **Deny** check box always takes priority over the **Allow** check box (you must be careful of this consequence of using the **Deny** check box).

To add a group or a user, click the **Add** button. To delete a user or a group, select the account concerned and then click the **Remove** button.

Windows 2000 Professional

You can create several share names for the same folder. To do this, you can click the **New Share** button (to make this button appear, you may need to click **OK** to close the dialog box, and then re-open it and reselect the **Sharing** tab).

Alternatively, you can use the Computer Management console to share a folder.

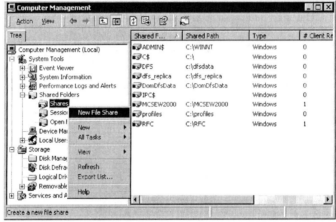

Right-click the **Shares** folder and then select **New File Share**.

Windows 2000 Professional

Fill in the different fields and then click **Next**.

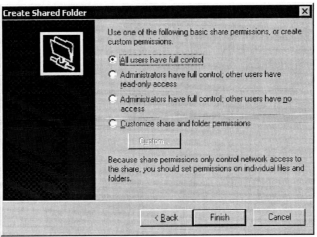

You can then specify the share permissions that must be applied to this folder.

d. Ceasing to share a folder

When you stop sharing a folder, you prevent access to this folder via the network, and you withdraw all its share permissions.

➨) Right-click the name of the shared folder concerned, and select the **Sharing** option.

➨) If there are several shares, then select the share(s) that you wish to remove.

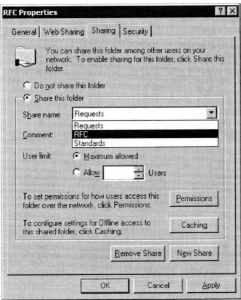

→) Click the **Remove Share** button, then click **OK**.

→) If you have only one share name for the folder, or if you want to stop sharing the folder, whatever the share name, then click the **Do not share this folder** option.

Alternatively, you can remove a share using the **Computer Management** console:

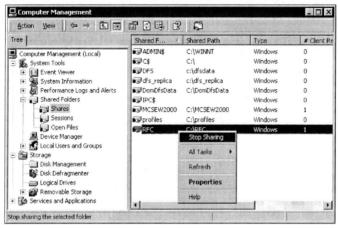

e. Connecting to a shared resource

Once a folder is shared, it is accessible via the network.

→) Double-click the **My Network Places** icon, followed by the **Entire Network** icon. Then select the machine on which the shared resource is located (select the domain or the workgroup, followed by the machine concerned).

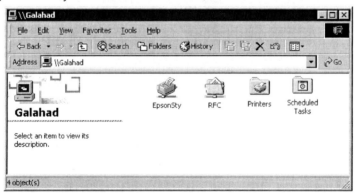

→) Double-click the icon that represents the computer concerned. You will be able to access a shared resource if you have the necessary permissions.

In order to connect a drive letter to a shared resource, right-click the **My Network Places** icon, or, go into **Windows Explorer** and open the **Tools** menu, then select the **Map Network Drive** option.

The following dialog box appears:

→) Choose the drive letter that you want to use as a reference to the shared resource on the target computer.

→) Enter the path that leads to the resource concerned. This must be a UNC path (**server****share**).

→) Enable the **Reconnect at logon** check box if you want to continue using this drive letter the next time that you log on.

→) You can connect to the resource using the permissions of another user account. In order to do this, click **different user name**, and then, in the dialog box that appears, enter the user name and the password for the account that you want to use for this connection.

→) The **Web folder or FTP site** link allows you to add the connection to this shared folder into **My Network Places**.

You can now access the shared directory by double-clicking the **My Network Places** icon. You can also add network places using the **Add Network Place** icon. Network places are not necessarily paths that lead to shared directories: you can also add URLs that point to Web sites or to FTP sites.

f. Checking shares

Checking shares allows a user or the administrator to display the list of network users who are accessing the shared resources, and to control the access to these resources.

→) Open the **Computer Management** console.

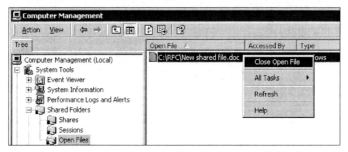

– The **Open Files** folder allows you to view the list of all the files from shared folders that are open on the server. It also allows you to close these shared resources. If you close a file that was open in read/write mode, then any modifications that had been made will be lost. However, as the user still has the right to access the resource, the disconnection is temporary since he or she can re-access it immediately.

⊙ This passive disconnection technique allows the system to ensure fault tolerance even when the network temporarily fails.

- The **Sessions** folder allows you to view all the sessions that are open on the computer. It lists all the people who are logged onto the computer via the network. All the connections that a user has made are represented by a single session, no matter how many times the user has logged onto the machine. This feature is particularly useful when you want to shut down a computer, as it allows you to warn all the users who are currently logged onto it.

- The **Shares** folder allows you to share, or to stop sharing a resource (as discussed earlier in this chapter).

This console allows you to connect to remote computers in order to administer them. For example, you can create new shares remotely, or stop sharing remote resources.

Sending administrative messages

If you want to stop a service in order to carry out maintenance work, then you must warn the users who are connected so that they will be able to save their data.

You can send a message to all the users who are connected to your server.

→) Open the **Computer Management** console, and right-click **Shared Folders**.

→) Select **All Tasks**, followed by **Send Console Message**.

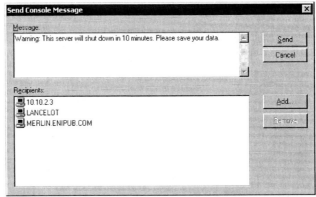

Your message will be sent to all the machines that are listed under **Recipients**.

g. Advice for sharing folders

In order to ease the access to resources via the network, you must take into account the following points:

- Choose share names carefully and provide comments on the shares. On the client machines, specify that explorers and browsers should use **Detail** view so that your comments are visible.

- Remember that if the share name exceeds 8.3 characters, then the users of machines that run MS-DOS, Windows 3.x or Windows for Workgroups will not see the shares and will not be able to access them.

h. Optimizing file and folder access

Sharing folders for network applications

According to the size of the company network, at least one server will be needed to store the applications that are used.

→) Wherever possible, create a shared folder (called APPS, for example) that contains one subdirectory per application.

→) For each application, create a group with a name that represents the application in question (for example, WORD or EXCEL). These groups will simplify the management of the users who have access to the specific applications concerned.

→) Attribute the following permissions:

Read   for the users group that must use the application,

Change   for the users group that must update and troubleshoot the application,

Full Control for the administrators.

Sharing data folders

Data folders allow users to exchange information via a centralized folder that is reserved for this purpose.

Data folders can be divided into two categories:

Public data folders

These folders allow users from different groups to exchange information.

→) You could apply **Change** permission to the **Domain Users**, for example,

→) Create a tree structure so that you can back up the data very easily.

Working data folders

These folders allow specific user groups to share a private data space.

→) Create a basic directory, which you can call DATA, for example.

→) You could apply **Change** permission to specific groups on specific DATA subfolders. For example, the ACCOUNTANTS subfolder could be created for the **Accountants** group.

Sharing home directories

The home directories of all the users can be grouped together into one folder.

→) Create a folder that is called USERS and share this folder using the same share name.

→) Create a subfolder for each user and give it the name of the user in question.

→) If you are working in NTFS, create a **USERS** share with **Full Control** permission for **Everyone**. On each of the user's subfolders, grant **Full Control** permission for the user alone.

◉ When you create the user, if you specify %username% to create the user's home directory on an NTFS volume, (specifying the path **\servername\users\%username%** for example) then the appropriate permissions will be applied automatically.

➜) If you are working in FAT, then you must share each user's home directory with **Full Control** permissions for the user alone.

2. Access security

The permissions that this chapter has described so far, are applied to enable users to access resources via the computing network. They do not provide protection when users access a computer locally.

This chapter will now cover the security features that allow users to protect their own data from unauthorized access, both locally and via the network. These security features also allow you to protect the operating system from accidental deletion by uninformed users, or by users who are insensitive to system warnings when the system is about to delete files. In order to use these Windows 2000 features, you must be using the NTFS file system. Only NTFS allows you to implement security and to audit attributes on folders and files.

NTFS allows you to keep each file and folder up to date with an Access Control List, or ACL. This ACL maintains at file system level, the user numbers (SID) and the user permissions on the resource.

a. NTFS Permissions

NTFS distinguishes between folder permissions and file permissions.

Conditions for attributing NTFS permissions

To apply NTFS permissions for a file or for a folder, you must either be the owner of the item concerned or you must be the administrator or you must have the necessary permissions. The permissions that are required are **Full Control**, **Change Permissions** or **Take Ownership** (which allows you to become the owner of the object).

Permissions for a folder

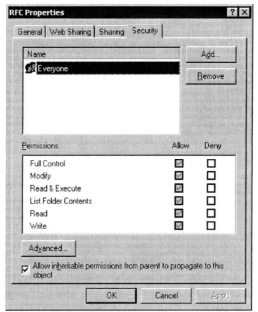

In order to apply NTFS permissions for a folder, right-click the folder concerned, select **Properties**, and then select the **Security** tab.

The following permissions appear:

- **Write**: users who have this permission can create files and folders, and they can also modify the attributes of these items (for example: **Read-only**, and **Hidden**).

A user who has this permission must also have read permission so as to be able to access the folder.

- **Read**: users who have this permission can read the contents of the folder and also the contents of the files that are in the folder. This permission also allows users to read the attributes.
- **List Folder Contents**: this permission covers **Read** permission, plus the right to browse the folder's contents
- **Read & Execute**: this permission covers Read permission, plus **List Folder Contents** permission, plus the right to navigate across folders so as to reach other folders and files.
- **Modify**: this permission covers **Read & Execute** permission, and it also allows you to delete the folder.
- **Full Control**: this permission allows you to change permissions for the folder, to take ownership of the folder, to delete the folder, and it covers all the other NTFS permissions as well.

If permissions are not applied explicitly to a user's account, or to one of the groups to which the user belongs, then the user will not be able to access the resource.

In reality, each of these permissions is an association of NTFS attributes. In order to find out the list of attributes, apply a single permission to a user, and click the **Advanced** button. Then, select the **Permission Entry** for the user that has this permission and click the **View/Edit** button.

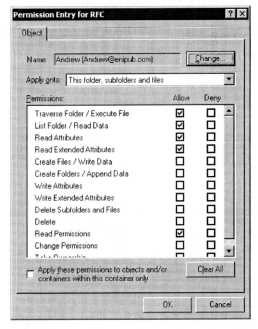

Permissions for a file

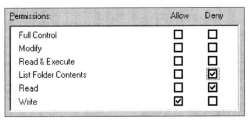

- **Write**: allows you to write in the file, to change its attributes, and to display the permissions and the owner of the file.
- **Read**: allows you to read the file contents, its attributes, the permissions that are associated with the file, and the name of its owner.
- **Read & Execute**: This permission provides **Read** permission, and it also allows you to run programs.

- **Modify**: This permission provides **Read & Execute** permission, and it also allows you to delete the files.
- **Full Control**: This permission covers **Modify** permission, and it also allows you to take ownership of the file and to change its permissions.

Advanced permissions

If the standard permissions do not fully meet your needs, then you can create your own permissions by combining NTFS attributes. However, you must ensure that your new permission is coherent.

You can customize your permissions as follows:

➜ Display the properties of the resource for which you want to apply NTFS permissions.

➜ Under the **Security** tab, add the user, or the user group, to which the permission must apply.

➜ Select this user, or group, and then click the **Advanced** button.

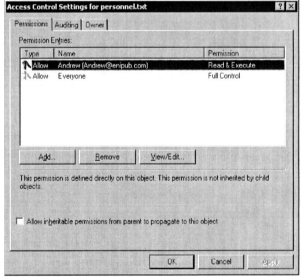

➜ This dialog box shows the list of all the NTFS attributes that have been granted to each user.

➜ Click the **View/Edit** button.

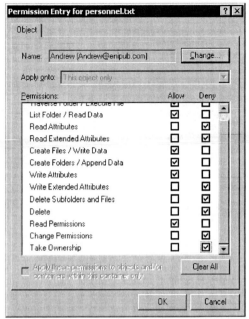

→) Choose the NTFS attributes that you require.

→) You can also specify the scope of your permissions.

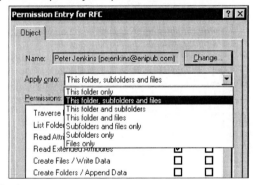

Applying NTFS permissions

Multiple application

You can apply NTFS permissions for a file or for a folder, to users or to groups of users.

When a user is a member of several groups to which different permissions have been attributed, then the permissions that will be applied to the user will be the combination of all the permissions that are applied to the user's groups.

Chapter 7

An exception to this rule occurs when a permission has been denied to the user or to one of the user's groups. In this case, the deny always takes priority.

For example: suppose you want all domain users to have **Full Control** permission for a file. You apply this permission:

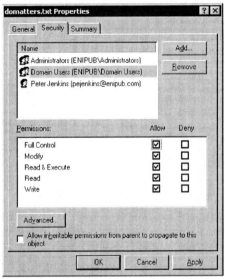

However, you do not want the user Peter Jenkins to be able to access this file. You deny **Full Control** permission for this user:

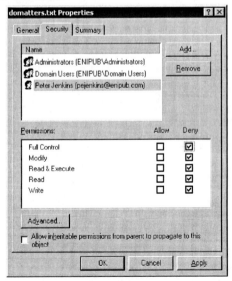

Windows 2000 Professional

Inheriting permissions

When you create a file or a folder, the file or the folder inherits the permissions of the parent container. This inheritance is re-presented by a series of check boxes that are grayed-out.

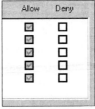

To cancel this inheritance, disable the following check box:

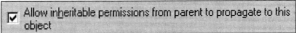

The following message then appears:

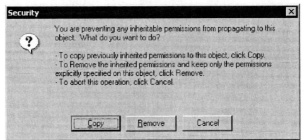

In response to this dialog box, you can choose one of several options:

– You can choose to keep the inherited permissions, and to make their check boxes appear with a white background so that you will be able to change them. In this case click **Copy**.

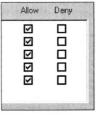

– Alternatively, you can choose to remove the inheritance, and to keep only those permissions that you have attributed for the file or the folder. In this case click **Remove**.

If you remove an inheritance, you can recover it again by re-enabling the **Allow inheritable permissions from parent to propagate to this object** check box.

By default, the permissions for folders and for files are inherited from the parent container.

b. Taking ownership of files and folders

Each file or folder that is located on an NTFS volume has an owner. By default, the owner of a resource is the user that created the resource, who is automatically a member of the **CREATOR OWNER** group. When a user is the owner of a resource, he/she can always modify the permissions, such as those that allow users to read or to write.

A user cannot become the owner of a resource, unless he/she has the special **Take Ownership** permission. Although a user that has this permission can become the owner of a resource, he/she cannot make another user the owner of the resource.

Here are the steps that you must follow in order to take ownership of a resource:

→) Right-click the name of the file, or of the folder, of which you want to take ownership, and select the **Properties** option.

→) Select the **Security** tab and then click the **Advanced** button.

→) Select the **Owner** tab.

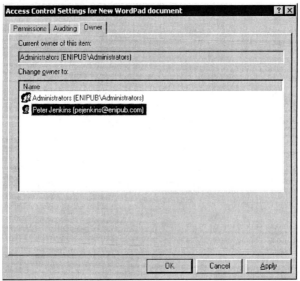

If the user has **Take Ownership** permission, then the user's account will appear in the list under **Change owner to**. The user must select his/her account and then click the **Apply** button.

Notice a difference between Windows 2000 and NT 4.0: when a Windows 2000 user who belongs to the **administrators** group takes ownership of a resource, then it is the user's account that becomes the owner.

c. Copying and moving files and folders

In order to copy or move an item to an NTFS partition, a user must have the necessary permissions.

For example, a user can move a file between NTFS partitions only if the user has **Write** permission for the destination folder, and **Modify** permission for the source folder.

If you copy a file or a folder to a different NTFS partition, or to the same NTFS partition, the file or the folder will inherit the permissions of the destination container folder.

If you move a file or a folder to a different NTFS partition, the file or the folder will also inherit the permissions of the destination container folder. However, if you move a file or a folder to the same NTFS partition, then the file or the folder will keep the same permissions.

If you copy or move files or folders from an NTFS partition to a non-NTFS partition, the file or the folder will lose its permissions, as these permissions are supported only on NTFS partitions.

When you copy a file or a folder, you become the owner of the copy that you have made.

When you move a file or a folder from one partition to another, you copy the item first, and then you delete the source item.

3. Encrypting documents

a. Introduction

In order to enhance resource security, Windows 2000 allows you to encrypt your data, in the context of NTFS file systems. This technique ensures that the contents of your documents will be accessible only by those users who have the key that decrypts them.

Once you have encrypted a document, users who are authorized to decrypt it will be able to access it transparently. Although this encryption is applied according to NTFS permissions, it is independent of the NTFS permissions that are applied to the same document.

For this purpose, Windows 2000 uses EFS (*Encrypting File System*). In response to increasing security requirements, EFS allows improved protection of sensitive data. Although it is difficult to by-pass NTFS permissions, an element of risk is always present. For example, on the Internet you can obtain utilities that allow you to access NTFS partitions by booting your computer on a simple MS-DOS diskette. In this case, NTFS permissions no longer apply.

EFS uses symmetric encryption (this means that the same keys are used for encryption and for decryption). The list of these keys itself is encrypted with a user's public key from the X.509 v3 certificate. This list is integrated into the document. In order to decrypt the document, you must use the user's private key that was used to encrypt the document so that you can extract the list of keys that are used. Only the user knows this private key. This technique is known as asymmetric encryption (the public key that is used in order to encrypt the document is different from the private key that is used in order to decrypt the document).

◐ Files are encrypted block by block, and each block is encrypted using a different encryption key.

◐ EFS allows you to encrypt files or folders that are on a computer. It does not allow you to encrypt data that is transferred via the network. For this purpose, Windows 2000 offers solutions such as IPSec and SSL (Secure Sockets Layer).

b. Implementation

Encrypting

→⟩ Open **Windows Explorer** and then right-click the file or the folder that you want to encrypt (this must be on an NTFS partition or volume). Then select **Properties**.

→⟩ Click the **Advanced** button.

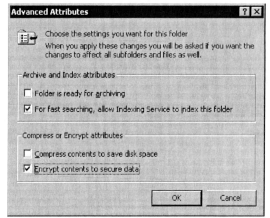

→⟩ Activate the **Encrypt contents to secure data** option, and then click **OK**.

If you encrypt a folder that contains files or subfolders, then you must choose whether you want to encrypt only the folder, or whether you want to encrypt the folder along with its subfolders and files.

💿 You cannot encrypt a file or a folder, and compress it as well. If you encrypt a file that is compressed, then the file will lose its compression attribute.

You can also use a command prompt utility in order to encrypt or decrypt files or folders. This utility is called **cipher.exe**.

Using cipher.exe

/e   Encrypts the folders that are specified, and encrypts also any files or folders that will be added later to the specified folders.

/d   Decrypts the specified folders. Any folders or files that are added to the specified folders later will not be encrypted.

/s:dir   When combined with **/e** or **/d**, this switch encrypts or decrypts the folders and subfolders that are specified in the command line.

/i   By default, **cipher** stops when an error occurs. This switch forces **cipher** to carry on running.

/q   Reports only important information.

/k   Generates a new encryption key for the user who is running **cipher**.

If you run the **cipher** utility without specifying any switch, then **cipher** will return the status of the current encryption.

```
E:\>cipher /e /s:data1
 Setting the directory data1 to encrypt new files [OK]
 Encrypting directories in E:\data1\
data2                    [OK]
 Encrypting directories in E:\data1\data2\

2 directorie(s) within 3 directorie(s) were encrypted.
E:\>
```

If you decide to encrypt a file that is located in a directory that is not encrypted, then you can choose either to encrypt only the file, or to encrypt the file and its parent folder.

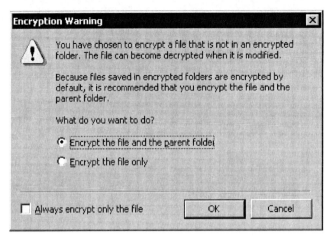

Stopping encryption

If you want to stop encrypting (decrypt) a file or a folder, go into **Windows Explorer**, right-click the folder or the file that you want to decrypt, select **properties** and click the **Advanced** button. Then, deactivate the **Encrypt contents to secure data** option.

If you decrypt a folder that contains files or subfolders, then you must choose whether or not you want to decrypt the contents of the folder.

You can also use the **cipher.exe** utility for this purpose, specifying the switch **/d**.

Copying and moving

When you copy or move an encrypted document, then the document will stay encrypted, whether the destination folder is encrypted or not.

Similarly, if you back up encrypted documents using the Windows 2000 backup utility, then these documents will remain encrypted after you have restored them.

If you copy, or move, an unencrypted file to a folder that is encrypted, then the file will also be encrypted. You can apply a policy that will prevent the encryption of files that are moved to an encrypted folder that is situated on the same volume.

In order to do this, you must use the policy:

Do not automatically encrypt files moved to encrypted folders

that is situated in the **Group Policy** snap-in, in the folder **Computer Configuration - Administrative Templates - System**.

You must note that if you copy or move an encrypted file to a file system other than NTFS, then the file will not be encrypted at the destination. You may find this technique useful for distributing a document that you have encrypted.

⚫ When another user has encrypted a document, you can copy or move it only to an NTFS file system.

⚫ A user who has the right to delete a file will be able to delete an encrypted file.

c. Recovery agents

Only the user who has encrypted a document can read it. But what happens if the user account of the person who encrypted the document is deleted? Is the data permanently lost?

To deal with such situations, **recovery agents** allow you to decrypt documents. Each encrypted document contains the list of the keys that were used to encrypt the document. This list is itself encrypted with the user's public key, and normally, it can be decrypted only with the private key of the user who encrypted the document. However, this list is also encrypted with the recovery agent's public key. Consequently, it can be decrypted by the recovery agent's private key. Thereby, when a user's private key fails, you can use the recovery agent to recover the documents concerned.

Who are they?

The first administrator who logs onto a domain after the domain has been created becomes the recovery agent for that domain.

The first administrator who logs onto a workstation, or a stand-alone server, becomes the recovery agent for the workstation or the server.

Recovering a document

A recovery agent decrypts a document using his/her private key:

- either you must copy the recovery agent's private key onto the computer on which you want to recover the encrypted document (you are strongly advised not to use this method for security reasons),
- or you must send the document that must be decrypted to the recovery agent, so that the recovery agent can use his/her private key on its own machine.
- If you decide to send the document to the recovery agent, back up the document using the Windows 2000 backup utility, then send the backup to the recovery agent, who can restore it on his/her own machine. Once this is done, the recovery agent will be able to open the document transparently.

4. Compression management

a. Introduction

The NTFS file system supports the compression of files and of folders. The purpose of this compression is to optimize disk space. A file that is compressed takes up less space than the same file when it is not compressed.

You can compress a whole partition as well as a file or a folder.

b. Compressing

To compress a file or a folder that is situated in an NTFS partition, right-click the file or the folder and select the **Properties** option.

Click the **Advanced** button to display the following dialog box:

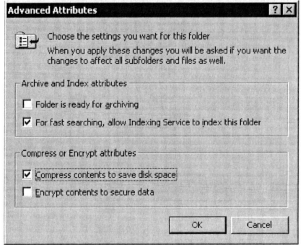

Activate the **Compress contents to save disk space** check box, and click **OK**.

> 🔊 You can choose either to compress a file or a folder or to encrypt the file or the folder. You cannot choose both at once!

When you have compressed a file, the users can continue to use the file, just as they did before. You can access these files from any type of client, whether it is a Windows client or an MS-DOS client.

To recognize a file or folder that has been compressed more easily, without having to look at its attributes, you can make your compressed file or folder appear in your **Windows Explorer**, in a different color than that in which non-compressed items appear.

→) Open the **Tools** menu of your **Windows Explorer**, select **Folder Options**, and then select the **View** tab.

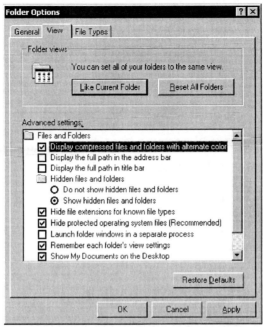

→) Activate the **Display compressed files and folders with alternate color** option.

The names of compressed files and folders now appear in blue.

If you choose to compress a folder, you must indicate whether you want to compress only this folder, or whether you want to compress any files and subdirectories that are contained in the folder, as well.

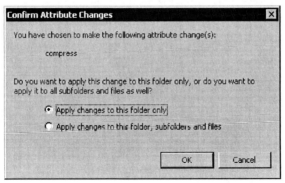

c. Copying and moving compressed files

Here are some rules concerning the compression attribute when you copy or move a file or a folder:

	Onto the same NTFS volume	Between different NTFS volumes
Copy	Inherits the compression attribute of the destination	Inherits the compression attribute of the destination
Move	Retains its compression attribute	Inherits the compression attribute of the destination

For example, if you move a compressed file that is located on the path **c:\data\file.txt**, to the path **d:\applications \file.txt**, and the destination folder, "**applications**", is not compressed, then the file "**file.txt**" will lose its compression attribute.

On the other hand, if you move the same file, **c:\data\file.txt**, to **c:\backup\file.txt** and the destination folder, "**backup**" is not compressed, then the file "**file.txt**" will keep its compression attribute.

d. Compressing from a command prompt

The **compact.exe** utility allows you to manage your compression operations from the command prompt.

```
E:\>compact /?
Displays or alters the compression of files on NTFS partitions.

COMPACT [/C | /U] [/S[:dir]] [/A] [/I] [/F] [/Q] [filename [...]]

  /C        Compresses the specified files.  Directories will be marked
            so that files added afterward will be compressed.
  /U        Uncompresses the specified files.  Directories will be marked
            so that files added afterward will not be compressed.
  /S        Performs the specified operation on files in the given
            directory and all subdirectories.  Default "dir" is the
            current directory.
  /A        Displays files with the hidden or system attributes.  These
            files are omitted by default.
  /I        Continues performing the specified operation even after errors
            have occurred.  By default, COMPACT stops when an error is
            encountered.
  /F        Forces the compress operation on all specified files, even
            those which are already compressed.  Already-compressed files
            are skipped by default.
  /Q        Reports only the most essential information.
  filename  Specifies a pattern, file, or directory.

Used without parameters, COMPACT displays the compression state of
the current directory and any files it contains. You may use multiple
filenames and wildcards.  You must put spaces between multiple
parameters.
```

When you copy a non-compressed file into a compressed folder, then the file will be compressed after it has been copied. Consequently, the partition that contains the destination folder must have enough available disk space to receive the initial non-compressed file.

5 Accessing shared FTP and WWW resources

a. Introduction

The core version of Windows 2000 provides a service that allows you to use Web features, either within your company or on the Internet. When you install Internet Information Services on a Windows 2000 machine, you transform it into a Web and FTP server.

A Web server is a computer that runs the TCP/IP protocol and that sends Web pages to clients that ask for them. The HTTP (*HyperText Transfer Protocol*) protocol is used, for this purpose. HTTP is encapsulated within TCP/IP. Your Windows 2000 computer can accommodate Web sites so that they can be consulted all over the world via the Internet network. However, providing information via a Web server does not necessarily imply that that the information will be available on the Internet. IIS 5.0 (*Internet Information Services 5.0*) allows you to provide information within a company, in the same way as you provide information on the Internet. This type of configuration is called an **intranet**.

When you implement an intranet, you use the techniques used on the world network, except that they are limited to a network (which generally belongs to a company) without an entry point via the Internet. Users consult the information using a **browser**. A browser is an application that you can use to consult Web pages. Some browsers, such as Internet Explorer, also allow you to view graphics, listen to sounds, read video and run programs such as Java applets or ActiveX controls.

When you consult a Web site using your browser, you can enter the name of the Web server that you want to consult, a name like **www.eni-publishing.com**. Such addresses are used because they are easier to remember than addresses such as 132.145.0.1. However, when you run a query on a full name such as **www.eni-publishing.com**, a DNS server transforms this name into an IP address.

The Windows 2000 Internet Information Services are a great improvement over previous versions. This chapter will provide you with some key points concerning IIS administration, but it is by no means an in-depth study of this service. A complete book would be necessary to allow you to master this service.

b. Installing

For the Web server, you must use the TCP/IP protocol with a static IP configuration. It is preferable to use a DNS server so that you will be able to resolve Internet names and an NTFS partition to secure the data that your computer will accommodate.

Unlike Windows 2000 Server, Windows 2000 Professional does not install Internet Information Server 5.0 automatically, by default.

You can install these services as follows:

→) Go into the **Control Panel** double-click the **Add/Remove Program** icon and then click the **Add/Remove Windows Components** button.

→) Enable the **Internet Information Services (IIS)** check box, then click the **Details** button to select the IIS options that you wish to install.

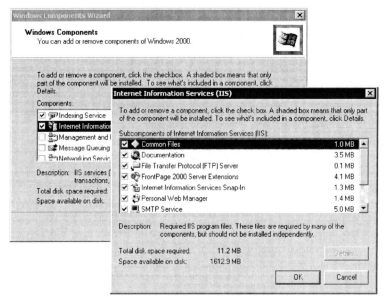

→ Click the **OK** button, followed by the **Next** button.

→ When the installation is finished, you will be able to use a console that allows you to manage **Internet Information Services**: ![Internet Services Manager]

⊙ When you install **Internet Information Services**, you create a tree in which the parent directory is **Inetpub**.

c. Accommodating Web sites

You can create a Web site using the **Internet Services Manager** console. This is the first step that must be taken in order to allow users to access your computer.

By default, an example site is created in the **Inetpub\wwwroot** directory when you install IIS. This site allows you to test your installation of Internet Information Services on your server by using a browser to connect to the local address.

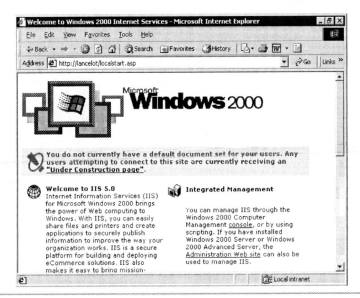

In the **Address** box, you can enter the name of your computer, or you can specify its IP address (for example, **http://10.0.1.38**) or you can enter **http://localhost**.

IIS 5.0 provides online help in HTML format at the **http://localhost/iishelp** address.

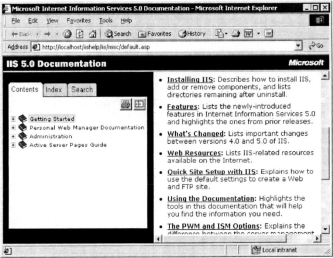

You can create a new site, or **subweb**, as follows:

→) Open the **Internet Services Manager**.

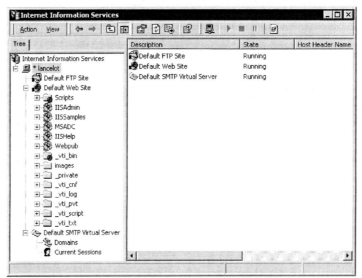

You can then choose to create a new subweb.

You must specify the **Subweb Name**.

Windows 2000 Professional

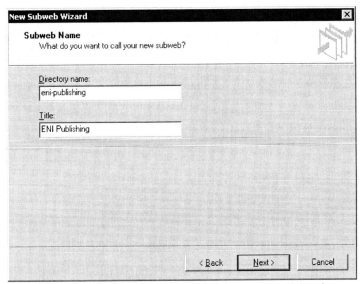

Finally, the wizard asks you to confirm the creation of your new subweb.

The wizard creates a subtree in the **Inetpub** hierarchy.

You can also create a virtual directory (a www path to a specific folder) by right-clicking your subweb and choosing **New - Virtual Directory**.

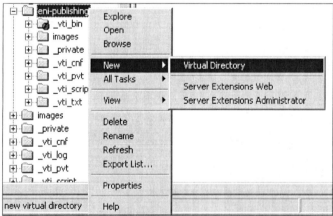

➜) Enter an **Alias** for your virtual directory (this is the **www** equivalent of a share name).

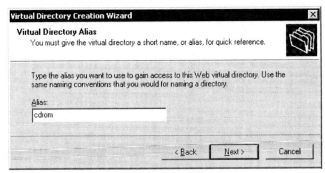

→) Use the **Browse** button to specify the physical **Directory**.

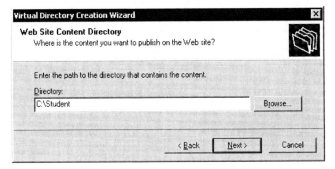

You must then specify the access permissions that you want to grant for your virtual directory.

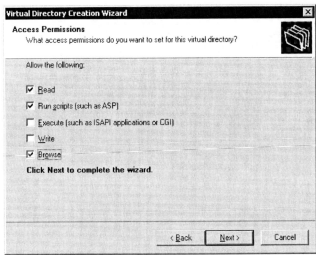

The **Internet Information Services** console then shows a link to your directory.

Windows 2000 Professional

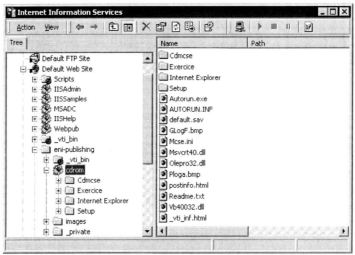

You can now access this directory using your web browser.

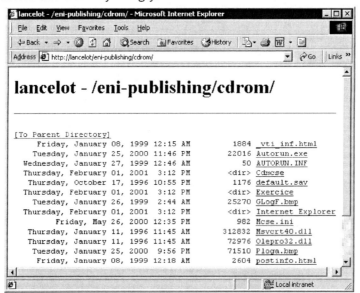

In addition, you can modify the properties of a site. To do this, right-click the site concerned, then select **Properties**.

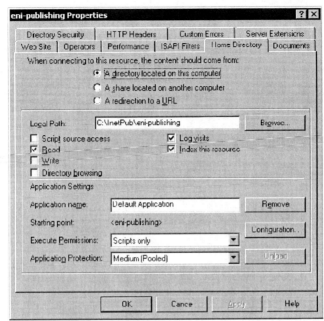

- The **Home Directory** tab allows you to specify where the site information must be stored. If the folder that contains this site is not located on the Web server, you must indicate **A share located on another computer**.

- The **Performance** tab allows you to limit the bandwidth used for this Web site. This feature is especially useful if your Web server accommodates several sites. In addition, you can limit the percentage of the CPU that this site will use. When you activate the **Enable process throttling** check box, the system will add an event into the **Event Viewer**, as soon as the site uses more CPU than it is allowed to use. You can force the site to keep within its CPU limit by enabling the **Enforce limits** check box.

- The **Documents** tab indicates the page that must be loaded when users connect to the site.

- The **Custom Errors** tab allows you to modify error messages to make them more understandable by the users who receive them.

d. Authenticating access

When you install Internet Information Services, you create an account called **IUSR_your-computer-name**. This account allows users to consult information without having to enter a name and a password. This account uses anonymous authentication. This means that anonymous users can access documents for which permissions have been granted to the **IUSR** account: you must be careful not to grant too much permission to this account.

If you do not want to allow anonymous access to your site, you can choose other authentication methods.

Basic authentication

When you define basic authentication, you force users to enter a user account and a password before they can access the information. You can apply such "filtering" at site level or at folder or file level. This authentication method is based on Windows 2000 accounts. The user can access the resource only if he/she supplies the name of a user account and the corresponding password.

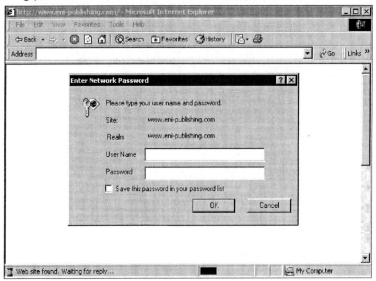

It must be noted however, that this method does not encrypt the account information when it is transmitted from the client to the server.

You can configure this authentication method as follows:

→) Go into the **Internet Services Manager** console, right-click the Web site that you want to secure, then select **Properties**.

→) Select the **Directory Security** tab, then click the **Edit** button under **Anonymous access and authentication control**.

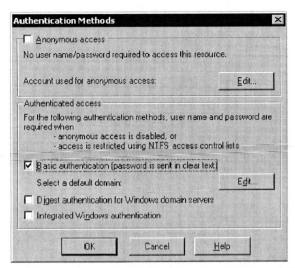

→) Deactivate the **Anonymous access** check box and the **Integrated Windows authentication** check box and enable the **Basic authentication** check box. Click **Yes** in response to the warning message that appears and then click **OK** twice to complete the operation.

Integrated Windows authentication

As with the previous method, this integrated Windows authentication forces users to enter the name of a user account and the password that is associated with it before they can access the database concerned. In this case, passwords are not transmitted on the network and authentication information is encrypted.

To use this method, you need a browser that will support it. At the time of publication, Internet Explorer (version 2.0 or later) was the only browser that supported this authentication method.

Digest authentication for Windows domain servers

This method runs only with accounts that are in Windows 2000 domains. It requires that passwords are stored in clear text. The password is not transmitted on the network and only a hashed value is sent to the server. At the time of publication, only Internet Explorer 5 was able to use this method.

e. Setting up an FTP (File Transfer Protocol) site

FTP is a file transfer protocol. You can create an FTP site using IIS 5. This means that you can provide users with access to documents and you can even allow them to download applications.

By default, you create an FTP site when you install IIS. This site is empty when it is created and you can add documents that you wish to publish by copying them into the directory **inetpub\ftproot**. You can also create a new FTP site by right-clicking the name of your server, then selecting **New** followed by **FTP site**. A wizard then helps you to create your site.

You can modify the configuration of the FTP site created by default by right-clicking **Default FTP Site** in the **Internet Services Manager** console, then selecting **Properties**.

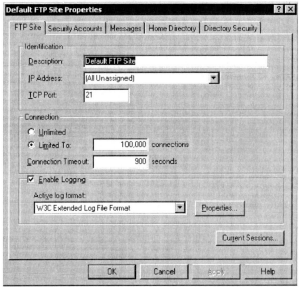

- The **FTP Site** tab allows you to configure the port that FTP uses (port 21 by default) and the maximum number of simultaneous connections that can be made to the FTP site.
- The **Security Accounts** tab allows you to set up the access to the FTP site (by default, anonymous connections are allowed).
- The **Messages** tab allows you to indicate a message that must be displayed when a user connects to, or disconnects from, the FTP site.

- The Home Directory tab allows you to specify the path to which users are directed when they connect to the FTP site. This tab also allows you to display the results of FTP queries in either an MS-DOS.i.MS-DOS; or a UNIX listing style.

Here is an example of the Unix listing style:

```
E:\WINNT\System32\cmd.exe                                    _ □ X

E:\>ftp merlin
Connected to merlin.enipub.com.
220 merlin Microsoft FTP Service (Version 5.0).
User (merlin.enipub.com:(none)): administrator
331 Password required for administrator.
Password:
230 Welcome to my FTP site
230 User administrator logged in.
ftp> dir
200 PORT command successful.
150 Opening ASCII mode data connection for /bin/ls.
-r-xr-xr-x   1 owner      group                  4 Mar 21 11:30 RFC1812.txt
-r-xr-xr-x   1 owner      group                  4 Mar 21 11:31 RFC2131.txt
-r-xr-xr-x   1 owner      group                  4 Mar 21 11:31 RFC2136.txt
226 Transfer complete.
ftp: 216 bytes received in 0.01Seconds 21.60Kbytes/sec.
ftp> quit
221 See you later
```

- The **Directory Security** tab allows you to specify IP addresses that will be granted or denied access to the FTP site.

Make sure that you apply suitable NTFS permissions to documents that can be accessed via FTP.

You do not have to copy or move the documents that you want to appear on your FTP site. You can create virtual directories pointing elsewhere in the network. Users who connect will not notice any difference. To create a virtual directory, right-click your FTP site, then select **New** followed by **Virtual Directory**. Enter an alias (this is the name that the users will see) and enter the path where the data is located. Finally, you must grant suitable permissions. To make this virtual directory operational, you must create a directory with the alias name in the directory that accommodates the FTP site (on the IIS server).

f. Troubleshooting IIS

If you have a problem with your Web server then check the following points.

Testing your Web site

- Check that the files associated with your Web site reside in a Web shared folder. To do this, open **Windows Explorer**, right-click your root directory, activate the **Web Sharing** tab and check that it is shared as "/".
- Check the home directory of your Web site. To do this, go into the **Internet Information Services** console, right-click your Web site and access the **Home Directory** tab.
- Open your Internet browser and enter the URL of your site, for example **http://localhost**.
- Try connecting from another machine by opening its Internet browser and entering the IP address of the Web server in the **Address** field: for example **http://192.168.100.2**.

- Check that a name resolution service, such as DNS or WINS is available. In addition, check that the client machines needing to access your Web site have been configured as DNS clients (or possibly as WINS clients).
- Try accessing the IIS 5.0 online documentation by entering the following URL in the **Address** field of your Internet browser: **http://localhost/iisHelp**.

6 Using Briefcase

a. Introduction

Briefcase is a special folder that allows you to memorize the origin of a file when you make a copy of it. This technique provides data access to a roaming user, even when the user no longer has any physical connection with the company network. In addition, when the user reconnects to the company network, this tool automatically synchronizes the information for which it provided offline access, with the source files on the company network. This approach means that you do not need to copy the latest file versions manually, nor do you need to delete old file versions manually .

You can use this technique with all types of non-permanent connections: for example, via the network, using serial or parallel cables, or using removable storage media.

b. Creating a new Briefcase

→) To create a new **Briefcase** on your desktop, right-click anywhere on your desktop, and select **New - Briefcase**.

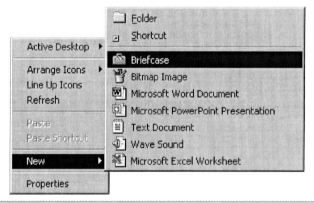

You can create your **Briefcase** anywhere in your file hierarchy.

You can open your **Briefcase** by double-clicking it:

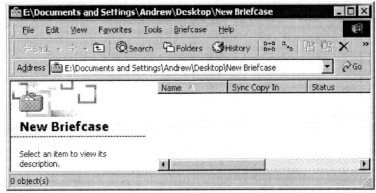

When you open your **Briefcase** for the first time, the **Welcome to the Windows Briefcase** dialog box appears with instructions on how to use your **Briefcase**.

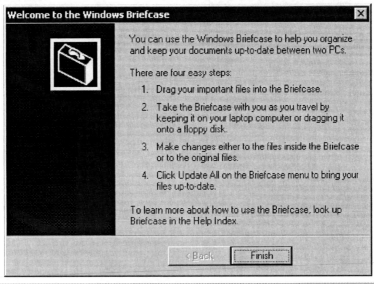

If you use several profiles on the same workstation, then you are advised either to create your **Briefcase** directly in the root of a drive or to create a shortcut on each desktop of the users concerned.

c. Working offline

The advantage of **Briefcase** is that it allows you to work with documents from the network when you are no longer connected to the network.

However, first you must clearly define the files and folders that must be available offline.

Then, before you disconnect your workstation, or eject your removable storage medium, or unplug your serial cable, you must copy the documents that you want to use offline to your **Briefcase**.

To make a file or a folder available offline, you can simply drag the file or the folder onto your **Briefcase**.

If you want to make a shortcut, and the file to which it points available offline, then you must first create the shortcut and then drag your shortcut onto your **Briefcase**, making a synchronization copy.

In the example below, two shortcuts have been created to an executable program that is located on a remote drive. The first shortcut was created directly from the program file, by selecting the **Create Shortcut(s) Here** option. On the other hand, the second shortcut was created first on the remote drive, and then it was copied into the **Briefcase** using the **Make Sync Copy** option.

These shortcuts were created by right-clicking the remote file, dragging it onto the **Briefcase**, and then selecting the corresponding option from the shortcut menu, as with this third shortcut for which the **Make Sync Copy** option is selected:

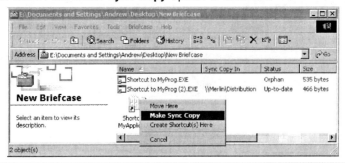

Important note: If you create **only** a shortcut to a file or a folder in your **Briefcase**, then you will not have offline access to the file or the folder. If you want to access the file or the folder offline, then you must create a **copy of** the file or the folder in your **Briefcase**.

Briefcase is all the more deceptive in this respect when it displays a shortcut **Status** as **Up-to-date**:

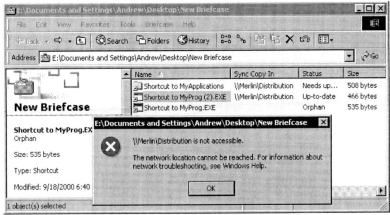

Briefcase is not the only tool that allows you to work with documents offline.

You can use the **Offline Files Wizard** to make data available in **Windows Explorer** after you have disconnected from your network. However, when you no longer have a network connection, you will be able to access only those files and folders that you made available beforehand.

The first step is to enable the Windows 2000 **Offline Files** feature. If this option is disabled, although you will still be able to work with your **Briefcase**, you not be able to work with offline files in either **My Computer** or in **Windows Explorer**.

➙) Go into **Windows Explorer** or **My Computer**. Open the **Tools** menu and choose **Folder Options**.

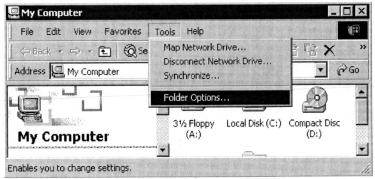

➙) Select the **Offline Files** tab, and activate the **Enable Offline Files** check box.

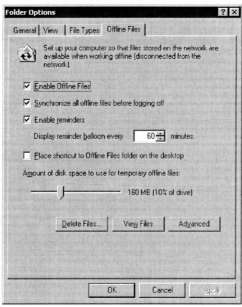

→) Confirm this setting by clicking **OK**.

The next step consists of selecting the folder or the file that you want to make available offline. To do this, go into **Windows Explorer** or **My Computer**, right-click the folder or the file concerned and select the **Make Available Offline** option:

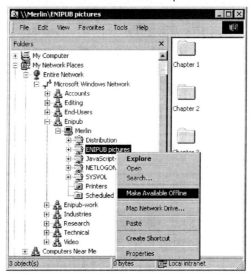

The **Offline Files Wizard** starts. This wizard provides information and allows you to specify settings:

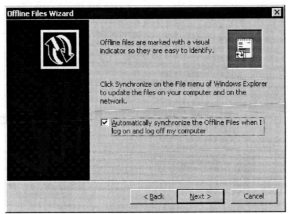

It then allows you to choose various options:

If you selected a folder, then you must indicate whether you want to make the folder and all its subfolders available offline, or whether you want to make available only the first folder level:

The synchronization process starts.

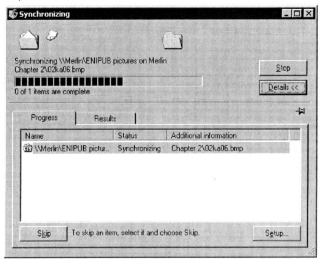

Then, when you are connected to the source of the files, you can work normally:

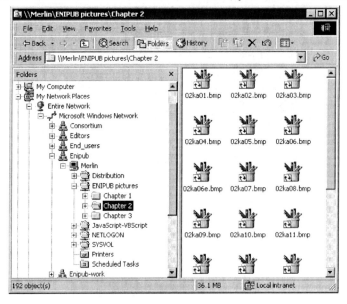

However, as soon as the connection is broken, the display changes, and you can access only those files that you made available offline:

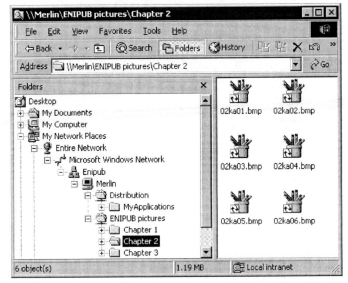

⊙ Permissions that were defined for a file or for a folder will continue to apply when you work in offline mode.

⊙ When you are disconnected from the network, you cannot print to shared printers on the network, but you can still print to your local network printer: in fact when you request your printing offline, Windows 2000 will first queue your file, and then it will print your file when you reconnect to the network.

d. Synchronizing files

The **Synchronization Manager** allows you to specify how Windows 2000 must synchronize your files.

First, you must open the **Synchronization Manager**. To do this, go into **My Computer** or into **Windows Explorer**, open the **Tools** menu and select the **Synchronize** option:

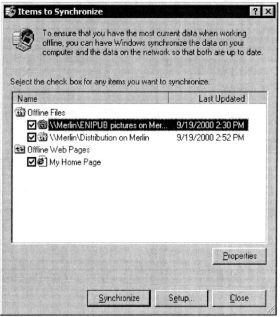

You can then consult the **Properties** of a your offline files:

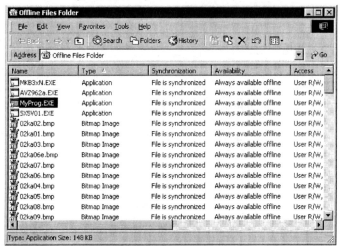

As the previous section describes, before you can use **Synchronization Manager** to manage the synchronization of your files, you must have activated the **Enable Offline Files** option on the **Offline Files** page of the **Folder Options** dialog box (to access this dialog box select the **Tools - Folder Options** menu option in **My Computer** or in **Windows Explorer**). In addition, you must have selected the files and folders concerned and activated the **Make Available Offline** option.

You can synchronize a specific folder by activating the corresponding check box in the **Synchronization Manager** (the **Items to Synchronize** dialog box) and then clicking the **Synchronize** button.

In addition, you can specify that Windows 2000 must synchronize some or all of your offline folders when you log on, and/or when you log off.

→) Go into the **Synchronization Manager** and click the **Setup** button:

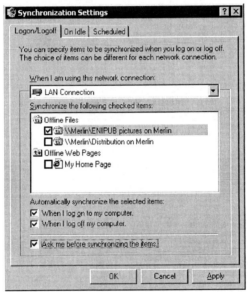

You can then request file synchronization when you log onto or when you log off from your computer.

When you are working with a slow connection, it is often useful to disable the automatic synchronization options.

e. Checking the status of your files

You can check the status of the files that are in your **Briefcase**:

→) Go into your **Briefcase**:

You can then check the overall status of all the files that your **Briefcase** contains.

→) To obtain a more detailed, up-to-date status of an individual item, right-click the item concerned, select the **Properties** option, and then activate the **Update Status** tab.

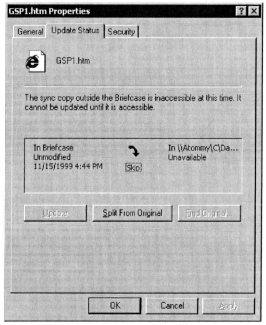

To update all the files in your **Briefcase**, go into the **Briefcase** menu and select the **Update All** option.

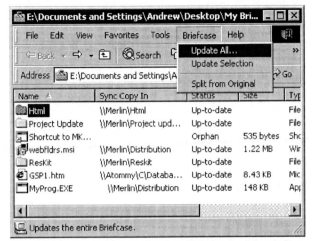

Then, click the **Update** button to update all your **Briefcase** files (after you have done this you can then decide to update each item separately, by selecting the item concerned in the main **Briefcase** window and choosing the **Briefcase - Update Selection** menu option).

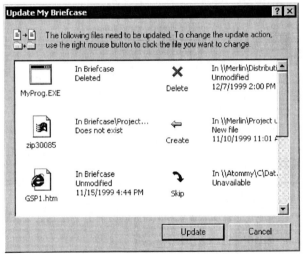

f. Choosing between Briefcase and the Offline Files Wizard

Both of these Windows 2000 tools allow you to work with a document when either your workstation or the machine that contains the source file, is disconnected from the network. However, as these tools have different characteristics, they are not equally suitable for use in all cases.

Briefcase

This tool is useful when you want to transfer files frequently, either between computers via a cable, or between a computer and a removable disk.

> ⊙ You are advised to create several Briefcases, as this will help you to manage your file synchronization.

Offline Files Wizard

This tool is more suitable for working with shared folders in a network environment.

g. Troubleshooting offline file synchronization

If your offline files have undergone separate modifications in both local and remote locations, then you may have problems when you synchronize them.

With an Access database for example, Windows 2000 handles the synchronization at record level. However, if two records have been modified separately, then you must explicitly define the action that Windows 2000 must take when you start the synchronization process. You will also have this problem if you modify files separately.

In these cases you must choose, either to keep your version of the data, or to keep that of the remote server, or to keep both versions.

If you choose to maintain both versions of a file, then you must change the name of one or both of the files in order to ensure that you do not lose the separate modifications.

If, when you are working offline, you delete a file whose source is situated on a remote server, then the source file will be maintained on the remote server.

On the other hand, if you modify a file while you are working offline, and the file is deleted on the remote server in the meantime, then you will be able to choose either to save your version on the remote server or to delete the file on your workstation.

Finally, if a file is added in one of the remote folders while you are working offline, then Windows 2000 will add this new file onto your workstation automatically, when you reconnect to the network.

Chapter 8: Printer management

A. Terminology

First, this chapter will define a few terms that are used in the Windows 2000 environment:

Print server

> This is the Windows 2000 computer that receives the documents that must be printed.

Printer

> The printer is defined on the print server. It is the software interface between the application and the print device.

Print device

> This is the physical peripheral that produces the final document. It can be either a **Local device** or a device that is equipped with a network interface card: a **network-interface print device**.

A print device can have two types of connection:

Local connection

> With this type of connection, your device is physically connected to the parallel port, or to the serial port of your computer.

Remote, network connection

> With this type of connection, the device is connected either to another network computer, or to a Windows 2000 server, or to a print server. Several users can use such a connection to send their documents for printing.

B. Installing a printer

With Windows 2000, all the operations that can be carried out on the printers located in the **Printers** folder or in the **My Computer** console of your computer, can also be carried out remotely, via the network, from other Windows NT or Windows 2000 machines (provided that you have sufficient permissions). Thus, an administrator can remotely install or configure printers from his/her machine, just as if he or she had logged on to each of the machines concerned.

In order to do this you must open **My Network Places** and access the **Printers** icon of the remote computer.

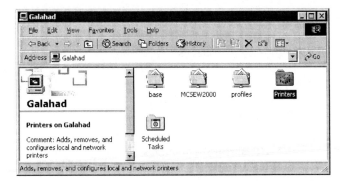

1. Local printer

→) Open the **Control Panel**, and double-click the **Printers** icon. Alternatively, you can click the **Printers** folder that is situated in the **Start - Settings** menu.

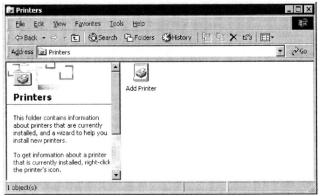

→) Double-click the **Add Printer** icon in order to start up the Add **Printer Wizard**.

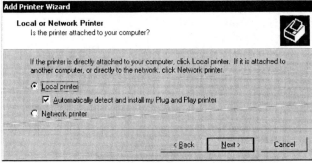

→) To install a printer that is connected to this computer, select **Local printer**, and then click **Next**.

⊙ Note that the Add Printer Wizard can automatically detect your Plug-and-Play printers.

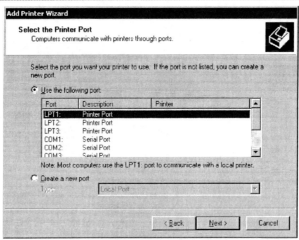

The dialog box shown above, allows you to specify the port on which your print device is connected. You can choose one of the different parallel ports (LPT1, LPT2, LPT3), or one of the different serial ports (COM1, COM2, COM3). Alternatively, you can choose to print to a file, or to the Microsoft FAX port if you are sending a fax.

You can also add other ports. If you have a network-interface print device, then you should add the port that corresponds to this peripheral. Such print devices are more convenient to use, because they do not require your server to act as a print server, and the information transfer is quicker on a network cable than on a parallel cable.

Windows 2000 supports the following ports:

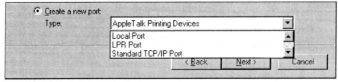

Apple Talk Printing Devices

As the title indicates, this option allows you to use Apple Talk print devices.

Local Port

This option allows you to connect a print device either to a parallel port or to a serial port, or to specify a file. This port also allows you to redirect print jobs either to a UNC path (*remote_computer**device_share_name*) or to the NULL port.

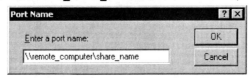

LPR Port

This option allows you to connect print devices that are attached to UNIX servers. It also allows your server to act as an LPD server.

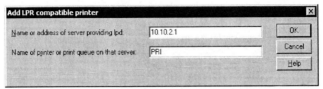

Standard TCP/IP Port

This option allows you to connect print devices that are directly attached to the network.

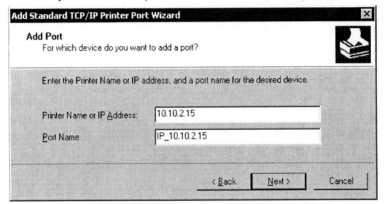

Port for Netware

This option allows you to use Netware print devices. It becomes available after you have installed the NWLink protocol and the client service for Netware.

Hewlett-Packard Network Port

This option allows you to use print devices using old HP Jetdirect adapters. This option is available only after you have installed DLC protocol.

By default, only the **Local Port** and the **Standard TCP/IP Port** are available. If you want to use the **LPR** or the **Apple Talk** port, you must install the corresponding services. Here are the steps that you must follow in order to do this:

→) Open the **Control Panel** and double-click the **Add/Remove Programs** icon.

→) Select the **Add/Remove Windows Components** icon. Then click the **Components** button, and select **Other Network File and Print Services**.

Chapter 8

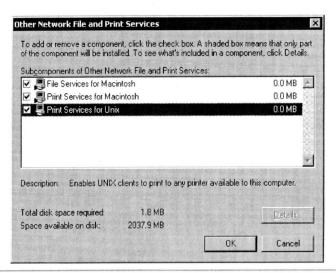

⊙ In UNIX, LPR is used to send print requests to a remote spooler. These print requests are received by the remote LPD service. When you have installed print services for UNIX, Windows 2000 is equipped with the following two services: LPDSVC.DLL which receives the requests that come from UNIX hosts, and LPRMON.DLL which allows you to send print jobs to the LPD service of a UNIX host.

→) When you have chosen the port that you wish to use, click **Next**.

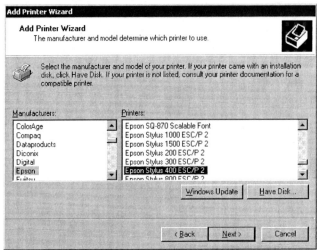

→) In the left hand pane, select the manufacturer of your print device. Then, in the right-hand pane, select its model reference. Click the **Next** button.

→) Enter a name for your printer (by default, the model reference will be used). Click **Next**.

Windows 2000 Professional

→) For the operation that is shown here, on the next screen select the **Do not share this printer** option (printer sharing will be discussed later on in this chapter). Then click the **Next** button.

Windows 2000 then offers to print a test page, made up of graphics and the list of drivers that are used. This option allows you to check that the drivers are suitable for your printer.

→) Click the **Next** button, followed by the **Finish** button.

If you decide to use your computer as a print server, then it is strongly recommended that your machine play only this role, if it will be required to handle large volumes of print jobs. You can use Windows 2000 Professional as a print server, provided that you will not have more than 10 simultaneous connections, including any that are set up by UNIX clients. If you will have a large number of connections, including Macintosh, UNIX and Netware connections, then you must use Windows 2000 Server, Windows 2000 Advanced Server or Windows 2000 Datacenter Server.

2. Network printer

Once a printer is shared, network clients can use it.

a. Connecting from a Windows 2000, 95/98 or NT machine

In order to install a network printer on a Windows 2000 machine, you must first locate the printer using **My Network Places**, or using **Active Directory**. When you have located the printer, right-click its icon and then select **Connect**.

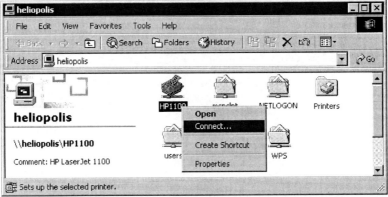

The driver is then automatically downloaded and the printer is installed. When this has been done, the printer appears in the **Printers** folder where it is represented with a network printer icon.

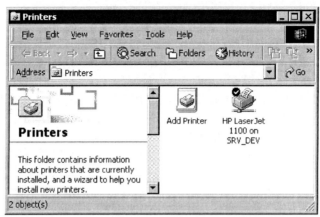

For other clients, such as machines that run Windows 95/98, Windows NT 4.0 or Windows NT 3.5x, you must install the drivers that correspond to the system on the print server. This will allow clients to download the driver automatically.

To add other drivers, go into the **Properties** of the printer, and select the **Sharing** tab. Click the **Additional Drivers** button to display the following dialog box:

The drivers for Windows 2000 versions that run on Intel platforms are installed. In order to add additional drivers, activate the check boxes that correspond to the drivers you wish to add.

b. Connecting from other clients

In order to allow other clients (such as those that run Windows 3.x or MS-DOS, for example) to use a shared printer, then you must manually install the appropriate driver on the machines concerned.

For non-Microsoft clients, you must install the appropriate services on the print server.

c. Connecting via the Web

If the print server to which you want to connect runs Microsoft Internet Information Server 5, then you can install a printer via your company's intranet, or via the Internet.

To do this, open your browser, and go to the address **http://*IIS_server_name/printers***.

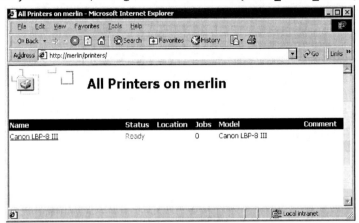

The browser displays all the printers that are installed on the target machine destination. Click the printer that you wish to install.

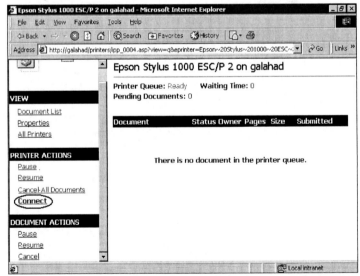

Then click the **Connect** link, in the left-hand pane of the browser window.

C. Configuring a printer

You can configure a printer by adjusting its properties:

→) Right-click the icon of the printer that you want to configure, and then select the **Properties** option.

1. General tab

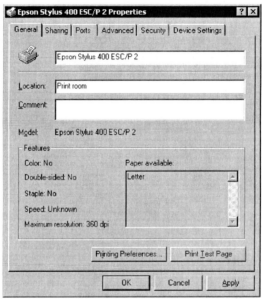

The **General** tab allows you to define the following items:

- **Name of the printer**: by default the printer name is that which was suggested when you installed the printer. However, you can specify any name that you like. Your choice of name is important as it may be used in order to search for this printer via Active Directory.
- **Location**: this information can help in an Active Directory search.
- **Comment**: this field allows you to indicate other information concerning the printer. This information can also help in an Active Directory search.

The **Printing Preferences** button allows you to specify the **Orientation** of your documents (**Portrait** or **Landscape**), the **Page Order** for printing and the number of **Pages per Sheet**. In addition, you can indicate **Advanced** options concerning a certain number of settings that are specific to the printer concerned.

As the name suggests, the **Print Test Page** allows you to print a test page at any time in order to check that your printer is working properly. Following your print attempt, you can start up the Print Troubleshooter, in order to solve any problems.

2. Sharing tab

The **Sharing** tab allows you to make the printer available for clients who want to print via the network (by connecting to the printer).

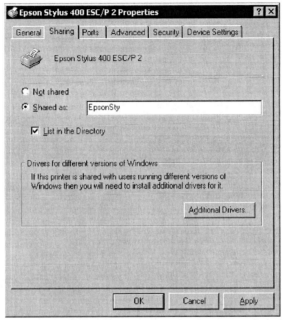

The name that you enter in the **Shared as** text box is the name that the clients will see via the network.

As mentioned above, the **Additional Drivers** button allows you to add other drivers so that machines which do not run Windows 2000 can automatically download the drivers that they will need in order to connect to this printer. The clients will automati-cally download the appropriate driver from the shared directory on the print server (the **print$** directory, under **%systemroot%\system32\spool\drivers**).

The **List in the Directory** check box, allows you to include the printer in the Active Directory database. This check box is enabled by default. This approach allows you to find a printer easily without needing to know the name of the print server on which it is connected.

3. Ports tab

This tab allows you to configure the printer ports (cf. B. Installing a printer).

This tab also allows you to redirect print jobs to another printer, in case you need to disconnect your printer for maintenance work.

→) Select the port that you wish to redirect, and then click the **Add Port** button.

→) Select **Local Port**, and then click **New Port**.

→) Enter the UNC path that leads to the new printer.

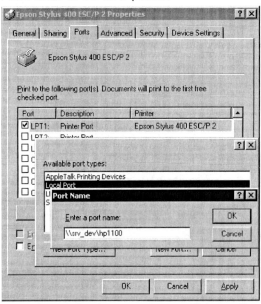

All the print jobs that are sent to the former printer will be redirected to the new share, without the users noticing any difference.

4. Advanced tab

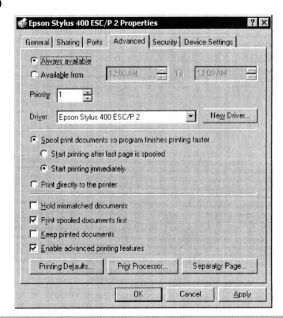

a. Availability

You can restrict the time periods during which print jobs can be sent to the printer. This is particularly useful if some of your users print large documents that can prevent other users from printing. In this case, you can install, on the same print server, two identical printers that point to the same print device. Connect the users who have high volume print jobs onto one of the printers, and connect the other users onto the other printer. Then, leave the default option, **Always available**, for the printer that will be used by the other users and, for the printer that will be used by the high volume print users, apply a time period restriction so that their documents will be printed only at night. With this approach, these large documents will be placed in the print queue, and they will be printed only during the time period that you specify.

b. Priority

You can assign a priority level for the documents that are sent to the printer. Windows 2000 will compare this priority level with that of an alternative printer (see the example above). The lowest priority level is priority 1, and the highest priority level is priority 99.

c. Changing the driver

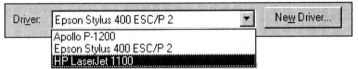

You can change the driver that is associated with your print device. You can also add a new driver, by clicking the **New Driver** button.

d. Spool

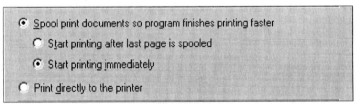

A spool is also known as a **queue**. When you start printing a large document, the computer processes your document first, in order to convert it into the language format of the printer concerned. Then, your document is processed again so that it can be sent page by page at the printing rhythm of the print device. By putting your document into a queue, the system can allow the application to resume processing quicker. Windows 2000 puts the document into the background, to allow current processes to continue working normally.

On the other hand, the **Print directly to the printer** option makes you wait until the printing has finished, before you can carry on working with your application. This option is possible only if your printer is not shared, as only in this case is the spool by-passed.

The **Spool print documents so program finishes printing faster** option allows two sub-options:

Start printing after last page is spooled

Allows you to specify that the printing can be started only after the entire document has been put into the spool.

Start printing immediately

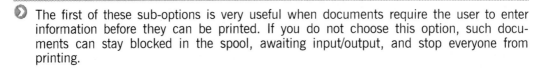

The first of these sub-options is very useful when documents require the user to enter information before they can be printed. If you do not choose this option, such documents can stay blocked in the spool, awaiting input/output, and stop everyone from printing.

Clients of Windows 2000, Windows NT and Windows 95/98 can use a second local spooler. Unlike the drivers of other clients, which process documents completely into a format that the print device can understand, the drivers of Windows 2000, Windows NT and Windows 95/98 clients process the document only partially before forwarding it to the remote spooler. As soon as it can be accommodated, the document is transmitted to the remote spooler, where it is processed completely. Then the document is placed in the print queue before being sent to the print device.

When a document is blocked in the spool, you can no longer delete the document. You often have to stop and then restart the **Print Spooler** service using the **Services** console in the **Administrative Tools** menu.

e. Options

There are four options that help you to manage your documents:

Hold mismatched documents

This option is useful with Postscript documents, for which different language versions can provoke minor errors.

Print spooled documents first

This option allows you to optimize print processing. With this option, the priority of a document is based only partially on the priority level that you specified further up in this dialog box. In addition, a document that has already been placed in the spool will have priority over documents that have yet to be placed in the spool (even if the new documents have higher priority levels).

Keep printed documents

This option allows you to specify that all documents that have already been printed will be kept in the print manager (in the spool). If this option is disabled then when the document has been printed, it will be deleted from the print queue, and its equivalent in printer language will be deleted from the hard disk.

Enable advanced printing features

This option allows you to use advanced features such as **Page Order** and the number of **Pages per Sheet**. You must disable this option if you have any compatibility problems.

The **Printing Defaults** button allows you to view the advanced features. It also allows you to view and to modify the properties that are available by clicking the **Printing Preferences** button under the **General** tab.

The **Print Processor** button allows you to select the data type of the print processor. The role of the print processor is to send the spooled document from the hard disk to the print device, with the help of the driver. For PCL printers the print processor data type by default is EMF (*Enhanced MetaFile*). Postscript printers use the RAW (ready to print) data type. Windows 2000 supports five different print processor data types.

The **Separator Page** button allows you to add separator pages between documents. This technique helps you to find your document amongst all the other documents that have been printed by the device. Separator pages also allow you to modify the printing mode.

Four separator pages are available. They are located in **%systemroot%\system32**:

- **sysprint.sep**: adds a separator page before each document. This separator page is compatible with Postscript printers.
- **pcl.sep**: allows HP printers to go into PCL mode, and adds a separator page before each document.
- **pscript.sep**: allows HP printers to go into Postscript mode, but does not add separator pages.
- **sysprtj.sep**: is similar to **sysprint.sep**, except that it uses Japanese characters.

You can modify the code of each page in order to customize the separator page.

5. Security tab

The **Security** tab allows you to specify the actions that users, and user groups, can carry out on the printer.

By default, the **Everyone** group has **Print** permission.

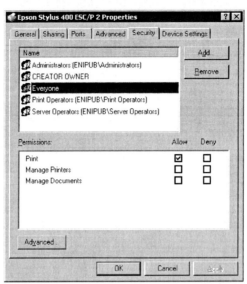

Printers that run on Windows 2000 offer three standard permissions:

Print

This permission allows users to connect to the printer and to manage their own print jobs (for example, they can remove their documents from the spool).

Manage Documents

This permission does not allow users to print, but it does allow users to manage all the documents.

Manage Printers

This permission provides full control on all documents that are submitted to the printer. It also provides full control on the printer itself. Users that have this permission can share the printer, change its permissions, delete the printer, change its properties, pause the printer, and manage all the documents that are submitted to it (including deleting the documents, and modifying their properties).

As with permissions on shared or NTFS folders, you can choose from two options for each permission: **Allow** and **Deny**.

If a user belongs to a group with permissions that are different from the user's own permissions, then the user will have the combination of all these permissions, with the exception of any permissions that have been denied, as the **Deny** option takes priority.

The **Advanced** button allows you to view access control settings including the attributes of the permission entries. It also allows you to create your own permissions by combining attributes together.

The **Owner** tab of these access control settings allows you to designate a user with **Manage Printers** permission as the new owner of the resource.

The **Auditing** tab of the access control settings allows you to monitor the use of the printer (the implementation of audits is covered in Chapter 6 - F).

6. Device settings tab

The **Device Settings** tab allows you to adjust the settings that are specific to the printer. These settings vary according to the printer model concerned.

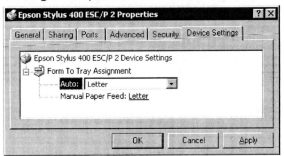

D. Implementing a printer pool

1. Introduction

A printer pool allows you to have a logical printer pointing to several print devices that work with the same driver.

This technique provides printing power suitable for large networks. It allows you to manage several print devices (with identical properties) using a single print queue (or a single printer).

With this approach, it is the printer that decides which of the available ports to use, according to their order of creation.

For example, if you have a fast print device, you should associate it with the first printer port so that it will have precedence.

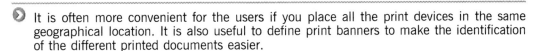

It is often more convenient for the users if you place all the print devices in the same geographical location. It is also useful to define print banners to make the identification of the different printed documents easier.

2. Configuring the pool

➙⊃ Open the **Start** menu, then select **Settings** followed by **Printers**.

➙⊃ Right-click the icon that represents the printer for which you want to create a print pool.

➙⊃ Select **Properties**, then select the **Ports** tab.

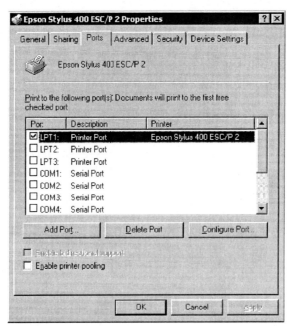

→) Activate the **Enable printer pooling** check box. Activating this check box allows you to select several ports.

→) Select all the ports that must be used in the pool and click the **OK** button.

E. Managing priorities

1. Introduction

On the same print server, you can create several printers accessing the same print device.

This technique allows you to specify different accesses to the same device, to accommodate a certain number of constraints:

- Printing during specific time periods.
- Defining printing priorities (by granting permissions for specific groups on each of the printers).
- Changing the print processing mode for the document (for example, you can choose to **Start printing immediately** for one printer and to **Start printing after last page is spooled** for another printer).
- Defining specific print formats (for instance, for photocopy printers equipped with different paper trays and using different paper formats).

For example, if you want to assign different priorities to two different user groups, for the same print device, you must create two printers that point to the same physical device.

Then, assign different priorities on the printers and apply specific permissions to the user groups.

These printers must be created on the same print server. However, you can locate the devices in different places (you can even place these devices on different shared local ports).

2. Configuring the priorities of two printers

Whether you have one printer, or whether you have several printers, the operating principle stays the same. You can even work with several printers that access several print devices. This approach combines the technique of priority management with that of the printer pool.

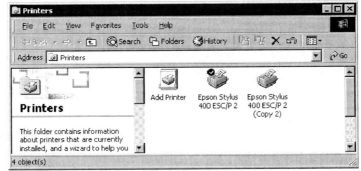

For each printer, associate a specific priority (using the **Advanced** tab) and apply specific permissions.

Example: The **Accountants** group must use the **Epson Stylus 400 ESC/P 2** with **Priority** level 12.

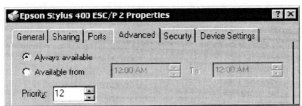

On the **Epson Stylus 400 ESC/P 2 (Copy 2)** you must set the **Priority** to level 99 for the **Managers** group.

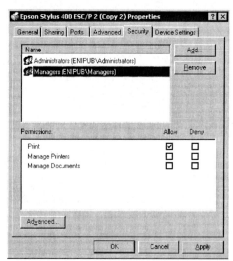

Then, you must connect the members of the **Managers** group onto the **Epson Stylus 400 ESC/P 2 (Copy 2)** printer and the members of the **Accountants** group onto the **Epson Stylus 400 ESC/P 2** printer.

F. Print management

When you print a document, it is first placed in the print queue. Each printer is associated with a print queue, which itself is managed by the print manager.

When the document is placed in the print queue it is in fact stored on the hard disk of the computer on which the logical printer is situated. The spool folder on the disk grows larger and the extent to which it is accessed will vary according to the sizes of the documents that are placed in the queue. In order to reduce any disc access delays due to printing operations, it may be useful to move the spool directory from the system disk onto another volume. This will help to spread the disk access work-load.

There are two ways of changing the path of the spool folder:

→) Open the registry.
HKEY_LOCAL_MACHINE\SYSTEM\CurrentControlSet\
Control\Print\Printers.
Modify the DefaultSpoolDirectory value.

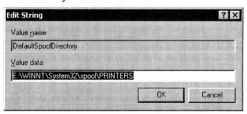

Alternatively:

→) Open the **Printers** folder, then open the **File** menu, and select **Server Properties**.

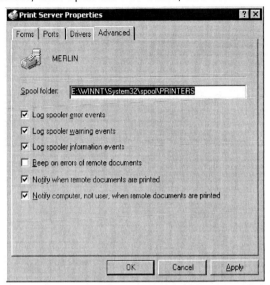

→) Click the **Advanced** tab. Note the different options that you may choose. For example, these options allow you to receive the following type of message when a document has been printed:

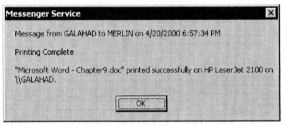

In order to access the print manager, double-click the icon that represents the printer concerned.

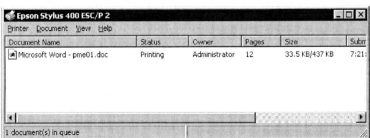

The print manager provides a menu bar and a display pane that provides details concerning the documents that have been placed in the print queue.

Each entry in the print queue is made up of the name of the document, the status of the document (for example **Printing, Paused printing, Spooled, Printer offline**), the owner of the document, the number of pages, the size of the document, the date and time at which the document was submitted, and the physical port.

The **Document** menu allows you to:

- pause a print job (so that you can insert the correct envelope, or change the ink cartridge, for example).
- resume a print job.
- restart the printing of documents, provided they are not deleted from the print queue after they have been printed.
- cancel the printing of a document.
- display the properties of a document.

The properties of a document cover all the settings that are used for the document. These settings concern not only the processing of the print job. They also concern the physical configuration of the printer.

You can specify that a user must be notified when the document has been printed, you can alter the priority of the document, and you can even define a printing schedule.

Amongst other options, the **Printer** menu allows you to:

- pause the printing for all the documents (**Pause Printing**). This option stops the physical printing, but it still allows new print jobs to be submitted to the printer, and placed in the print queue. This option is useful when you must carry out maintenance work on the print device.

– **Cancel All Documents**: this option removes all the documents from the print queue.

In order to suspend printing rapidly, you can put the printer offline.

G. Publishing and finding printers in Active Directory

One of the roles of the Windows 2000 directory database is to allow you to find network objects easily. You can locate print devices very easily and very quickly, without needing to know the name of the server onto which the device is connected.

By default, when you share a printer, it is automatically published in Active Directory (the **List in the Directory** check box is enabled).

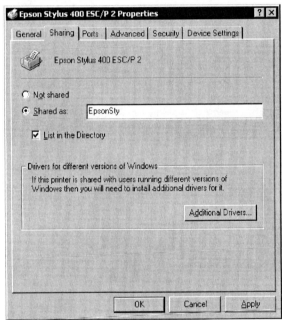

You can find a printer as follows:

→) Open the **Start** menu and select **Search**.

→) Then select **For Printers**.

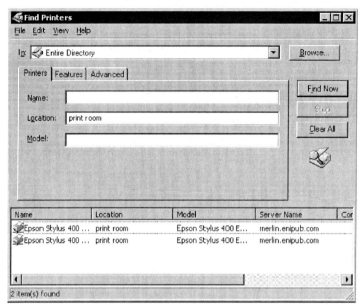

→) You can search by one or another of the fields that you entered when you configured the printer (for example, **Name**, **Location**, or **Model**). You can also search by items such as the server name or the owner name.

→) Click the **Advanced** tab to search by other fields:

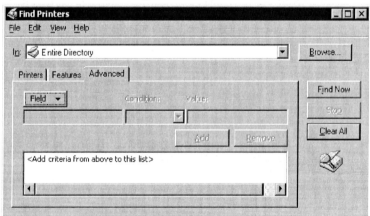

Click the **Field** button, to select the fields that you wish to use as criteria for your search.

When you have located the printer, provided that you have the necessary permissions, you can connect to it and view its properties and possibly modify them (for example, its ports or its permissions).

H. Administering a printer via the Web

One of the new features that Windows 2000 offers is to allow you to print via the Internet or via your company's intranet. Windows 2000 supports the IPP (*Internet Printing Protocol*) protocol that allows you to print to a URL address. This protocol is encapsulated in the http protocol.

To use this feature, IIS version 5 (*Internet Information Server*) must be installed on the server where the shared printers reside. On small networks (with up to 10 connections) you can also use Peer Web Services (PWS) on a Windows 2000 Professional machine.

Here are the steps that you must follow to connect to a printer via the Internet or via intranet :

➜) Open the **Printers** folder and double-click the **Add Printer** icon.

➜) Select **Network printer**, followed by **Next**.

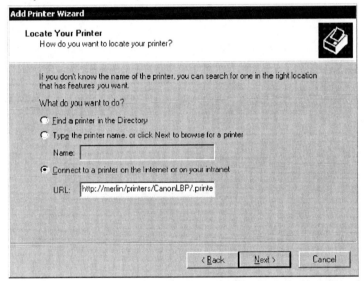

➜) Enter a URL address in the format: **http*://servername/printers/printer_sharename*.prin-ter**, then click **Next**.

➜) Select whether or not this printer must be your default printer.

➜) Click **Next**, followed by **Finish**.

➜) The printer appears in the Printers window in the following format:

When you access a printer via the Web, you use the authentication that is supplied by the IIS server.

Provided that you have the necessary permissions, you can manage your documents and your printers using your Web browser. When you install IIS 5, you create a virtual directory that points to **%systemroot%\web\printers**. You can access this directory by entering the URL address: **http://*web_server_name*/Printers**.

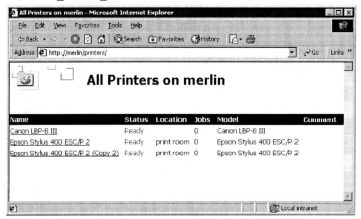

→) Select the printer that you wish to manage.

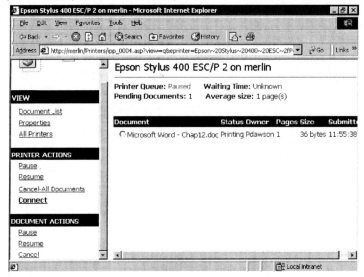

You can then manage documents that are on the spooler and on the printer itself.

If you attempt to carry out an action for which you do not have the necessary permissions, you will be asked to provide authentication.

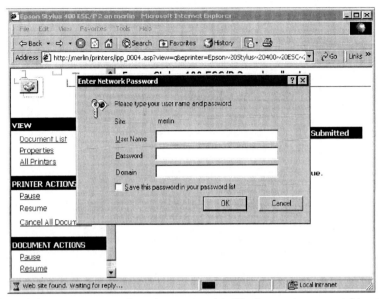

→) If you do not have an account and password with the necessary rights, the following message will appear:

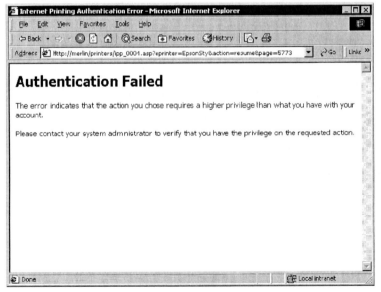

I. Troubleshooting print problems

If you are unable to print a document, here is a list of possible causes:
- The port is incorrect.
- The device is disconnected.
- The driver that is being used is unsuitable.
- The device has no more paper, or no more ink, or the paper is jammed.
- The format that you have selected is incorrect for the paper tray.
- The printer is paused.
- The spooler that is on the servers does not work or has not been declared.
- The printing period is badly configured.
- The user does not have the required permissions, or the printer is not shared (or is no longer shared).

A document that you sent from an MS-DOS application does not print:
- Check that the local driver is installed.
- Some DOS applications will not print until the application is closed.

You have problems with 16-bit Windows applications:
- There is a "memory error" upon startup.
- You cannot select a font.
- No default printer is selected.

Your document does not print completely or the print is deteriorated:
- Check that you are using the appropriate driver.
- The print processor does not support the data type concerned, or the data type has been changed.

The hard disk starts racing and your document never reaches the server:
- There is not enough disk space on the print server. Move the spool directory, or free up some space on the partition concerned.

You are unable to print on the server. The print jobs do not execute and you cannot delete them:
- Stop and restart the Spooler Service.

PostScript text appears on the printer:
- Check that your print device is able to manage PostScript.
- Check that your print device is correctly configured in order to manage Postscript (you could possibly use PostScript.SEP in order to switch to PostScript mode).

Chapter 9: System monitoring and performance tuning

A. Event Viewer

Windows 2000 traces many actions and events in the operating system. The **Event Viewer** console can be started from the **Administrative Tools** menu.

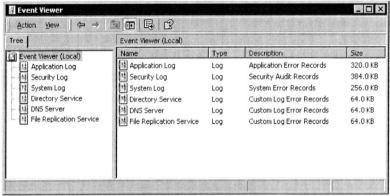

Several logs are available that allow you to record the events:

- **Application Log**: application developers use this log to write the information that is returned by their applications.
- **System Log**: This log contains information that is returned by the system, such as a notification that the system is unable to find a domain controller.

Both of these logs generally contain error records, which are represented by the icon: **⊗Error** , information records, which are represented by the icon: **ⓘInformation** and warning records, which are represented by the icon: **⚠Warning** .

- Security **Log**: This log contains the return messages from your audits (**⫿Success Audit** and **🔒Failure Audit**).

The **Action - Properties** menu allows you to set up the recording of events in the log that you have selected.

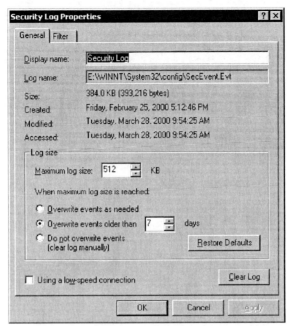

By default, the maximum size of the log is 512 KB. You can change this maximum size, and you can define the actions that must be taken when the log is full. These actions are as follows:

- Overwrite events.
- Overwrite events that are older than a specific number of days. However, you must note that if the log is full and no event that is recorded in it is older than this number of days then new events will not be written to the log.
- Do not overwrite events. This option implies that you must clear the log manually.

You can define a group policy that will stop the machine as the log becomes full. The objective of this technique is to ensure that no audit records will be lost.

If you have many records, then you can apply filters in order to help you to find the items that you seek. For this purpose, you must go into the **Properties** of the log concerned and select the **Filter** tab.

You can find out the cause of an error by double-clicking the event concerned.

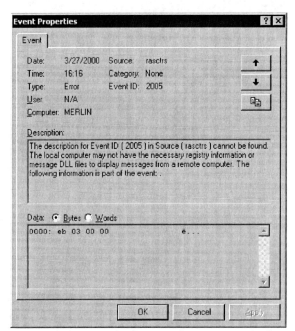

If you implement an audit policy, you must remember to consult the security log regularly. You can save the security log as a means of monitoring the security. To save a log, right-click the log concerned and then select **Save Log File As**. The file will be saved in **.evt** format (you can also save it in text format if you prefer). This allows you to read it later using the **Event Viewer**. Alternatively, you can save your logs in **.csv** format, which allows you to use these files with applications that handle delimiters.

B. Performance utility

The performance utility allows you to monitor the activities of one or more computers, in a detailed way. The monitored information is stored in text files. You can view it in graphic form, and you can associate it with minimum and maximum alert thresholds. The **Performance** console can be started from the **Administrative Tools** menu.

1. Counters

Windows 2000 considers as objects, such items as devices, files, disks, processors and virtual memory.
You can monitor each object in a number of different ways. For example, for the **Processor** object, the **Performance** console offers different **counters** such as the number of Interrupts/sec, the percentage of processor use in **User** mode and in **Privileged** mode. Four objects are especially important: the processor, the physical disk, the memory and the network interface.

An object can be present several times with the Windows 2000 system. In this case it is said to have multiple instances: a dual processor computer will have two **instances** of the **Processor** object. If the **NetBEUI** protocol is linked to two network cards, then it will also have two instances. The purpose of detailed system analysis is to find bottlenecks. In other words, to find devices that slow down the whole system because they do not have enough performance in order to deal with the workload that the system is asking of them.

One bottleneck can hide another bottleneck. For example, heavy disk activity will slow down the running of Windows 2000. This slowing down may concern the hard disk (due to disk fragmentation or poor access time and data transfer time, for example). On the other hand, it might also be masking a lack of RAM, for which the system must compensate with excessive paging between the swap file and volatile memory.

2. Graphs

Graphs are useful for short term monitoring.

The Performance utility provides many counters by default. You can add other counters by installing a program or by installing extra features.
The first counter that you must monitor for a given object is the counter that is most general for the object. This is also the most meaningful counter for the object. For example, for the **Processor** object, you must choose the **%Processor Time**; for NetBEUI, you must choose **Bytes Total/sec**.

To monitor a counter, click the ➕ button:

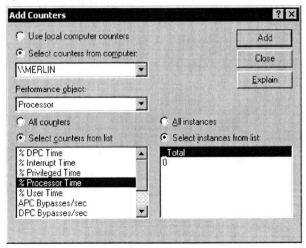

This dialog box allows you to choose the network computer that you want to monitor and the counter of the object instance. For each new counter, the **Performance** console displays a different description entry.

When you want to measure network performance on a computer, it is often useful to configure the **Performance** utility on the remote machine.

> It is advisable to start the Performance utility with a Realtime priority level in order to ensure that you do not distort the measurements.

You can delete a counter from the graph by selecting it and then clicking the [X] button.

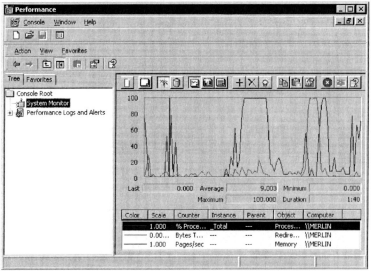

To highlight a counter, you can select it in the counter list and then press the shortcut key [Ctrl] **H**.

Finally, you can access the properties of the graph using the button. This button allows you to configure such settings as the type of view (**Graph, Histogram** or **Report**) and the counter measurement interval.

3. Alerts

You can apply alerts to the measurements that are made on Windows 2000 objects. Each measurement can trigger an alert according to maximum and minimum thresholds that you define as the administrator. A useful feature of these alerts is that you can associate them with an action: for example, you can send a warning message across the network, or you can stop a process.

To use alerts, go into the **Performance** console, and carry out the following steps:

→) Right-click the **Alerts** folder.

→) Select **New Alert Settings** and enter a meaningful name for your alert.

→) Click the **Add** button to add a counter onto which you want to apply your alert.

For example, the **Processor** object and the **%Processor Time** counter characterize processor workload. When the system carries out some operations, this counter can reach 100%. However, if the processor then returns to an activity level of between 0% and 80%, with a few occasional peaks, then the processor is certainly not a bottleneck for the system.

On the other hand, if the **Processor Queue Length** counter (the number of threads that are waiting to run) of the **System** object is permanently greater than 2, then the processor may be a bottleneck.

Each of the counters that you add allows you to monitor with respect to a maximum and a minimum threshold. For each alert, you can run a program, either upon the first alert that is associated with the counter, or upon each alert that is associated with the counter.

→) Specify the action that the system must carry out if the threshold is reached, by selecting the **Action** tab. You can specify actions such as: sending a message to a user or to a computer, adding an entry in the event viewer and running a program.

→) Indicate when the scanning must start and when it must stop, using the **Schedule** tab. You can choose to start and to stop scanning manually, at any time. In this case, right-click the alert that you want to start or to stop, and select **Start** or **Stop**.

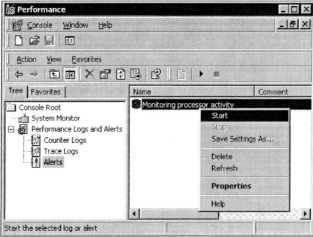

A red icon indicates that the scanning is stopped, and a green icon indicates that the scanning is running.

4. Reports

You can also view counter activity in text format. In this view mode, you configure and use the Performance utility in the same way as in Graph view mode.

To switch to Report mode:

→) Click the 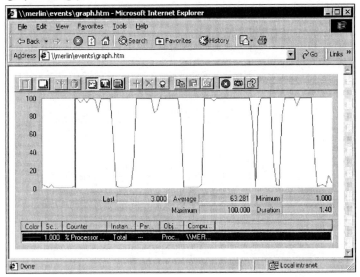 button.

→) The ⊞ and ☒ buttons respectively allow you to add and to delete the counter that you have selected.

5. Exporting data

Exporting data allows you to work with your measures using another application, such as a spreadsheet or a word-processor.

→) Right-click the graph, the histogram or the report and select **Save As**.

→) You can save your data in **.tsv** format (in this format the fields will be delimited using tabs). Alternatively, you can save your data in **.htm** format. In this case you can remotely run your graph using your browser.

C. Task Manager

Loss of control on your system is rarely caused by failure of the system itself. It is generally caused by the failure of an application. This does not prevent the other applications from running, but it can affect system performance. To remedy this situation, you must stop the process that is causing the problem. In order to do this, run the **Task Manager**, using the shortcut key sequence Ctrl ⇧ Shift Esc. Then click the **Task Manager** button in the **Windows Security** dialog box that appears. You can also access the **Task Manager** by right-clicking the taskbar.

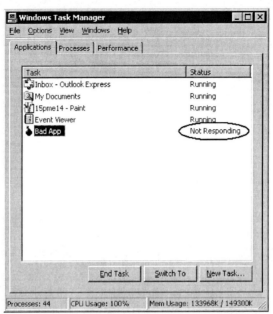

→) Click the **Processes** tab, or right-click the name of the application that has failed, and then select **Go To Process**.

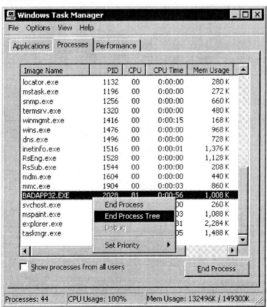

→) Right-click the process that corresponds to the application that has failed and then select **End Process**.

⮞ Note that you can also select **End Process Tree**, which allows you to delete all the processes that are associated with the process that you have selected.

Each process has a run priority level. There are 6 different priority levels:
- Realtime
- High
- AboveNormal
- Normal
- BelowNormal
- Low

By default, every application that you start has a **normal** priority level. You can set different priority levels so that one application will run faster than another. In order to do this, right-click the process for which you want to change the priority level, and select **Set Priority**.

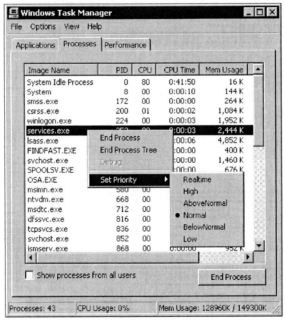

Then, select the priority to which you want to set the process.

⮞ Be careful not to set a process priority level to **Realtime**, as, if this process fails, the system would not be able to regain control.

D. Dr. Watson

1. Introduction

Dr. Watson is a program debugger for Windows 2000. It allows you to log any problems that occur in order to provide vital information concerning the cause of these errors. Dr. Watson operates at application level. It generates a log when an error occurs in an application.

Technical support personnel need the information that Dr. Watson obtains and generates to diagnose errors in programs running on Windows 2000 computers. When the system detects an error, Dr. Watson generates a text file called **Drwtsn.log**. This log can then be sent to technical support personnel by any method that they choose.

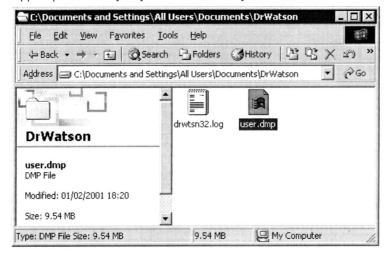

2. Setting-up Dr. Watson

You can create a **Crash Dump File** for an incident. This is a binary file that a programmer can load into a debugger in order to analyze it.

◉ By default, the crash dump file is called **user.dmp**.

To set up Dr. Watson, select the **Start - Run** menu option and enter **drwtsn32**.

➜ The dialog box that appears enables the **Create Crash Dump File** option by default. You can enter a specific name for this file in the **Crash Dump** box.

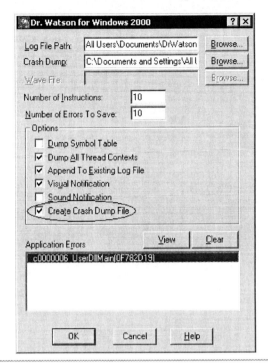

🔹 Dr. Watson starts up automatically when an error occurs in an application.

3. Consulting the log files

When an error occurs in an application, you can consult the log file and the crash dump file.

→) To consult the log file, double-click the last line in the **Application Errors** list.

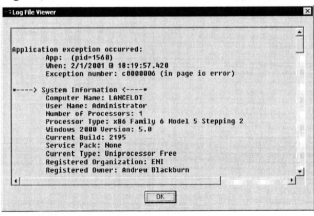

→) Use the scroll bars to move about in the log file.

The Windows 2000 online help provides more information on this subject. In particular, it explains how you can interpret the log file that Dr. Watson generates. To consult these online help pages, select the **Start - Help** menu option, select the **Index** tab and enter the keywords: **Dr. Watson**.

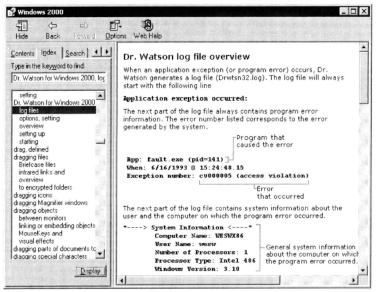

E. Performance tuning

Although Windows 2000 is configured to make the best general use of the system resources, you can adjust a certain number of settings in order to tune the system performance to your specific configuration.

1. Optimizing processor time

First, you can specify how the system must share its processor time between the foreground application, and the background applications.

For example, you could minimize processor time for a backup that runs in the background. Alternatively, you may want to speed up the printing of a document in the background. To make either of these adjustments, go into the **Control Panel**, open the **System Properties** dialog box, select the **Advanced** tab and click the **Performance Options** button.

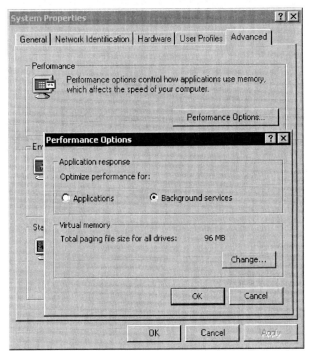

In the **Performance Options** dialog box, if you choose to **Optimize performance for Applications** then the system will assign more processor resources to the foreground program (the active window) than it will to the background programs.

On the other hand, if you choose to **Optimize performance for Background services** then the system will share the processor resources equally amongst all the programs that are running. Nevertheless, the system will still take into account the initial priorities that were assigned to the applications. In other words, if you choose this option then the system will not penalize execution of the background applications.

2. Setting affinity on a multiprocessor computer

When you are working on a multiprocessor platform, the **Performance** page of the Windows Task Manager describes the workload on each of your processors:

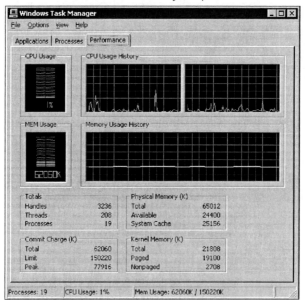

In certain cases, the system may not share the workload equally between its processors, even in an environment that is based on **SMP** (*Symmetric Multi-Processing*) architecture: in other words, even if the system does not definitively assign the processes to specific processors.

→) To assign a process to a processor, right-click the taskbar to open the **Windows Task Manager** dialog box and select the **Processes** tab. Then right-click the process that you want to assign and select the **Set Affinity** option.

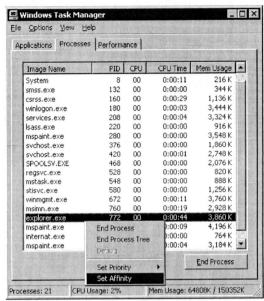

You can then select the processor(s) on which you authorize your system to run your process:

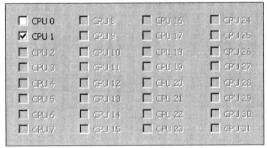

3. Optimizing the virtual memory

Virtual memory allows an operating system to work with a memory space that is greater than the physical memory (volatile memory, or RAM) that is available.

On Windows systems, the management of one or more paging, or swap, files provides this extra memory. The paging file is situated in the root directory of a volume.

Several techniques allow you to optimize the use of the paging file(s).

a. Sizing the paging file

First, you must ensure that the size of your paging (swap) file suits the applications that you will run on your computer.

🔷 By default, Windows 2000 sets the paging file size to one and a half times the size of the RAM on your computer (Chapter 3 of this book contains more details on configuring the paging file).

b. Preventing paging file growth

Another optimization technique is to prevent the paging file from growing dynamically (when a paging file grows it becomes fragmented, which can slow down the system considerably). To prevent paging file growth, go into **System Properties**, select the **Advanced** tab, click the **Performance Options** button, and then click the **Change** button in the **Virtual memory** frame. Then, set the minimum size of virtual memory to the same value as the maximum size of virtual memory. You must set this value in order to ensure that the system will not create paging file extensions. By doing this you will ensure that the paging file will not become fragmented.

🔷 You should have a good idea of how big your paging file needs to be, after the first few days of working on your machine.

c. Creating several paging files

You can create several paging files and, wherever possible, place them on the volumes that are used the least (in particular, you should avoid placing a paging file on the boot volume).

🔷 Important note: in Microsoft environments, the boot volume is the one which contains the Windows kernel and the Windows system files.

Remember that choosing not to create a paging file on the boot volume may be incompatible with the recovery settings that are defined in the **Write Debugging Information** frame of the **Startup and Recovery** dialog box (**System Properties, Advanced** tab, **Start-up and Recovery** button). The **Write Debugging Information** frame allows you to choose the level of detail you require for your debugging information. Each of these levels of detail requires a different size of paging file on the boot volume:

Type of dump	Minimum size of paging file on the boot volume
Small Memory Dump	2 MB
Kernel Memory Dump	50 MB or more
Complete Memory Dump	Size of RAM + 1 MB

By creating several paging files on separate volumes, you can balance the workload over the different volumes. In order to balance this workload correctly, you must not have more than one paging file per physical disk.

d. Using a striped volume

If you place the paging file on a striped volume then the system will balance the workload over several disks automatically.

F. Identifying bottlenecks

1. Memory

With Windows 2000, the component that is the most likely to cause bottlenecks is the RAM.

a. Paged and non-paged memory

Windows 2000 memory is divided into two categories: **paged** and **non-paged**.

Paged memory is virtual memory.

Unlike paged memory, data that is stored in non-paged memory stays in RAM and is never written to disk. Examples of such data are the internal structures used by the operating system.

b. Principle of virtual memory

On Windows 2000, virtual memory covers the RAM, the filesystem cache and the disk, as a single means of storing information.

Unused code and data are transferred to disk when the RAM space is needed. The more the system lacks RAM, the more the system uses the disk, and the more the system slows down. In this case, the memory is a bottleneck for the system.

c. Hardware page faults

A high rate of **Page Faults** is a sign that the memory is a bottleneck. A page fault occurs when a program needs data that is not in the physical memory and that must be read from the disk (from the swap file).

If you obtain a report with:

Memory   Page Faults/sec**5**

then you have a clear indication that the memory is a bottleneck for the system.

You can use other counters to identify a bottleneck:

Memory   Pages/sec**5**

This counter indicates the number of requests for pages that are not immediately available in RAM and must be read from disk, or that must be written to disk in order to free the RAM so that it can be used by other pages. If this value stays over 5, then the memory is certainly a bottleneck for the system.

d. Processor

Most of what happens on a server involves the processor. The CPU on an applications server is generally more heavily used than on a file server, or on a print server. Thus, whether processor activity on a server is *normal* or not, will depend on the role that the server plays.

The two most common causes of processor bottlenecks are calls made by applications and by device drivers, and excessive interrupts generated by unsuitable disks or by unsuitable network subsystem components.

The counters associated with the **Processor** object will help you to find out whether or not the processor is a bottleneck:

Processor	**% Processor Time**	**>>80**

This counter measures the time that the processor is occupied. A value of this counter that is constantly over 80%, indicates that the processor is a bottleneck.

You can then fine-tune your measures to identify the process that is using the processor. To do this, you must monitor each process individually.

If the system has several processors, you must use the counter:

System	**Processor Queue Length**	**>>2**

This counter indicates the number of requests waiting to be handled by the processor. In other words, it shows the number of threads that are ready to run and that are awaiting the processor. In general, a value of this counter greater than 2 indicates a bottleneck. In this case, you will need to look for the component that is overloading the processor.

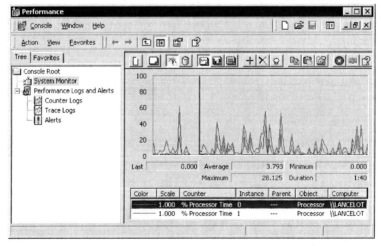

Windows 2000 Professional

2. Disk

Disks store the programs and the data used by the applications. A disk can often become a bottleneck when it is waiting for a response from the computer.

a. Activating disk counters

By default, the disk counters are activated (with disk management set up for automatic startup). If this is not the case, you must activate the counters or else they will stay empty. To do this you must use the **diskperf** command from a command prompt.

This command allows you to activate or to deactivate the disk performance counters at physical drive level for a logical drive or for a volume.

Here is the syntax for this command.

```
diskperf [-y[d|v]|-n[d|v] [\\computername]
```

in which:

-y

Specifies that the system must start both physical and logical disk performance counters when you restart it.

-yd

Activates the disk performance counters that the system will use for measuring the performance of physical drives when you restart it. This is the default setting.

-yv

Activates the disk performance counters that the system will use for measuring the performance of logical drives when you restart it. This is the default setting.

-n

Specifies that the system must not use any disk performance counters when you restart it.

-nd

Specifies that the system must not use any disk performance counters for physical drives when you restart it.

-nv

Specifies that the system must not use any disk performance counters for logical drives when you restart it.

\\computername

Specifies the computer on which you want to use disk performance counters. If you do not specify a computer name, then **diskperf** will assume that you want to work with the local computer.

◗ If you want to monitor the disks of a remote computer from your Windows 2000 Professional workstation, activate the disk performance counters on the remote system only.

◗ You must restart your computer for any changes to take effect.

When you study the disk subsystem, you must use the following counters:

%Disk Time

This counter indicates the activity level of the disk: it shows the time that is spent reading and writing information.

A **%Disk Time** that approaches **100%**, indicates that your disk is very heavily used. In this case you must identify the process that is responsible for the disk activity.

Current Disk Queue Length

This counter indicates the number of input/output requests that are waiting. A **Current Disk Queue Length** that is constantly over 2 indicates that the disk is a bottleneck.

b. Solutions when the disk is a bottleneck

If you find that your disk subsystem is a bottleneck, you can take a number of actions:

- You can add a quicker controller, such as a FAST SCSI-2, or a controller that has an integrated cache.
- You can add extra disks, if you are working in a RAID environment. This approach allows you to distribute the data workload over several physical disks. It also allows you to enhance performance, especially read performance.
- You can offload your system by distributing certain users, certain applications and even certain services onto other computers in the network.

3. Network

A Network bottleneck is one of the most difficult bottlenecks to analyze. Several elements can disrupt the smooth running of a network.

You can use a certain number of objects to monitor the network: **Server**, **Redirector**, and **Network Interface** along with the protocols. The object that you must analyze depends essentially on the environment.

Here are the counters that are most commonly used:

Server   **Bytes Total/sec**

This counter indicates the number of bytes that are sent and received by the server via the network. It shows the activity level of the server concerning reception and transmission of data.

Server   **Logon/sec**

The Logon/sec counter shows the number of instantaneous logon attempts. This counter is useful for finding the number of validations that a domain controller is carrying out.

Network segment   **%Network Usage**

This counter indicates the percentage of the network bandwidth that the local network uses. It is useful for adding a service onto a server.

Windows 2000 Professional

Chapter 10: Backing up, Restoring and Troubleshooting

A. Backing up and restoring

1. Backing up

Windows 2000 provides a tool that allows you to back up and to restore system data (such as the Active Directory, and the registry). This utility is called **Backup** and is located in the **Start - Programs - Accessories - System Tools** menu. The Backup utility is very easy to use and provides a graphic interface that is user friendly and intuitive. Not only does it allow you to back up and to restore, but also it allows you to schedule these activities. This tool has been greatly improved since the Ntbackup tool of Windows NT 4.0.

You can backup to tape devices, to logical drives, to removable disks or to CD-ROM writer drives. You can backup from volumes that are formatted either in FAT or in NTFS.

You can back up and restore manually. Alternatively, you can use a wizard that will guide you step by step through the procedure of creating the necessary jobs. This wizard also allows you to create an emergency repair disk.

It is, of course, extremely important that you back up system data and other essential information regularly. In addition, it is just as important that you test your backups. You must carry out restore tests regularly, to be sure that your storage devices will operate correctly on the day when you need to restore.

a. Backing up data

Every file and every folder has an archive attribute. When this attribute is set, it indicates that the file or the folder has been modified since the last backup. When you modify a file, the system sets this attribute, and will backup this file when it runs the next backup procedure.

You can access this attribute by opening the properties of the file, or of the folder, and then clicking the **Advanced** button.

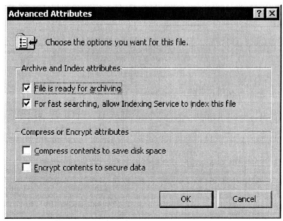

If the **File is ready for archiving** check box is enabled, then the archive attribute is set. If this attribute is disabled for a file or a folder then the system will automatically enable it when you modify the file or the folder.

You can make five types of backup:

Normal

Backs up all the files that you have selected and resets their archive attribute.

Copy

Backs up all the files that you have selected and does not reset their archive attribute.

Incremental

Backs up all the files that you have selected that have been modified since the last backup. This type of backup resets the archive attribute.

Differential

Backs up all the files that you have selected that have been modified since the last backup. This type of backup does not reset the archive attribute.

Daily

Backs up all the files that have been modified during the day that the backup is made. This type of backup does not reset the archive attribute.

A differential backup takes longer than an incremental backup. However, a differential backup takes less time to restore than an incremental backup.

In order to back up data you must carry out the following steps:

➜ Go into the **Start - Programs - Accessories - System Tools** menu, and then select **Backup**.

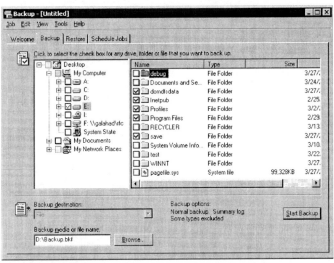

→) Activate the **Backup** tab, and then select the folders and the files that you want to back up.

→) Open the **Tools** menu and select **Options**.

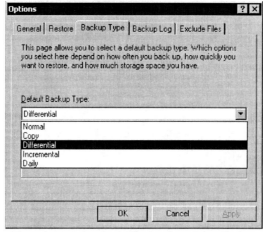

→) Activate the **Backup Type** tab and select the backup type that you want to implement.

→) The **Backup Log** tab allows you to specify the level of detail that you want to log during the backup process.

→) Click the **OK** button.

→) Enter the name of the backup file, along with the identification of the drive onto which you want to back up.

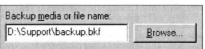

→) Click the **Start** button in order to start the backup.

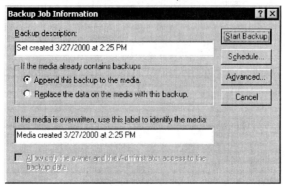

→) Enter a description for your backup (the description by default includes the creation date and time). The **Advanced** button allows you to select the backup type. This button is useful if you have not already selected the backup type using the **Tools** menu.

→) Click the **Start Backup** button. When your backup has finished it is represented by an ⚙️ icon.

💿 If you back up NTFS files, the NTFS permissions that are associated with the files and the folders will be maintained when these files and folders are restored onto an NTFS partition. Similarly, files that have been encrypted will remain encrypted after you have restored them.

💿 Before you carry out your backup, make sure that nobody is using the files that you have selected. The backup process will ignore any files that are being used. These files will be indicated in the backup log. Nevertheless, Windows 2000 can backup files that are being used by the system when it backs up the System State.

b. Backing up the system state

The Windows 2000 Backup utility allows you to back up the data that concerns the state of your system. On your Windows 2000 Professional workstation, this comprises the registry database, the system startup files and the COM+ Class Registration database.

You cannot back up these components individually.

In order to back up these components, go into the **Backup** utility, and activate the **System State** check box.

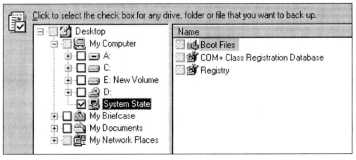

c. Scheduling

One of the improvements that the Windows 2000 Backup utility offers, with respect to the Windows NT version, is that Windows 2000 Backup allows you to schedule your backup jobs, using a graphic interface.

→) Click **Schedule Jobs**, in the **Backup** utility.

→) Click the **Add Job** button in order to start the **Backup Wizard**.

→) Follow the steps of the **Backup Wizard**.

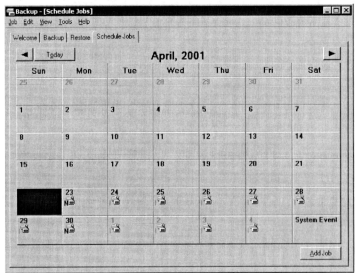

In this schedule, the system will carry out a normal backup every Monday, and an incremental backup on the other days of the week.

2. Restoring

a. Restoring data

You can use the **Restore Wizard**, or you can restore manually. To restore manually, activate the **Restore** tab in the **Backup** utility. Then, select the backup that you want to restore. If no backup media appear in the list, then this is probably because you have deleted the catalog that corresponds to the media catalog by selecting **Delete Catalog** from the **Tools - MediaTools** menu. In this case you must import the catalog that corresponds to the backup. You can do this by opening the **Tools** menu and then selecting **Catalog a backup file**.

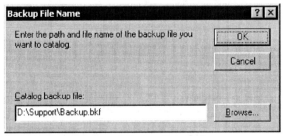

→) Enter the path to your backup files and then click **OK**.

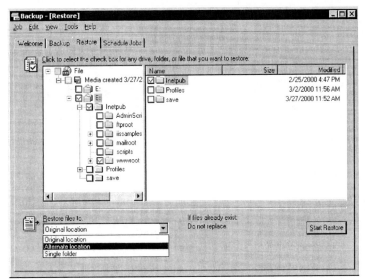

→) Open the media and select the files that you want to restore from the backup set. Then, indicate whether you want to restore your backup to the original location, or whether you want to restore your backup to an alternative location.

→) Click the **Start** button.

→) Click the **Advanced** button if you want to specify advanced settings, and click **OK** in order to start restoring.

b. Restoring the system state

When you restore the system state, Windows 2000 deletes the current system state and replaces it with the system state from the backup. Consequently, you must back up the system state regularly in order to avoid losing data.

If your workstation fails to such an extent that you must re-install your system, then you can restore the system state from your old system onto your new one. In this way you will ensure that your new system has exactly the same characteristics as the old one (the same name, and the same registry database).

To do this, re-install the Windows 2000 system, allowing all the default installation options (these will be updated when you restore your old system state). Then, re-install all your applications. Finally, use the **Backup** utility, in order to restore the system state from your most recent backup.

B. Troubleshooting

1. Startup steps

After your computer has tested its hardware components (using the POST, or Power On Self Test, sequence on Intel platforms), the first action that it will carry out is to read the MBR (Master Boot Record). Then, this MBR will examine the partitions table in order to find the active partition in this table, which contains four entries. The boot sector in the active partition is run: this is the operating system preloader. The preloader then loads the operating system loader, which will then load the operating system.

Here are the steps of a Windows 2000 boot:

- **Step 1**
  Reading NTLDR (for MS-DOS, IO.SYS is the first file that is read). **Ntldr** switches the processor from real mode to 32-bit linear memory mode. Then it starts up the FAT and NTFS system drivers, which allow it to access the file systems in order fully to start up Windows 2000. **Ntldr** then reads **BOOT.INI** so as to build the boot loader menu.
- **Step 2 - BOOT.INI**: This is a text file that allows Windows 2000 to boot, or to start up on another operating system.

Here is an example of the **boot.ini** file. You can use this file to boot Windows 2000:

```
[boot loader]
timeout=30
default=multi(0)disk(0)rdisk(1)partition(1)\WINNT
[operating systems]
multi(0)disk(0)rdisk(1)partition(1)\WINNT="Microsoft Windows 2000
Professional" /fastdetect
```

ARC Names

ARC names have the following structure:

```
SCSI(x)disk(y)rdisk(0)partition(n)
or
MULTI(x)disk(0)rdisk(z)partition(n)

SCSI(x)  or  MULTI(x)
```

The value x denotes the SCSI hardware controller numbers in their initialization order. It must be noted that some SCSI discs appear with the name MULTI (those for which the SCSI controller BIOS has not been disabled), according to the BIOS management mode.

DISK(y)	For Multibus SCSI adapters, this corresponds to the bus number. It is always equal to zero for MULTI controllers.
RDISK(z)	For MULTI components, z indicates the disk number on the adapter. For SCSI disks it is always equal to zero.
PARTITION(n)	n indicates the partition number on the disk, from 1 to n.

On a disk that is handled by an IDE controller, or by a SCSI (BIOS activated) controller, the second partition that is on the second physical disk of the first controller will be referenced by: multi (∅) disk (0) rdisk (1) partition (2). In this case disk (∅) is a constant.

◉ Important note: an incorrect ARC name will generate the following message, "Windows 2000 could not start because the following file is missing or corrupt:
%Systemroot%\System32\ntoskrnl.exe
Please re-install a copy of the above file"
In most cases, you can solve this problem simply by editing the **boot.ini** file.
An incorrect ARC name can occur after you have created a new main partition, when the Windows 2000 boot partition is in a logical drive of an extended partition.

– Step 3
NTDETECT.COM: hardware detection program.

◉ NTDETECT.COM allows you to generate the HARDWARE volatile key.

◉ If you select an operating system other than Windows 2000, then the BOOTSECT.DOS file allows you to run the preloader of this other system (BOOTSECT.DOS is a copy of the former boot sector before Windows NT was installed).

– Step 4
The **Hardware Profile/Configuration Recovery** startup menu, followed by loading of the Windows 2000 system.

2. Contents of the BOOT.INI sections

This file is hidden, and is in read-only mode (S, H, R attributes). With Intel platforms, it is created automatically on the system partition when Windows 2000 is installed.

a. [boot loader] Section

`timeout` Defines the number of seconds that must elapse before Windows 2000 loads the default operating system.
A value of 0 causes the system to start immediately.

◉ You can modify **boot.ini** directly, and set a value of -1. In this case the system will wait indefinitely for you to select an option.

◉ In most cases, you should use the **Control Panel - System** icon, activate the **Advanced** tab, and then click the **Startup and Recovery** button, in order to modify this value.

◉ If you want to modify this file after you have started MS-DOS, then you must simultaneously disable the three attributes S, H, and R. Before you modify the file, you must reset these attributes using the following command: **attrib -S -H -R BOOT.INI**. After you have modified the file, you must reset these attributes using the following command: **attrib +S +H +R BOOT.INI**.

default   This parameter corresponds to the path of the default operating system. This path must be present in the (operating
systems) section.

b. [operating systems] section

This section allows you to define the paths to the boot sectors of the different operating
systems that are available, such as: Windows 2000, Windows NT, Windows 95/98,
MS-DOS and OS/2.

3. Last known good configuration

Internally, Windows 2000 manages several sets of system configurations (it manages three
in general).
In most cases, Windows 2000 starts up with the default configuration, or **CurrentControl-
Set** (see HKEY_LOCAL_MACHINE\
System).

In fact, Windows 2000 records a configuration as the **Last Known Good Configuration**
as soon as a user is able to log on with it (even if it generates many errors!)

When a problem occurs following a new installation, then the message **At least one driver
or service failed during system startup** will warn you of the problem, before you log on. In
this case, you must stop and restart the machine, without logging on, so as to restart using
the **Last known good configuration** option.

You can access this option as follows:
- When you start up Windows 2000, press the ⌷F8⌷ key when you are prompted to do so.
  Then, use the arrow keys in order to select the **Last known good configuration** option.

When you apply the **Last Known Good Configuration**, you lose all the configurations from
the previous session.

4. Starting from a floppy disk

You can start up Windows 2000 using a FAT diskette, whether Windows 2000 uses FAT
or whether it uses NTFS!

For this purpose, you must use a diskette that you have formatted on a Windows NT 4.00
system, or on a Windows 2000 system (this is necessary so that the NT preloader will be
installed on the diskette, and ready to load **NTLDR**). You must then copy the files **NTLDR**,
BOOT.INI, **NTBOOTDD.SYS** (if the BIOS of the SCSI controller is deactivated) and
NTDETECT.COM, which are situated in the root of the Windows 2000 system partition.
Startup steps 1 to 3 are carried out on the diskette instead of the hard disk.

5. Using an emergency repair disk

As the administrator, you can repair the system by starting up on the Windows 2000 installation startup diskettes. You can create these 4 diskettes by selecting the bootdisk directory on the Windows 2000 CD-ROM, and entering the command **makeboot a** in a command prompt:

After you have inserted the fourth diskette, you can carry out an emergency repair by pressing the **R** key. However, in order to do this you need previously to have created an emergency repair diskette on the system that you want to repair. You can create this diskette using the **Welcome** tab of the **Backup** utility. You can also repair the installation using the recovery console (by pressing the **C** key).

After you have pressed the **R** key, you can repair manually, so that you can choose the options that you want to use. Alternatively, you can choose to carry out a fast repair. In this case the following options will be chosen for you:

Inspect startup environment

This option checks the presence of the files that are needed in order to start up Windows 2000 (such as **boot.ini**, and **ntldr**).

Verify Windows 2000 system files

This option is needed if any Windows 2000 files have been deleted, or if the disk has been altered. The **SETUP.LOG** file that is contained on the emergency repair disk allows the program to copy the files from the CD-ROM onto the hard disk.

Inspect boot sector

This option recreates the boot sector (so that it will point to the first **NTLDR** file).

ⓘ You can also run an emergency repair by booting on the Windows 2000 CD-ROM, without using the startup diskettes.

6. Other startup options

Windows 2000 can run in different modes. This feature allows you to troubleshoot any operational problems that the system may have. You can access the menu that allows you to choose these modes by pressing the F8 key when you are prompted to do so during the startup process of your system.

Safe Mode

This option allows you to start up your system by loading the essential drivers that you need for this purpose. A file called **Ntbtlog.txt** is created in the **%systemroot%** directory. This file allows the system to detect the drivers that have been loaded, and the drivers that have not been loaded.

Safe Mode with Networking

This is the same as **Safe Mode**, except that the drivers that the system needs for networking are loaded as well.

Safe Mode with Command Prompt

When you choose this option, Windows 2000 runs in **Safe Mode** without loading the graphic interface.

Enable VGA Mode

With this option, Windows 2000 runs with the standard VGA graphic drivers. You must choose this option when you have a problem with you graphic card driver.

Enable Boot Logging

When you choose this option Windows 2000 starts up normally, and produces a report on all drivers and services that have been loaded during the start up. This report is written to the **Ntbtlog.txt** file that is located in the **%systemroot%** directory.

Directory Services Restore Mode (Windows 2000 domain controllers only)

This mode allows you to start up Windows 2000 without loading Active Directory, so that you will be able to restore it on the domain controller concerned.

Debugging Mode

When you choose this option, the system sends debugging information to another computer via a serial cable.

7. Recovery console

a. Introduction

The recovery console is a text mode interface that allows you to repair your system when you can no longer boot Windows 2000. You can use this console to stop or to start services that could prevent the system from starting up, format hard disks and read data that is situated on FAT or NTFS disks. In order to go into this console, you must indicate the installation that you wish to repair, along with the password of the local administrator of the workstation.

You can run the recovery console in two ways:

- You can start up the system, either using the four startup diskettes, or using the Windows 2000 CD-ROM. Then, when you are prompted to do so, you must press the **C** key so as to start up the recovery console.
- Alternatively, you can access the recovery console using the Windows 2000 startup menu. However, before you can do this, you must first install this console.

b. Installing the recovery console

→) Start up a command prompt.

→) Access the **I386** directory of the Windows 2000 CD-ROM.

→) Input the command **winnt32 /cmdcons**.

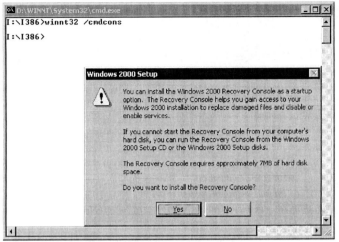

→) Click the **Yes** button.

→) Restart your computer. You will notice that the **Microsoft Windows 2000 Recovery Console** option now appears in the startup menu along with other options (such as **Microsoft Windows 2000 Professional**, for example).

The **boot.ini** file has been modified and will now look like the following example:

```
[boot loader]
timeout=30
default=multi(0)disk(0)rdisk(1)partition(1)\WINNT
[operating systems]
multi(0)disk(0)rdisk(1)partition(1)\WINNT="Microsoft Windows 2000
Professional" /fastdetect
C:\CMDCONS\BOOTSECT.DAT="Microsoft Windows 2000 Recovery Console" /cmdcons
```

c. Starting up the Recovery Console

To start up the **Recovery Console**, choose the **Microsoft Windows 2000 Recovery Console** option when you start up your computer.

A screen appears similar to that shown below. You must select the Windows 2000 system on to which you want to log (even if you have installed only one on your computer), and you must enter the administrator's password.

You can then start entering commands (the **Help** command allows you to consult the list of available commands).

```
Microsoft Windows 2000(TM) Recovery Console.

The Recovery Console provides system repair and recovery functionality.

Type EXIT to quit the Recovery Console and restart the computer.


1: C:\WINNT

Which Windows 2000 installation would you like to log onto
(To cancel, press ENTER)? 1
Type the Administrator password: ********
C:\WINNT>
```

d. Recovery Console commands

When you have opened the Recovery Console, enter the **Help** command to display the Recovery Console commands.

Here is a list of the commands that the console provides:

Attrib

This command allows you to modify file and folder attributes.

```
attrib [+r|-r]  [+s|-s]  [+h|-h]  [+c|-c]  [[drive:][path] filename]
```

+	sets an attribute
−	clears an attribute
r	specifies the read-only file attribute.
s	specifies the system file attribute.
h	specifies the hidden file attribute.
c	specifies the compressed file attribute.

To display the attributes of a file or a folder, use the **Dir** command.

Batch

This command runs the commands in a text file.

```
batch input_file [output_file]
```

input_file	specifies the text file containing the list of commands that you want to run.
output_file	specifies the file that must store the output of the commands in the input_file. This parameter is optional. If you do not specify an output_file, then the commands will output to the screen.

Chdir (Cd)

This command displays the name of the current folder, or it changes the current folder.

```
chdir [drive:]
chdir [path]
chdir [..]
cd [drive:]
cd [path]
cd [..]
```

cd..	allows you to move to the parent directory.

➜ Enter **chdir drive:** to display the current directory on the specified drive.

➜ Enter **cd** without any parameters to display the current drive and the current directory.

Chdir interprets spaces as delimiters. If a directory name contains spaces, you must enter this name between quotation marks. Here is an example:

```
cd "\Documents and Settings\Administrator\My Documents"
```

Chdir operates only in system directories of the current Windows installation, in removable media, in the root directory of each hard disk partition or in local installation sources.

Chkdsk

This command creates and displays a status report.

```
chkdsk [drive:] [/p] [/r]
```

drive:	Specifies the drive you want to check.
/p	Specifies that chkdsk must make a full check even if the drive that you specified is not marked for chkdsk to run.
/r	finds bad sectors and recovers any readable information. When you specify /r, you also specify the /p parameter, implicitly.

You can use chkdsk without any parameters. In this case, chkdsk shows the status of the disk in the current drive.

Chkdsk needs the Autochk.exe file. First, Chkdsk looks for this file in the startup directory. If it cannot find this file in this directory, then it will look for it on the Windows 2000 Installation CD-ROM. If Chkdsk cannot find the Windows 2000 Installation CD-ROM, then it will ask you to specify the location of the Autochk.exe file.

Cls

This command clears the screen.

```
cls
```

Copy

This command copies a file to a different location.

```
copy source [destination]
```

source	specifies the file that you want to copy.
Destination	specifies the name of the destination folder and/or the name of the destination file.

As the source you can specify removable media, or the root of any drive, or the local installation sources, or any subfolder in the system directories of the current Windows installation, or the **Cmdcons** directory.

As the destination you can specify the root of any drive, or the local installation sources, or any subfolder in the system directories of the current Windows installation, or the **Cmdcons** directory.

However, you cannot specify removable media as the destination.

If you do not specify a destination, then this command uses the current directory by default.

You may not use wildcard characters with this command.

If the destination file already exists, then **Copy** asks you to confirm your action.

If you ask this command to copy a compressed file from the Windows Installation CD-ROM, it will automatically decompress the file when it copies it.

Delete (Del)

This command deletes a file.

```
delete [drive:][path] filename
del [drive:][path] filename
```

[drive:][path] filename	specifies the file that you want to delete.
Delete	operates only in system directories of the current Windows installation, in removable media, in the root directory of each hard disk partition, or in local installation sources.

Dir

This command lists the files and the subfolders that a directory contains.

```
dir [drive:][path][filename]
```

[drive:][path] [filename]	specifies the drive, the directory and/or the files that you wish to view.

Dir lists all the files concerned, including system files and hidden files.

The files may have the following attributes:

d	Directory
r	Read-only
h	Hidden file
a	File is ready for archiving
s	System file
c	Compressed
e	Encrypted
p	Reparse point

Dir operates only in system directories of the current Windows installation, in removable media, in the root directory of each hard disk partition, or in local installation sources.

Disable

This command disables a Windows system server or device driver.

```
disable service_or_device_driver_name
```

service_or_device_driver_name	specifies the system service or the device driver that you want to disable.

Windows 2000 Professional

Disable	displays the name of the current startup type for the system service or for the device driver, before it sets this startup type to SERVICE_DISABLED. You should make a note of the previous startup type in case you need to reactivate the system service or the device driver concerned.

Here are the different startup types that the disable command displays:

- SERVICE_DISABLED
- SERVICE_BOOT_START
- SERVICE_SYSTEM_START
- SERVICE_AUTO_START
- SERVICE_DEMAND_START

Diskpart

This command allows you to manage partitions on your hard drive partitions.

```
diskpart [/add | /delete] [device_name | drive_name | partition_name]
[size]
```

/add	creates a new partition.
/delete	deletes an existing partition.
device_name	specifies the device on which you want to create or to delete a partition. The output of the **map** command provides this name. Here is an example of a correct device name: \Device\HardDisk1.
drive_name	specifies the partition that you want to delete as a drive letter. Here is an example of a correct drive name: E:
partition_name	specifies the partition that you want to delete, as a partition name. You can use this parameter instead of the drive_name. Here is an example of a correct partition name: \Device\HardDisk1\Partition1.
size	specifies the size in MBs of the partition that you want to add.

> If you use the **diskpart** command without any parameters, a partition management user interface will appear.

Enable

This command enables a Windows system service or device driver.

```
enable service_or_device_driver_name [startup_type]
```

service_or_device_driver_name	specifies the system service or the device driver that you want to enable.
device_driver_name	The name of the device driver you want to enable.

startup_type	specifies the startup type for the system service or device driver. You can specify one of the following startup types: - SERVICE_BOOT_START - SERVICE_SYSTEM_START - SERVICE_AUTO_START - SERVICE_DEMAND_START

The enable command displays the name of the current startup type for the system service, or for the device driver, before it sets this startup type to the new value that you specify. You should make a note of the previous startup type in case you need to restore this setting to its previous value.

If you do not specify a startup type, the enable command will display the current startup type for the system service or the device driver concerned.

Here are the different startup types that the enable command displays:

- SERVICE_DISABLED
- SERVICE_BOOT_START
- SERVICE_SYSTEM_START
- SERVICE_AUTO_START
- SERVICE_DEMAND_START

Exit

This command closes the Windows 2000 Recovery Console and restarts your computer.

Expand

This command decompresses a compressed file.

```
expand [/y] source [/F:filespec] [destination]
expand [/d] source [/F:filespec]
```

/d	specifies that expand must not decompress the files. With this option, expand displays only the files contained in the source.
/y	specifies that expand must overwrite any existing files without asking for confirmation.
source	specifies the file that you want to decompress. You cannot use any wildcard characters in this specification.
/f:filespec	specifies files that you want to extract when the source contains more than one file. You can use any wildcard characters in this specification.
destination	specifies the destination folder for the decompressed file. If you do not specify a destination then expand will write to the current folder.

As destination you can specify the root of any drive, or the local installation sources, or any subfolder within the system directories of the current Windows installation, or the **Cmdcons** directory.

However, you cannot specify removable media as the destination.

In addition, the destination file must not be in Read-only mode.

To deactivate the Read-only attribute, use the Attrib command.

Expand will ask you to confirm your action before it overwrites any existing files, unless you use the **/y** option.

Fixboot

This command writes a new partition boot sector onto the system partition.

```
fixboot [drive]
```

    drive   specifies the drive to which you want to write the new partition boot sector. By default, this is the system partition onto which you are logged.

Only x86 computers support the fixboot command.

Fixmbr

This command repairs the master boot record of a hard drive.

```
fixmbr [device_name]
```

    device_name   specifies the drive onto which you want to repair the new master boot record. If you do not specify this parameter, then fixmbr will write a new master boot record to the boot device.

If fixmbr detects an invalid or nonstandard partition table signature, it will ask you to confirm your action before it replaces the MBR (master boot record).

Only x86 computers support the fixmbr command.

Format

This command formats a drive so that you can use it with Windows 2000.

```
format [drive:] [/q] [/fs:file-system]
```

    drive: specifies the drive that you want to format.
    /q   specifies that the command must carry out a quick format on the drive.
    /fs:file-system   specifies the file system that format must use (FAT, FAT32 or NTFS).

Help

This command gives online information on the Windows 2000 Recovery Console commands. For information on a specific command, enter either **help ?**, or **help** *commandname*.

Listsvc

This command lists the services and the device drivers provided by the computer.

Logon

This command logs you on to a Windows installation.

```
logon
```

The `logon` command will list all detected Windows 2000/NT installations. To log you on, it requests the local administrator passwords for these installations.

Map

This command displays the mapping of drive letters to the names of the physical devices that are currently active.

```
Map [arc]
```

     arc   specifies that map must display Advanced RISC Computing (ARC) device names instead of Windows 2000 device names.

Mkdir (Md)

This command creates a folder or subfolder.

```
mkdir [drive:]path
md [drive:]path
```

`Mkdir` operates only in system directories of the current Windows installation, in removable media, in the root directory of each hard disk partition, or in local installation sources.

More / Type

This command displays the contents of a text file on the screen.

```
more filename
type filename
```

Rename (Ren)

Renames a file.

```
rename [drive:][path] filename1 filename2
ren [drive:][path] filename1 filename2
```

For the destination file, you cannot specify a new drive or a new path.

`Rename` operates only in system directories of the current Windows installation, in removable media, in the root directory of each hard disk partition, or in local installation sources.

Rmdir (Rd)

This command deletes a folder.

```
rmdir [drive:]path
rd [drive:]path
```

`Rmdir` operates only in system directories of the current Windows installation, in removable media, in the root directory of each hard disk partition, or in local installation sources.

Set

This command allows you to display and to define Recovery Console environment variables.

```
set [variable=[string]]
```

For example:

```
set AllowWildCards = true
```

If you use `set` without any parameters, this command will display the current environment settings.

Here are the environment variables that the Recovery Console supports:

AllowWildCards	Allows wildcard support for certain commands, such as the **del** command, for example.
AllowAllPaths	Allows you to access all files and folders on the system.
AllowRemovableMe-dia	Allows you to copy files to removable media, such as floppy disks.
NoCopyPrompt	Specifies that the system must not prompt your confirmation before it overwrites existing files.

Set is an optional command. To activate this command you must use the **Security Templates** snap-in.

Systemroot

This command defines the current directory as the **systemroot** folder.

```
systemroot
```

See **More**.

For further information on the Recovery console commands, consult the Windows 2000 online Help.

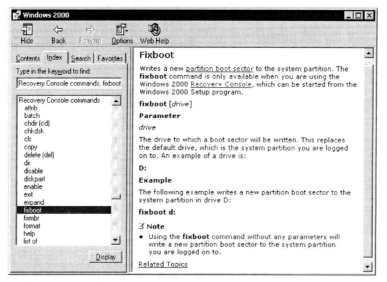

e. Examples of Recovery Console command execution

Here are a few examples of Recovery console command executions.

Example 1: Dir command

```
C:\dir
  The volume in drive C has no label
  The volume Serial Number is 3819-21dd

  Directory of C:\

12/07/99   02:00p   -arhs---       148992  arcldr.exe
12/07/99   02:00p   -arhs---       162816  arcsetup.exe
01/19/01   07:33p   ---h----            0  AUTOEXEC.BAT
01/19/01   07:04p   -a-hs---          192  BOOT.BAK
02/06/01   04:46p   -arhs---          268  boot.ini
02/06/01   04:46p   d-rhs---            0  cmdcons
12/07/99   02:00p   --rhs---       229264  cmldr
01/19/01   07:33p   ---h----            0  CONFIG.SYS
01/25/01   04:33p   -a------          182  debugLog.txt
01/22/01   10:03a   da------            0  Documents and Settings
02/01/01   12:51p   d-------            0  Inetpub
01/19/01   07:33p   -arhs---            0  IO.SYS
01/25/01   03:40p   d-------            0  LOGITEMP
01/19/01   07:33p   -arhs---            0  MSDOS.SYS
12/07/99   02:00p   -arhs---        34468  NTDETECT.COM
12/07/99   02:00p   -arhs---       214416  ntldr
01/23/01   07:56p   d-------            0  Office
```

```
01/25/01   05:05p   dar-----       0 Program Files
01/25/01   04:18p   d-------       0 QcamWeb
01/23/01   08:22p   d--hs---       0 RECYCLER
02/01/01   05:24p   d-------       0 Student
01/25/01   10:03a   d--hs---       0 System Volume Information
02/06/01   06:18p   da------       0 WINNT
             23 file(s)     790598 bytes
          1529536512 bytes free
```

Example 2: Listsvc command

```
C:\listsvc
Abiosdsk        Disabled
abp480n5        Disabled
ACPI            Disabled
ACPIEC          Disabled
adpu160m        Disabled
AFD             Auto        AFD Networking Support Environment
agp440          Boot        Intel AGP Bus Filter
Aha154x         Disabled
aic116          Disabled
aic78u2         Disabled
aic78xx         Disabled
Alerter         Manual      Alerter
ami0nt          Disabled
amsint          Disabled
AppMgmt         Manual      Application Management
asc             Disabled
asc3350p        Disabled
asc3550         Disabled
AsyncMac        Manual      RAS Asynchronous Media Driver
atapiBoot       Standard    IDE/ESDI Hard Disk Controller
Atdisk          Disabled
Atmarpc         Manual      ATM ARP Client Protocol
audstub         Manual      Audio Stub Driver
Beep            System
Browser         Auto        Computer Browser
...
...
...
UPS             Manual      Uninterruptible Power Supply
usbhub          Manual      Microsoft USB Standard Hub Driver
UtilMan         Manual      Utility Manager
VgaSave         System
W32Time         Auto        Windows Time
W3SVC           Auto        World Wide Web Publishing Service
Wanarp t        Manual      Remote Access IP ARP Driver
```

```
wdmaud        Manual     Microsoft  WINMM  WDM  Audio  Compatibility
Driver
WinMgmt       Auto       Windows  Management  Instrumentation
Winsock       Manual
Wmi           Manual     Windows  Management  Instrumentation  Driver
Extensions
```

Example 3: Map command

```
C:\map

?              0MB       \Device\Harddisk0\Partition0
C:  NTFS       3075MB    \Device\Harddisk0\Partition1
?              4MB       \Device\Harddisk0\Partition0
?              3099MB    \Device\Harddisk1\Partition0
A:                       \Device\Floppy0
D:                       \Device\CdRom0


C:\map arc

?              0MB       multi(0)disk(0)rdisk(0)partition(0)
C:  NTFS       3075MB    multi(0)disk(0)rdisk(0)partition(1)
?              4MB       multi(0)disk(0)rdisk(0)partition(0)
?              3099MB    multi(0)disk(0)rdisk(1)partition(0)
A:                       \Device\Floppy0
D:                       \Device\CdRom0
```

Example 4: Set command

```
C:\set

AllowWildCards = FALSE
AllowAllPaths = FALSE
AllowRemovableMedia = FALSE
NoCopyPrompt = FALSE
```

8. Additional tools

You can also install additional tools from your Windows 2000 Professional CD-ROM. To install these tools, go into the **\Support\Tools** folder of this CD-ROM and run the **Setup.exe** program.

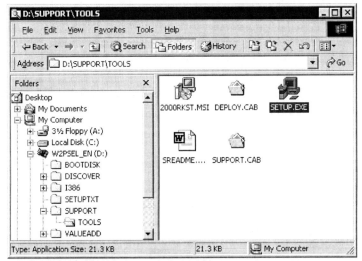

A wizard starts up to help you with your installation.

When you have finished installing these tools you can access new programs from the
Start - Programs menu.

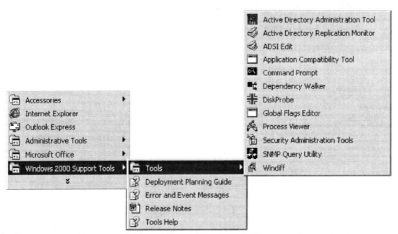

The **Tools Help** menu option provides online documentation on these tools.

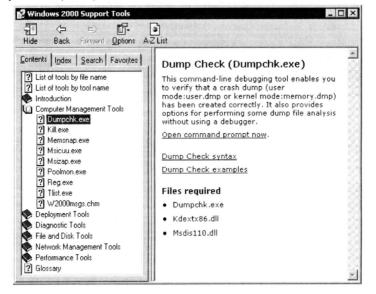

The Resource Kit **Error and Event Messages Help** is another useful online help module. This module groups together the most common error messages according to category.

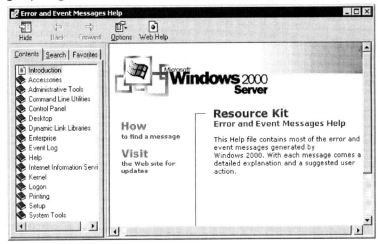

E

G

H

I

I386 folder, *26, 41, 195, 466*
IDE controller, *462*
IEEE 1394
    devices, *125*
    troubleshooting, *172*
IETF (Internet Engineering Task Force), *12, 248*
IIS (Internet Information Server Services), *10, 377, 411, 427*
    authentification, *385*
    installing, *377*
    services, *194*
    WEB sites, *378*
Image Color Management (ICM)
    managing colors, *137*
    troubleshooting, *138*
Imagecast, *24*
Incoming connections, *253*
Incremental backup, *457*
Infrared
    installing, *160*
Infrared Data Association protocols
    IrLPT, *157*
    IrTran-P, *157*
Infrared devices, *157*
    maximum connect rate, *167*
    setting up an infrared connection, *163*
Input Locales, *204*
input/output ports, *20*
Installing
    components, *40*
    from the network, *41*
    problems, *45*
    setup switches, *42*

Installing from a local CD-ROM, *32*
Installing Windows 2000 Professional, *62, 427*
Integrated Services Digital Network (ISDN), *250*
Integrated Windows authentification, *387*
Intel systems, *16, 21*
Intellimirror, *109*
Interactive group, *295, 312*
Interconnection services
    at application level, *235*
    at network level, *235*
Internet, *427*
Internet addressing, *236*
    drawbacks, *238*
Internet connection sharing, *275*
Internet Connection Wizard, *261, 264*
Internet Information Server, *10, 411*
    see also IIS
Internet mail account
    setting up, *270*
Internet Options, *201*
Internet Printing Protocol
    see *IPP*
Internet Service Provider (ISP), *261, 267*
Internet Services Manager console, *378, 386, 388*
Intranet, *377*
IO.SYS, *462*
IP Address, *239, 264*
IP address class
    class A, *237*
    class B, *237*
    class C, *237*
    class D, *237*
IP configuration
    IP Address, *239*
    subnet mask, *239*

M

Windows 2000 Professional

Windows 2000 Professional

T

V

VGA
    Enable VGA mode, *466*
Virtual memory management, *449*
Virtual Private Networks
    see VPN
Volumes, *339*
    extending a simple volume, *342*
    managing, *330*
    mirrored, *339*
    mounting, *346*
    RAID 5, *339*
    simple, *339, 341*
    spanned, *339, 343*
    striped, *339, 344*
VPN (Virtual Private Networks), *11, 15, 250-251, 255, 261, 291*

W

WAN, *250*
WAN link protocol, *250-251*
WAN protocol, *268*
WDM (Windows Driver Model) architecture, *10*
Web printers, *427*
Web services, *16*
Web sites, *358, 378*
Welcome screen, *91*
welcome.osc file, *92*
WHQL (Windows Hardware Quality Lab), *154*
Windiff, *479*

Windows 2000 Advanced Server, *16*
Windows 2000 Datacenter Server, *16, 187, 409*
Windows 2000 kernel, *22*
Windows 2000 range, *11*
Windows 2000 Server, *13, 409*
Windows 3.x, *284, 330, 359*
Windows 95/98, *11, 22, 24, 32, 235, 284, 298, 330, 350, 410, 464*
Windows Explorer, *154, 335, 356, 398*
Windows for Workgroups, *235, 350, 352, 359*
Windows Hardware Quality Lab (WHQL), *185*
Windows Installer, *109*
Windows Installer package, *195*
Windows NT, *109, 284, 306, 330, 350, 410, 456, 464*
Windows NT 4.0, *11*
Windows NT LAN Manager (NTLM), *284*
Windows NT3.51/4, *24*
Windows sockets, *234*
Windows update, *184*
WinINSTALL LE tool, *109*
Winlogon process, *284*
Winnt.exe, *26, 41 - 42*
Winnt32.exe, *26, 42 - 43*
Winnt32.log, *45*
WINS (Windows Internet Naming Service), *244*
Winsock, *158*
Wireless devices
    Installing an infrared printer, *168*
Wireless Link, *162*
With Command Prompt, *466*
With Networking, *465*
Work offline technology, *11*
Workgroup, *40*
Workgroup domain, *23*

X